www.wadsworth.com

wadsworth.com is the World Wide Web site for Wadsworth and is your direct source to dozens of online resources.

At *wadsworth.com* you can find out about supplements, demonstration software, and student resources. You can also send e-mail to many of our authors and preview new publications and exciting new technologies.

wadsworth.com
Changing the way the world learns®

Distant Mirrors

THIRD EDITION

Distant Mirrors

America as a Foreign Culture

Edited by

PHILIP R. DEVITA
State University of New York, Plattsburgh

JAMES D. ARMSTRONG
State University of New York, Plattsburgh

WADSWORTH

THOMSON LEARNING ™

Australia • Canada • Mexico • Singapore • Spain • United Kingdom • United States

WADSWORTH

THOMSON LEARNING ™

Anthropology Editor: *Lin Marshall*
Assistant Editor: *Analie Barnett*
Editorial Assistant: *Reilly O'Neal*
Marketing Manager: *Matthew Wright*
Project Manager, Editorial Production:
Jerilyn Emori
Print/Media Buyer: *Robert King*
Permissions Editor: *Joohee Lee*
Production Service: *Scott Rohr / Buuji, Inc.*
Copy Editor: *Linda Ireland*
Cover Designer: *John Odam*

Cover Image: Top row: *flag, Gazelle Technologies*
©1993; basketball player, Rubberball ©1996;
building, Cannon Information Systems Research
Australia ©1994–1996; car wheel, Artville ©1997.
Middle row: *guitar, Artville ©1997; picnic, Gazelle*
Technologies ©1991; gun, Metaphotos. Bottom row:
skateboarder, Rubberball ©1996; handshake,
Bodyshots, Digital Wisdom ©1994.
Text and Cover Printer: *Webcom, Ltd.*
Compositor: *Buuji, Inc.*

Library of Congress Cataloging-in-Publication Data

Distant mirrors: America as a foreign culture / edited
by Philip R. DeVita, James D. Armstrong. — 3rd ed.
    p.   cm.
    Includes bibliographical references.
    ISBN 0-534-55648-5 (alk. paper)
    1. United States—Social life and customs—
1971—Foreign public opinion.   2. Popular
culture—United States—Foreign public opinion.
I.DeVita, Philip R. II. Armstrong, James D.

    E169.04. D578 2001
    973.92—dc21   2001026063

Wadsworth/Thomson Learning
10 Davis Drive
Belmont, CA 94002-3098
USA

For more information about our products,
contact us:
Thomson Learning Academic Resource Center
1-800-423-0563
http://www.wadsworth.com

International Headquarters
Thomson Learning
International Division
290 Harbor Drive, 2nd Floor
Stamford, CT 06902-7477
USA

UK/Europe/Middle East/South Africa
Thomson Learning
Berkshire House
168-173 High Holborn
London WC1V 7AA
United Kingdom

Asia
Thomson Learning
60 Albert Street, #15-01
Albert Complex
Singapore 189969

Canada
Nelson Thomson Learning
1120 Birchmount Road
Toronto, Ontario M1K 5G4
Canada

Contents

FOUR

Professor Widjojo Goes to a Koktel Parti   32
Weston LaBarre

An eminent African anthropologist analyzes the apparently strange customs at American rituals, which he has directly observed, from the reference points of his own cultural background. The author shows how, in interpreting American behavior from his own value system Widjojo's understanding of the American "drinking season" may be ethnocentric.

FIVE

An Outsider's View of American Culture   37
Janusz L. Mucha

A Polish sociologist compares his European idea of the "city" to what he discovered in the United States. He discusses the immediate and informal cordiality of Americans, the prevalence of urban anonymity, and the naturalness of violence, patriotism, education, ethnocentrism, and potluck dinners.

SIX

Growing Up American: Doing the Right Thing   44
Amparo B. Ojeda

Professor Ojeda, now an anthropologist and linguist, describes her initial difficulty in adjusting to some American customs as a student on her first visit to America. Years later, after returning to the United States with her daughter, she faced a crucial conflict between the American value of individualism and the emphasis on respect of her own Philippine traditions.

SEVEN

My American Glasses   50
Francisco Martins Ramos

An anthropologist from Portugal examines such cultural traits as informal language use, social life, body ritual, and football and offers critical insights into customs that Americans take for granted.

EIGHT

American Graffiti: Curious Derivatives of Individualism   59
Jin K. Kim

Professor Kim, a scholar in the area of intercultural communication and communication theory, has spent more than twenty years in the United States. In a letter written to a close friend from his native South Korea, he writes entertainingly of American approaches to privacy, manners, sexual mores, individuality, and interpersonal relationships.

NINE

The Young, the Rich, and the Famous: Individualism as an American Cultural Value   68
Poranee Natadecha-Sponsel

From the point of view of a Thai scholar, Americans appear open and immediately friendly in their greetings. But if one looks very closely, these greetings seem superficial and ritualized, hiding the more important aspects of American cultural values.

Understanding Ourselves: About the Third Edition

JAMES D. ARMSTRONG
AND PHILIP R. DEVITA

BACKGROUND

Americans are known to prefer newness and bigness. In fact, this feature of American culture was recognized by Alexis de Tocqueville in his groundbreaking and still largely accurate observations made in 1832 and first published in 1835 as *Democracy in America.* So, it seems inevitable and very American for us to expand the first two editions of *Distant Mirrors,* edited volumes about American culture. Even though we have made a few changes based on the suggestions of colleagues and reviewers, the subject is the same, and our orientation is identical to that of the first two editions. We originally went searching for the startling freshness of outsiders' perspectives to enable us to understand ourselves better, and in these essays, both new and old, we think we have achieved this goal.

However, in this third volume we have opened with four new articles, each explicitly intended to orient the undergraduate reader to not only the breadth of issues relating to questioning and understanding from "within" (Lowell and Ellen Holmes', "The American Cultural Configuration"), but also to consider the contributions of the "other" to our everyday activities (Ralph Linton's, "One Hundred Percent American"). Further, the classic "Body Ritual among the Nacirema" by Horace Miner and Weston LaBarre's "Professor Widjojo Goes to a Koktel Parti" serve extremely well as pedagogical introductions (whether tongue-in-cheek or analytically astute) addressed to how truly strange we Usans might appear to outside observers. The remainder of the volume consists of fifteen essays written by anthropologists and other scholars using ethnographic perspectives to interpret aspects of American culture. As in the first two editions, the authors have situated themselves in their essays so the reader can identify with their experiences and know about the background and context affecting their interpretations.

Anthropology has a long history of concern with the "other," the different, the strange. This focus on others and their cultures gives anthropology a comparative perspective that provides a reflective lens for understanding ourselves and our own immediate world. However, the ethnographic spaces of today differ a great deal from the ones inhabited by exotic people seemingly untouched by Western influence who are considered by many to be the main subjects of anthropological scrutiny. The global village is a fact, and the romantic vision of ethnographic adventure in remote places among pristine people is gone. We are, therefore, compelled to look closer to home for the strangeness and similarity that is the compelling part of the ethnographic enterprise.

It is difficult, however, for young students of American culture to fully appreciate the strangeness and wonder of their own interactive arenas. The cultural assumptions we grow up with are powerful. As insiders—speaking the same language, following the accepted patterns of behavior, embedded in a way of life—we tend to take many aspects of our own social action for granted. We generally speak and behave most appropriately and seldom are compelled to analyze what we say or do prior to speaking or acting. We are wonderfully successful performers on this complex and often confounding stage of sociocultural life. Furthermore, when others around us are similarly embedded in a way of life, we are less likely to question their actions or see the underlying assumptions behind those actions. We see our own routine behavior as uninteresting or natural. As Americans, we often interpret that behavior as the product of our own individual choice, rather than as the product of a tradition of similar choices. We forget to ask the questions that reveal our own culture's underlying values and beliefs. In short, when looking at ourselves, our own mirrors may be clouded.

With this expanded edition of *Distant Mirrors,* we hope to throw American culture into sharper relief. This volume provides other mirrors, other reflections. Outsiders, having grown up in other cultures, will not take as much for granted about our behavior as we do. They will not share our assumptions about what is appropriate and accepted. They will attend to different things and ask different questions than we would. They will interpret our routine behavior in other ways and see significance in what for us seems meaningless. They will provide other ways for understanding how American behavior is culturally constructed. Their lack of emotional involvement and embeddedness in the contexts they encounter—and, hence, the freshness of their viewpoints—will provide us with understandings different from those we can gain by ourselves.

This is not to say that the insiders studying themselves do not have advantages. Certainly our self-knowledge and self-awareness give us a head start in studying ourselves. Many American scholars from various disciplines have written insightful interpretations and critiques of American culture, our institutions, and the events, rituals, processes, places, and people that give Americanness meaning. Still, cultural insiders studying their own culture, especially those using the ethnographic method of experiencing life firsthand, are required to manufacture distance from the subject they seek to understand in order to find the right questions. Cultural outsiders, by virtue of their otherness, do not have to manufacture distance. It is already there. Thus, they are keenly aware of what warrants explanation. In making sense out of what appears strange, outsiders can easily read between the cultural lines and contextualize our behavior in a broader comparative perspective. So what they might miss through lack of awareness is more than compensated for by their relative lack of familiarity and ready access to comparison.

To create the original collection, we asked anthropologists from many areas of the world to write essays. We told them that we wanted literate insights into everyday American life with no holds barred. Articles could be humorous, caustic, critical—but not heavily theoretical and certainly not written in the traditional academic style of journal articles. We asked that the authors give first-person accounts of their personal experiences, especially the ones that they thought revealed important insights into American culture(s), institutions, and social life. For this edition we maintained the same goals, seeking only to broaden the range of points of views.

This is not, of course, the first attempt to use foreign viewpoints to examine American culture. Indeed, several of the contributors to this collection are among the growing number of foreign scholars who have written eloquently about American culture. But this is one of the few books that brings together the perspectives of experts from a variety of homelands in a single volume.

ORGANIZATIONAL FRAMEWORK

Some reviewers of the first two editions suggested that the book could be improved by arranging the articles into categories based on some subset of those standard subjects covered in introductory cultural anthropology courses. We are resisting this suggestion for several reasons. First, not all the articles lend themselves to easy classification. In fact, most of them deal with more than one theme and could not easily be assigned to a single category, such as marriage, individualism, identity, or economics. Second, our experience as teachers informs us that the organization of a collection of articles usually has little impact on how instructors use the collection in practice. Both of us usually deviate from the structure of the books we use in our courses. We believe that most instructors will pick and choose articles in the order that best suits their purposes. Finally, we are not convinced that the subject-oriented approach to teaching introductory courses in anthropology is the best. Organizing these articles by subject matter, if we could agree on their classification, would serve to reinforce a habit in the discipline that we view as having negative pedagogical implications. The authors did not write these articles about particular subjects. They wrote them about coming to terms with a new cultural system either as visitors to the culture, students of the culture, or new residents in a new arena. All these articles are about solving research problems, about dilemmas of understanding, and about human interactions across cultural boundaries. To pigeonhole these articles would put us in the position of partially constructing their meaning for the reader.

At the same time, we did not randomly nor haphazardly make up the order in which the articles appear. In fact, we have organized the articles into subsets of topic similarity, recognizing that the differences between the sets are fuzzy at best. The first group of articles (Chapter 1 through Chapter 4) is what we view as "ice breakers." In its own way, each should generate some new awareness of how much of our lives are benefited and made easier from the historical contribution of others (Linton), what underlying configurations may apply to understanding ourselves (Holmes and Holmes), or how strangely we may appear to the outsider (Miner and LaBarre). In each of these introductory articles, we are led both intellectually and humourously beyond the taken-for-grantedness.

We remain concerned with American life in general. Each article presents a variety of ideas. Each one jumps from characteristic to characteristic and experience to experience. In a sense, these articles introduce the reader to the subject of study. They delineate it in broad strokes. Notably, certain themes are developed, such as individualism, superficiality, and diversity, which are repeated in later essays. To a certain extent, Chapters 5 through 10 are more forthrightly similar to Horace Miner's Body Ritual among the Nacerima. Other articles are focused more on particular facets of American life. Each article centers on a particular institution, social setting, or cultural characteristic. At the same time, they repeat the themes developed in the other essays. For example, Ojeda's and Natadecha-Sponsel's articles echo Kim's concern with the value of individualism in American life.

All of these articles can be useful complements to a variety of courses. The first volume of *Distant Mirrors* was used in English composition courses, American studies courses, and freshman seminars introducing new students to college life, as well as cultural anthropology and sociology courses. Because we teach cultural anthropology, we are more aware of how these articles connect with such courses. Although these articles can be used as supplementary readings for many of the subjects covered in introductory cultural anthropology, such as family, kinship, and class, they are especially valuable in teaching about ethnocentrism and relativism and in introducing students to the problematics of cross-cultural experiences and the ethnographic method.

SOME SUGGESTIONS FOR READING THIS BOOK

We did not merely think that a book like this would be an interesting accompaniment to the texts used in anthropology, sociology, American studies, or English composition courses. We had another agenda, stemming from our collective experience teaching American students in introductory level anthropology courses. We believe that for American students to get the full impact of ethnography, experience the cultural relativity important to anthropological interpretation, understand the power of culture as an influence on our understanding of the world around us, and have the substance on which to build informed comparisons, they need to have a solid grasp of their own cultural world. As several of these articles clearly establish (for example, Mucha, Dussart, and Kim), we are woefully unaware of the way of life of others, even the others that inhabit the United States.

The vast majority of our students come into anthropology courses as the products of American individualism, having almost no sense of how culture influences their way of being, believing that their behavior has been the outcome of their own almost privately made decisions. Few students see their behavior as the outcome of culture. They view their own behavior as the inevitable outcome of human nature. Sometimes they recognize culture in the behavior of others, but usually that recognition comes from representations of others made by Americans on television, in the movies, in newspapers, and in high school textbooks. Usually their appreciation is not much more profound than an idea that others like different food and music. Anthropology courses may serve as a corrective for the distortions and triviality of their understanding, but even in anthropology courses the representations of others come mainly from our perspective.

What we are trying to achieve is twofold. First, we want students to develop cultural self-awareness, the realization that they live in a culturally constructed world and their behavior and understanding of the world come from their embeddedness in a cultural system. This is necessary for them to appreciate the similarities and differences that exist between them and others. It is our view that introductory cultural anthropology courses should be as much about understanding ourselves as about understanding others. We think that this understanding is produced through critical reflection resulting from the questions students have about others that can be turned into questions about themselves. If this cultural self-reflection is encouraged by reading about others as we see them, then it will be further stimulated by the opportunity to read about Americans as others see us. Second, we want students to appreciate the fact that culture influences the way others are experienced, perceived, and represented. This allows them to better identify with the complexities of trying to understand others. The full impact of these realizations should be a much less ethnocentric view of the world, combined with a sense that culture is a dynamic force in our lives.

How can this book be used to achieve these goals? As Richard Deutsch (1994) states in his review of the first edition of *Distant Mirrors,* "readers will see their reflection with amusement, critical thought, and even outright defensiveness." It is the defensiveness, perhaps the product of our cultural arrogance, that we have found to be most productive. Not everyone gets defensive, but those who do often provoke reactions about the readings that pull their classmates into the discussion. A number of colleagues who have used the book report that many of the articles produce this kind of reaction.

Another idea that has been successful is to encourage students to engage with each article as if it were a conversation between the reader and the author. Teachers can create this kind of reading by providing students with questions about the readings or requiring students to write questions about the readings to share in class. Requiring students to consider the degree to which they agree or disagree with each author's conclusions is an easy and often critique-evoking exercise. For example, is American culture truly distinct from European culture, as Emanuel Drechsel argues in Chapter 19? Are all Americans neighborly strangers, or is the lack of involvement in neighbors' lives limited to the cluster homes project that Honggang Yang describes in Chapter 12? What is it about Thai child rearing that causes Poranee Natadecha-Sponsel to react to the independence of American children the way she does in Chapter 9? Does the perceived lack of community that Geoffrey Hunt recognizes in Chapter 18 really create the belief in therapeutic communities advocated by alcoholism and drug counselors?

It is also useful to encourage students to compare the experiences and conclusions of several authors. Do Francisco Martins Ramos's (Chapter 7) and Hervé Varenne's (Chapter 10) European backgrounds produce substantially different readings of American cultural practices than does Yohko Tsuji's (Chapter 11) Asian perspective? Is the individualism discussed by Jin Kim in Chapter 8 the same value that Amparo Ojeda is writing about in Chapter 6? Is the circus metaphor developed by Emanuel Drechsel in Chapter 19 appropriate to the discussions of diversity central to Janusz Mucha's (Chapter 5), Françoise Dussart's (Chapter 16), and E. L. Cerroni-Long's (Chapter 17) articles? What are the similarities and differences experienced by those who came to stay, such as Andrei Toom (Chapter 15) or Saleem Peeradina (Chapter 14)? Is Gisela Ernst's (Chapter 13) discussion of the divisiveness in ethnic labeling pervasive within this society?

The main pedagogical goals of this book are to create cultural self-reflection, reduce ethnocentrism, and create new ways for our predominantly American readers to understand their own culture. We want readers to better understand the stuff they are made of in order for them to better understand themselves and others. Because we saw this as a book directed primarily at an audience of undergraduate students, we wanted it to be one that would be appealing for them to read. To that end we instructed the authors to personalize their accounts and avoid overly theoretical and technical analyses. It was especially important for us to have the authors situate themselves in their accounts, both to make the articles more personal and to allow students to understand the experiences that led to the authors' conclusions. Thus, we were interested in having subject matter that was familiar to students—that is, everyday life in a setting they know—interpreted by writers who did not necessarily share the same worldview assumptions as the readers but with whom readers could identify. Occasionally, students might bristle at what they read, but a number of American experts have written much more scathing critiques of our society than anything in this book (See the references provided by Holmes and Holmes). In fact, it seems to us that most of these authors are exceptionally sensitive about the way we are, in much the way that most American anthropologists are sensitive to the people they study. We will both admit that we were hoping for more critical—even caustic—articles by the contributing scholars and wondered if the basic politeness was not in fact an effort to show the respect they maintain for their American host society.

Students should learn to appreciate that the perspectives of others constitute an indispensable ingredient in the development of a critical understanding of themselves. These essays, given the accessible, sensitive, and personal ways in which they are written, are excellent means for encouraging reflectiveness and critical awareness in our students.

We have added study questions to each article. These are in no way complete, and we were most careful not to overindulge in anthropologically based queries. Students of American culture, sociology, and English may discover more significant concerns than those we have developed. In the final assessment, it should be the individual instructor who determines which issues might best serve his or her pedagogical needs.

REFERENCES

Deutsch, Richard. 1994. Review of *Distant Mirrors: America as a Foreign Culture*. *American Anthropologist* 96: 1009–1010.

Miner, Horace. 1956. Body Ritual among the Nacirema. *American Anthropologist* 58: 503–507.

Tocqueville, Alexis de. 1966. *Democracy in America*. New York: Harper & Row.

Acknowledgments

There are a number of people who deserve our thanks. First, we would like to thank all the contributing authors for their patience with us and their cooperation on this project. Their cooperation has not only helped us to produce what we believe is a unique and significant collection, but it has also given us the opportunity and pleasure to get to know them. Both of us also recognize that our associations with a number of other non-Americans, who have shared their insights about our culture, helped us to realize the importance of this project. Many thanks are given to James Clifton, who encouraged Phil DeVita to put this collection together. Our close friend and colleague, Richard Robbins, read and commented on all of the manuscripts and often reinforced our commitment to this project.

A number of other colleagues, who have used this book in their courses and have encouraged us to work on a third edition, deserve our thanks. We also thank the reviewers, Barbara E. Cook, California Polytechnic State University, San Luis Obispo, Anna A. Hall, Delgado Community College, Michael D. Lieber, University of Illinois, Chicago, Chris Mayer, Cowley County Community College, and Michael C. Stone, Hartwick College, who offered meaningful insights and suggestions about the first two editions. In almost all instances we agreed with their critiques, especially with the fact that most of the articles focus on middle-class sociocultural contexts. That was not the original intent of this project but that is how it evolved.

One Hundred Percent American

RALPH LINTON

How much of the values and material aspects of our "American Way" do we take for granted? This very brief article by Ralph Linton, written in 1937, directs us to question our concepts of international superiority and ethnocentrism. Historically, we owe so much of our heritage to the ideas and inventions of people and cultures from distant lands. What does this article, as significant today as it was over sixty years ago, instruct us as to the issue of cultural relativism?

Ralph Linton (1892–1953) received his B.A. from Swarthmore College, and he earned his Ph.D. at Harvard in 1925. He taught at University of Wisconsin, Columbia University, and Yale University. Linton began his training as an archaeologist but, during his 1920 to 1922 research in the Marquesas Islands, developed an interest in living peoples and switched to cultural anthropology. From his broad-reaching studies in the South Pacific, Americas, Africa, and Madagascar, Linton developed insights into the process of acculturation and complex cultural-psychiatric relationships. He was the first to formally introduce the concepts of status and role to anthropological analyses. Among his most important works are The Study of Man *(1936),* The Cultural Background of Personality *(1945),* The Science of Man in the World Crisis *(1945), and* The Tree of Culture *(1955).*

There can be no question about the average American's Americanism or his desire to preserve this precious heritage at all costs. Nevertheless, some insidious foreign ideas have already wormed their way into his civilization without his realizing what was going on. Thus dawn finds the unsuspecting patriot garbed in pajamas, a garment of East Indian origin; and lying in a bed built on a pattern which originated in either Persia or Asia Minor. He is muffled to the ears in un-American materials: cotton, first domesticated in India; linen, domesticated in the Near East; wool from an animal native to Asia Minor; or silk, whose uses were first discovered by the Chinese. All these substances have been transformed into cloth by methods invented in Southwestern Asia. If the weather is cold enough he may even be sleeping under an eiderdown quilt invented in Scandinavia.

On awakening he glances at the clock, a medieval European invention, uses one potent Latin word in abbreviated form, rises in haste, and goes to the bathroom. Here, if he stops to think about it, he must feel himself in the presence of a great American institution: he will have heard stories of both the quality and frequency of foreign plumbing and will know that in no other country does the average man perform his ablutions in the midst of such splendor. But the insidious foreign influence pursues him even here. Glass was invented by the ancient Egyptians, the use of glazed tiles for floors and walls in the Near East, porcelain in China, and the art of enameling on metal by Mediterranean artisans of the Bronze Age. Even his bathtub and toilet are but slightly modified copies of Roman originals. The only purely American contribution to the ensemble is the steam radiator, against which our patriot very briefly and unintentionally places his posterior.

In this bathroom the American washes with soap invented by the ancient Gauls. Next he cleans his teeth, a subversive European practice which did not invade America until the latter part of the eighteenth century. He then shaves, a masochistic rite first developed by the heathen priests of ancient Egypt and Sumer. The process is made less of a penance by the fact that his razor is of steel, an iron-carbon alloy discovered in either India or Turkestan. Lastly, he dries himself on a Turkish towel.

Returning to the bedroom, the unconscious victim of un-American practices removes his clothes from a chair, invented in the Near East, and proceeds to dress. He puts on close-fitting tailored garments whose form derives from the skin clothing of the ancient nomads of the Asiatic steppes and fastens them with buttons whose prototypes appeared in Europe at the close of the Stone Age. This costume is appropriate enough for outdoor exercise in a cold climate, but is quite unsuited to American summers, steam-heated houses, and Pullmans. Nevertheless, foreign ideas and habits hold the unfortunate man in thrall even when common sense tells him that the authentically American costume of gee string and moccasins would be far more comfortable. He puts on his feet stiff coverings made from hide prepared by a process invented in ancient Egypt and cut to a pattern which can be traced back to ancient Greece, and makes sure that they are properly polished, also a Greek idea. Lastly, he ties about his neck a strip of bright-colored cloth which is a vestigial survival of the shoulder shawls worn by seventeenth-century Croats. He gives himself a final appraisal in the mirror, an old Mediterranean invention, and goes downstairs to breakfast.

Here a whole new series of foreign things confronts him. His food and drink are placed before him in pottery vessels, the proper name of which—china—is sufficient evidence of their origin. His fork is a medieval Italian invention and his spoon a copy of a Roman original. He will usually begin the meal with coffee, an Abyssinian plant first discovered by the Arabs. The American is quite likely to need it to dispel the morning-after effects of overindulgence in fermented drinks, invented in the Near East; or distilled ones, invented by the alchemists of medieval Europe. Whereas the Arabs took their coffee straight, he will probably sweeten it with sugar, discovered in India; and dilute it with cream, both the domestication of cattle and the technique of milking having originated in Asia Minor.

If our patriot is old-fashioned enough to adhere to the so-called American breakfast, his coffee will be accompanied by an orange, domesticated in the Mediterranean region, a cantaloupe domesticated in Persia, or grapes domesticated in Asia Minor. He will follow this with a bowl of cereal made from grain domesticated in the Near East and prepared by methods also invented there. From this he will go on to waffles, a Scandinavian invention, with plenty of butter, originally a Near-Eastern cosmetic. As a side dish he may have the egg of a bird domesticated in Southeastern Asia or strips of the flesh of an animal domesticated in the same region, which has been salted and smoked by a process invented in Northern Europe.

Breakfast over, he places upon his head a molded piece of felt, invented by the nomads of Eastern Asia, and, if it looks like rain, puts on outer shoes of rubber, discovered by the ancient Mexicans, and takes an umbrella, invented in India. He then sprints for his train—the train, not sprinting, being an English invention. At the station he pauses for a moment to buy a newspaper, paying for it with coins invented in ancient Lydia. Once on board he settles back to inhale the fumes of a cigarette invented in Mexico, or a cigar invented in Brazil. Meanwhile, he reads the news of the day, imprinted in characters invented by the ancient Semites by a process invented in Germany upon a material invented in China. As he scans the latest editorial pointing out the dire results to our institutions of accepting foreign ideas, he will not fail to thank a Hebrew God in an Indo-European language that he is a one hundred percent (decimal system invented by the Greeks) American (from Americus Vespucci, Italian geographer).

NOTE

Ralph Linton, "One Hundred Per-Cent American," *The American Mercury* 40 (1937): 427–29. Reprinted by permission of *The American Mercury,* Box 1306, Torrance, California.

STUDY QUESTION

1. Provide five examples of how, in your daily life, you employ something that had its historical origin in a culture that was not invented in the United States. Do not use examples provided in the article.

TWO

The American Cultural Configuration

**LOWELL D. HOLMES AND
ELLEN RHOADS HOLMES**
Wichita State University

As we learned in Professor Linton's article, Americans tend to conveniently take their beliefs and behaviors for granted. Perhaps, with national feelings of superiority, we remain unaware of the patterns . . . configurations . . . that may provide critical insights into what it is to be American. Professors Lowell and Ellen Holmes take us on a journey of introspection . . . a look into some issues that point to the paradoxical nature of American society. What is it to be an "Average American"? Who is the "Common Man or Woman"? Is our society youth-focused with an emphasis on individualism? What do authors and other respected scholars of American culture have to say about issues such as education, technology, nature of the family, and religion?

Lowell D. Holmes is *Distinguished Professor Emeritus of Anthropology at Wichita State University, where he taught anthropology for 32 years. He received his B.S. in English Literature and Ph.D. in Anthropology from Northwestern University, where his major professors were Melville Herskovits, William Bascom, and Francis Hsu. His research has been carried out in Samoa (1953–1954, 1962–1963, 1974, 1976, 1988) and among Samoan migrants in San Francisco in 1977 and 1992. Other interests have been in comparative gerontology and American culture, the latter leading to the development of a course called "The Anthropology of Modern Life," which has remained a popular course at Wichita State for over 25 years. Major publications include* Anthropology, An Introduction *(1965),* Samoan Village *(1974),* Jazz Greats Getting Better with Age *(1986), and* Quest for the Real Samoa *(1987).*

Ellen Rhoads Holmes *taught and served as Academic Coordinator of the gerontology program at Wichita State University until her retirement in 1997. She received her B.A. and M.A. from Wichita State University, and she earned her Ph.D. in Anthropology at the University of Kansas. Research interests and experience include cross-cultural aging, nonwestern homes for the aged, cultural change, the Samoan Islands, and American culture. In addition to articles on Samoan culture and the impact of modernization on the aged, she is coauthor of* Samoan Village Then and Now *(1992) and* Other Cultures, Elder Years *(1995).*

*A*nthropologists today commonly show as much interest in the cultural patterns and processes of their own society as they do in foreign, exotic ones. To non-scientists this might seem strange, and they might ask why, if you live in a society day after day, would you have to research its culture? The answer is, of course, that often the most significant things about the way a people behave are so taken for granted by them that they have difficulty talking about them. Individuals who grow up and live in a particular society are commonly the least aware of its culture.

While there is a significant number of anthropologists who believe that foreign cultures should be studied by one of their own rather than by an intruding foreigner, for many years most anthropologists assumed that it is difficult to be objective about or even fully aware of the details and patterns of one's own culture. It is the old problem of not being able to see the forest for the trees. Much of life for the average individual (of any culture) consists of following certain customary routines and procedures, almost without thinking. Robot-like, our Mr. or Ms. Average American rises at a prescribed hour, dresses in the appropriate way, eats the usual breakfast, and then drives an automobile along the regular route to the office or factory. If there is a detour on one of the streets usually taken, our subject will probably become upset and frustrated at having to utilize an alternate route.

Once at work our Average American participates in the usual job routine, which might have been difficult to learn at first but after a time can be performed with a minimum of thought or imagination. Our friend is quite conscious, however, of the impression he or she makes on the boss because, after all, the important thing is to "get ahead." On weekends it is likely that the family is loaded into the car, and they drive to the church of their choice—probably the denomination in which the parents were raised. The sermon reaffirms many of the beliefs that he or she has always ascribed to, and the phrases of the minister are familiar and orthodox.

Once every four years our Average American exercises a cherished rite that is guaranteed by the Constitution, but in most cases takes little notice of the real political issues at stake. If, for example, our Average American happened to be raised in a Republican family, this is probably the way he or she will vote, and there will be a tendency to find the looks and personality of the party candidate attractive and those of the opposite candidate offensive.

The point that we are trying to make is not that Mr. or Ms. Average American is stupid or abnormal in any way. The point is that he or she is a product of their culture and social environment, and culture provides ready-made solutions to almost all of one's problems. A person doesn't have to think about how and why one does things. It is easier and often more efficient to follow the regularly accepted procedure. That is what culture does for people.

Because it is natural for people to be like this, they find it fascinating when an anthropologist describes how and why they behave in a certain way. After reading about themselves in a monograph on American culture by Margaret Mead, or any number of other anthropologists, they might very well make the comment "She seems to have us pegged pretty well. I just never thought about it that way." The real point is that our Average American seldom stops to analyze his or her own values and motivations at all.

A   C U L T U R E   O F   P A R A D O X E S

The cultural pattern of the United States is one involving numerous paradoxes and ambiguities. This is probably the case in any complex civilization characterized by rapid change. Although we claim to be a peace-loving people, we have fought four major wars and over two dozen limited military actions during the twentieth century, and we spend more to maintain our military preparedness than all the other nations in the world put together. While some would characterize our society as a welfare state others would label it a warfare state. Americans believe in rugged individualism, and yet we have been described as a "nation of sheep." There is a basic belief in human equality and a lauding of the "common man," and yet there is great preoccupation with class, racial, and ethnic differences. On the one hand we express faith in the need for quality education, and on the other we exhibit a general undercurrent of anti-intellectualism and an unwillingness to meet the essential cost of mass education. Americans are great humanitarians full of missionary spirit, but they are frequently hostile to welfare programs, national health insurance, minimum wage legislation, or foreign aid programs designed to relieve human suffering.

The interesting thing about these cultural contradictions is that the opposing attitudes and behavioral patterns cited above do not necessarily represent the views of different subgroups but are found simultaneously in the value system and behavior of the "average" American.

T H E   A V E R A G E   A M E R I C A N

At this point we feel it proper to ask who the Average American is and how one can possibly single out a set of cultural ideas and behavior patterns and maintain that it represents the "American Way." America has long been called a melting-pot nation although it has literally hundreds of subcultures. There are class differences, ethnic differences, racial differences, regional differences, and even occupational differences, but social scientists have come to consider the relatively homogeneous values and customs of middle-class America as being most representative of the American pattern of culture. For example, Alan Wolfe cites polling data indicating that "at no time between 1972 and 1994 did more than 10 percent of the American population classify themselves as *either* lower class or upper class" (1998: 1) And in a 1992 poll, 75 percent of the respondents identified themselves as middle class (Wolfe 1998). In spite of the social and economic complexity of our society the vast majority of Americans like to think of themselves as middle class and to a large extent ascribe to a certain set of values and effect a particular lifestyle. Even those who identify with the lower classes either aspire to middle-class status or use it as a measuring stick for behavior. Robert Bellah et al. maintain that "not only are middle-class values understood and respected, but lower-class people explain their inferior position in terms of circumstances that have prevented them from behaving in a middle-class fashion" (1985: 151). And social scientists generally describe the middle class as having the "real American way of life." They are the families in the suburban row houses, with the brood of well-scrubbed children, the picture window with its ribbon-trimmed lamp, the 30-inch television set, the recreational vehicle parked in the driveway, and on the dinner table, hamburgers or other "bland foods." Such families are particularly puritanical about what they consider "proper," and this culture, with its stress on cleanliness, respectability, hard work, and conformity, is much the same all over the United States. Geographical or regional traditions affect this middle-class pattern very little, and in the South, for example, only the lower and upper classes eat typical Southern food. While visiting in the South the middle-class Northerner will have no trouble finding a meal exactly to his tastes at the local McDonald's, Pizza Hut, Bonanza Steak House, Burger King, Red Lobster, Taco Tico, or Long John Silver restaurant.

The middle class is the set of people who determine our lifestyle, pay the majority of state and federal taxes, vote in and out the politicians and dominate the local and national power structures. It is their support that is courted by the politicians. These are the people who have been referred to as the "silent majority" or the "Establishment" and who therefore are seen as representing what is "normal" and "proper" in American life. Theirs is a pattern of life which is expected to endure in spite of opposition from the radical pressures of the "far left" and the "far right" or from such special crusades as the National Organization for Women, the Gay Rights Movement, or the American Civil Liberties Union.

The middle-class pattern of respectability is primarily that of white, Anglo-Saxon, Protestant America but it has also been adopted by other racial and ethnic groups who have been fortunate enough to "make it." Although some black and brown faces are now evident in suburban areas, few corn-row or dreadlocks hairdos are found on commuter trains. Suburban America has still not completely accepted people of color, but it finds them somewhat more palatable if they keep their lawns well-manicured, drive late-model cars, barbecue in the back yard, and keep their children well-dressed and immaculate.

The middle-class lifestyle represents the image that is most frequently exported by way of U.S. Information Service brochures, World Trade Pavilions, movies and television series. This is also the pattern that social scientists from foreign countries seem to perceive as most typical when they come to America to study our way of life. Although a considerable number of middle-class America's offspring took excursions into the counterculture during the 1960s and early 1970s by "dropping out" or "sitting in," most of these temporary radicals have now returned to the fold, to the Chamber of Commerce, and to the mainstream of American values. The generation gaps have narrowed and the heated dinner-table debates over morality, militarism, ethics, and civil rights have greatly moderated. Young middle-class America has returned to professional educational interests—pre-med, pre-law, nurse's training, computer science, engineering, retailing, accounting—leaving the philosophy, world religions, and literary criticism courses to the more well-to-do or the more impractical of their peers.

CONFORMITY

Numerous American and European observers of American culture have noted the American compulsion to conform. This conformity is of a particular type, however. Margaret Mead (1978) describes our culture as *co-figurative*—meaning that the prevailing model for members of the society is the behavior of their contemporaries. David Reisman et al. (1950), on the other hand, describes our behavior as *other-directed*.

We are concerned primarily with what other people of our social position or age-set have, think, or do, and in order not to appear strange or peculiar, we tend to try to "keep up with the Joneses." We are careful to adhere to popular trends, to join book clubs so we will read the best sellers, to listen to top-20 radio stations so we are familiar with the most popular record releases, and we try to make sure our houses, clothing, and cars are acceptable to our particular social reference group. In the 1960s and early 1970s there was a pronounced pattern of dual conformity—one model for the Establishment and one model for the anti-Establishment or counter-culture. Both were concerned with identification with a particular group and style of life, and both had rigid standards in regard to appropriate dress, values, and loyalties to particular ethical and behavioral codes.

People of all cultures tend to conform, but not always in the ways found in America. Francis Hsu (1963) describes Chinese conformity as *situation-centered* and maintains that Chinese people are psychologically and socially dependent on, and conform to, the family, and not to unrelated peers as is the case in America. Europeans conform also, but more to standards and conventions of the past. While Paris and Rome may represent centers of innovation and vogue in dress design, art, and industrial design, most citizens of these countries seem more concerned with traditional ways than are most Americans. In America advertisers have learned that the way to sell a product is to convince the buyer that it is "new" and "everyone is buying it." Few items of tradition have an equivalent appeal. In England, however, one need only recall the British coronation ceremony with the ancient horse-drawn carriages and their footmen and military escorts in sixteenth-century costume to see how these people respect and dote on the past. Ancient castles, noble families, coats of arms, and ceremonies conferring knighthood are cherished elements of most European cultures. Peasants cling to ancient folk dances, time-tested recipes, and honored customs, and occasionally derive pleasure from donning the costumes of their ancestors. There is a great deal less of this type of thing in America. American centennial celebrations often feature beard-growing contests, but in most cases men neglect their razors on these occasions not so much because their ancestors did, but because everyone else is doing it.

Perhaps the American pattern of conformity is different from that of Europe because of our long-term love affair with the machine. Max Lerner (1957) has suggested that the machine and mass-production methods have certainly made conformism as a way of life easier. To buy and use what everyone else does and to behave and think like everyone else certainly reduces the strain of thinking for oneself. He writes:

> Most American babies are born in standardized hospitals with a standardized tag put around them to keep them from getting confused with other standardized products of the hospital. Many of them grow up either in uniform rows of tenements or of small-town or suburban houses. . . . They are sent to monotonously similar schoolhouses, where almost uniformly standardized teachers ladle out to them standardized information out of standardized textbooks. . . . As they grow older they dance to canned music from canned juke boxes, millions of them putting standard coins into standard slots to get standardized tunes sung by voices with standardized inflection of emotion. They date with standardized girls in standardized cars. . . . They spend the days of their years with monotonous regularity in factory, office, and shop, performing routinized operations at regular inter-

vals. . . .They die of highly uniform diseases, and to the accompaniment of routine plati-
tudes they are buried in standardized graves and celebrated by standardized obituary
notices. (1957: 260–261)

David Potter (1964), on the other hand, believes that America's style of conformity is associated with the belief that everyone is of equal worth and that no one has
a right to impose his/her will on anyone else. But if the majority have adopted an
opinion on a particular matter, anyone who questions the wisdom of that opinion
is, in effect, setting themselves up as being better than the majority. It is an accepted
fact that the majority must not force a person to conform, but it is also that person's
responsibility to voluntarily accept the will of the majority.

The American cultural configuration fosters, in Ashley Montagu's opinion, a
"rigid set of requirements to which children are forced to subscribe by their parents,
teachers, church, peer groups, and other socializing agencies. Under the pressures
of such socializing agencies it is difficult for most individuals to escape becoming
anything other than the echo of other people's voices" (1967: 35).

Not only is individual variation in behavior frowned upon in educational systems
but also in recreational activities. Such group-oriented organizations as Boy and Girl
Scouts, Camp Fire Boys and Girls, Little League, and 4H Clubs offer regulated programs of recreational and educational activities designed to meet the needs of the
"American boy and girl." The assumption is that all young people should enjoy
camping, group games, summer camps, team athletics, and handicrafts. The child
who does not enjoy this kind of program is considered somewhat abnormal, if not
even delinquent. And even young adults are subject to these kinds of pressures.

If Americans cannot make people conform to certain types of standards in any
other way they will pass a law. "There ought to be a law" is a well-known American
cry of anguish. A host of ordinances and laws regulate areas of life that most
European societies view as personal matters. City and state laws regulating adver-
tisement and sale of liquor and tobacco, litter laws, Sunday closing laws, curfews,
and movie and book censorship are but a few of the methods used to produce uni-
formity in thought and behavior. While on the one hand, Americans savagely
demand "liberty" and "freedom," on the other hand, they are constantly restricting
liberty through their own law-making devices.

THE COMMON MAN

The tendency to conform is associated to a certain extent with the American "cult of
the common man and woman." In America some people can admit they are more
fortunate than others but not that they are better than others. While the majority of
our citizens are motivated to "get ahead" socially and economically, it isn't nice to
make too big a point of it. "We are great ones for playing up regional differences,"
writes Robert Heilbroner (1976: 371), "but equally avid on playing down economic
ones. The banker goes out of his way to talk baseball to the gas station attendant.
The richer we are, the more we insist that we are just like everybody else (except
that we pay more taxes)." No one engenders greater enmity than the person who
makes it known that he/she is better than other people. Some of our most popular
public figures—people like Will Rogers, Pete Seeger, Garth Brooks, Willard Scott,
Bill Cosby—have been extremely successful but are admired because they identify

with the common people and in some cases give the appearance that "they haven't got a dime." While equal opportunity seldom is realized by racial minorities, the average American theoretically holds to the precept that all men are created equal. Americans have almost deified log-cabin-born Abraham Lincoln while the wealthy aristocrat George Washington runs far behind in national popularity even though he was the "father of our country."

Many a presidential candidate has learned that if he wishes to succeed in politics he must show the voters that he has something of the common man in him. This has often been achieved by developing a public image that will be well received by farm populations, blue collar workers, and "just plain folks." It would appear that the image of farmer is highly representative of the common man, and President Franklin D. Roosevelt often gave his occupation as "farmer" although his estate on the Hudson was hardly what the average person would consider a farm. Roosevelt was also very much aware that clothes (particularly old ones) can make a president. A common FDR symbol was his battered campaign hat. John F. Kennedy, as well as his brother Bobby, showed their lack of concern for fastidious grooming by wearing no hat at all and letting their hair fly free. President Roosevelt, however, had one urbane habit, and this was a vulnerable point of attack. He used a cigarette holder. No cartoon of criticism ever left out the cigarette holder. Presidential candidate Adlai Stevenson, definitely an urban intellectual, found great difficulty relating to the common man. In spite of numerous pictures of Adlai perched atop a tractor on his Illinois farm, he never quite convinced the people that he really belonged there.

Jimmy Carter presented himself to the voters as the peanut farmer made good with numerous "down home" attributes such as a less than intellectual brother who pumped gas for a living, an evangelist sister, and a personal commitment to a fundamentalist "old time religion" faith. His advisors were all "good old boys" from small towns in Southern states and their "poor but honest" approach to national problems was too much for the Gerald Ford campaign.

Ronald Reagan's 1980 campaign posters presented him in a worn and slightly soiled wide-brimmed felt hat appropriate for doing chores on a small ranch. Reagan's "Aw shucks" rhetorical style plus his stock of popular cliches such as "Win one for the Gipper," "Make my day," and "Tell it to the Marines" created the illusion that a multi-millionaire President was really just one of the common folk. And illusion is very important in politics. Weatherford writes in *Tribes on the Hill,* "When politicians become actors, actors also become politicians. At least the actor is a professional capable of making the performance look genuine" (1981: 268). President Clinton, an expert at down home rhetoric, not only stressed his small town Arkansas background but his capacity to "feel the common man's pain."

While everyone makes a great point of being the common man we also seem motivated to move up the social ladder and show that we are better than average, even if we do have the common touch. our nation abounds with "just plain Joes" trying to get into country clubs with exclusive memberships.

It is a fine line that must be walked. As David Potter observes, "It is permissible for an American to have servants (which is a matter of function), but he must not put them in livery (which is a matter of rank); permissible to attend expensive schools, but not to speak with a cultivated accent; permissible to rise in the world, but never to repudiate the origins from which he rose" (1964: 241).

An excellent example of the wealthy relating to the common man is Bill Gates, the head of Microsoft and the richest man in America, who in 1999 donated one billion dollars for college scholarships for the nation's minorities.

AUTHORITY

One drawback of the "common man" idea is that it makes the exercise of authority difficult when one's role demands it. Pulling rank has always been considered a cardinal sin against American democracy, and probably no army in the world has had greater difficulty in its officer-enlisted personnel relations than the American military. A common remark of GIs in World War II, in response to orders from superiors, was "Why should that guy tell me what to do? All he ever was in civilian life was a shoe salesman." In the Vietnam War, authority problems ranged all the way from movements among enlisted men to establish a practice of electing their officers to actual refusals to accept officers' orders under fire.

Arthur Asa Berger (1973), a social scientist who believes that comic strips are an excellent avenue to cultural value analysis, has examined how military authority is treated in American and Italian comics. Concerning Mort Walker's Beetle Bailey, Berger writes:

> In this strip, currently one of the most popular in America, the common soldier consistently engages in the battle of wits with his superiors and generally emerges victorious. . . .
> It is the enlisted men who have the "upper hand" most of the time because they have the brains and because authority is not seen as valid. The sergeant is a good-natured boisterous glutton, and the lieutenant is foolish and childish. (1973: 47)

But in a "contemporary Italian military strip dealing with the adventures of Gibernetta and Gedeone," writes Berger, there is humor but "a reverential and respectful attitude toward authority."

Some scholars have conjured up some very mystical explanations for this resentment of authority in Americans. They maintain that in rejecting authority, the American is symbolically rejecting the authoritarian European father. It would seem perfectly logical, however, to explain the phenomenon by the idea developed on the frontier and in the colonies that every man was his own master and no person had any right to exert his will over any other. In the New World, a man had to earn his place in society; he couldn't inherit it. An early observer (about 1840), Alexis de Tocqueville, was but one of many historians and social scientists who have pointed out that emphasis on personal autonomy and a distrust of authority are basic requirements in a working democracy. Americans, of course, think of themselves as devotedly democratic.

Not only do the enlisted ranks find it hard to respect the authority of their officers, but officers feel somewhat uneasy giving orders. Frequently, they are rendered completely inadequate for their job because they worry too much about being "democratic" or being viewed as a "good guy."

The problem of authority is also encountered in the world of business and industry. It is not unusual in our culture for the boss to take the office staff out for an evening and act like "one of the boys." Similarly, the factory picnic is a sort of day of atonement, when department heads, foremen, and even the boss take part in the inter-departmental baseball game in order to show that "bossing" is all part of getting the work done, but otherwise bosses are really people after all.

Of all the success stories in America those of the movie star, the pop music performer, and the sports hero are the most cherished by the public. Their appeal lies in the fact that the achievement connotes no authority but still dramatizes the possibility of a rapid rise to fame and fortune through hard work and the kind of opportunity available only in America.

YOUTH AND PROGRESS

America is a country where youth and change are valued on the one hand and distrusted on the other. "What's new?" is almost as frequently asked as "How are you?" and responses to the first question may bring discussions of new dances, new child-raising techniques, new hairdos, new kitchen gadgets, or new public personalities. To keep up with new trends and new ideas is to be young in spirit, and no one in America ever really looks forward to growing old. "Middle age" extends right up to senility or death. In a civilization where each generation is exposed to a whole new set of technological facts and social conditions, elderly people are not respected for their greater experience but rather considered "old fogies" and out of date.

Something of America's youth fetish can be inferred from the fact that Betty Crocker had her sixth face lift in 1986. The imaginary homemaker whose portrait has served as the General Mills trademark since 1936 has been getting younger and younger over the last sixty years. While the 1936 version was middle-aged, the most recent appears barely 30.

The American accent is on youth because the future belongs to the youth of a nation and America is future-oriented. There is no other nation in the world that dotes more over baby pictures, concentrates as much on developing new and different (and often educational) toys for children, or stresses as highly that parents should devote great amounts of their time and energy to seeing that their children are amused and provided with music and dancing lessons or programmed recreational activities. In America, parents usually play the role of spectators while their children take the spotlight. In England and in other European countries in general children are seen and heard as little as possible. When parents have guests, the small fry are relegated to the kitchen where they are expected to stay unless called by the parents, and they are seldom called.

Although America has been the land of the young for a long time, there are indications that this is beginning to change. Because we have greatly reduced the birth rate, and because people are living longer today, the median age of our population promises to rise gradually. In 1990, it was 32.8 years, but by the year 2025 it is expected to be 38.5 years (Kinsella and Taeuber 1992).

An aging population will result in a number of changes, besides the obvious ones involving Social Security financing. In 1977, James Mann and Alexander Astin suggested, for example, that a graying population would eventuate fewer fads in dress and pop music, a decline in junk food popularity, less childish programming on television, fewer traffic accidents and crimes, and revival of more sedate athletic pursuits. They predicted the return of ship cruising and ballroom dancing, and a movement of more and more people to the Sun Belt. As we approach the millennium, only a few of these predictions have come true, in spite of a greatly increased older population. Dress fads are still with us, but some of them are influenced by the preferences for casual clothing of the aging Baby Boom generation. There has been no decline in the popularity of junk food or fast food. A morning visit to almost any McDonald's restaurant will reveal a sizeable gathering of senior citizens having coffee and/or breakfast and conversation with friends. Television programming still caters more to youth than age. However, vacations on cruise ships are indeed more popular, and the Sun Belt states have experienced significant growth, including winter occupation by aging "snowbirds."

In most pre-industrial societies population profiles and culture remain remarkably stable over many generations. Change takes place slowly, and "youth" is synonymous with "inexperience." Government is frequently in the hands of village elders, and the older citizens of a "primitive" society serve as storehouses of tradition and as authorities on proper behavior. In such cultures individuals are secure in their knowledge of culture. There is no question about how children should be reared and disciplined. Proper methods are those their mothers and grandmothers employed.

Such confidence is seldom found in American culture. Each generation lacks confidence in the methods of the former but has no dependable solutions of its own. Since there is no faith in the old solutions, Americans turn to the "experts," but even they cannot agree on such things as how to rear, discipline, and educate children, or what the proper husband-wife relationship should be. There is no lack of advice, however. Every magazine for women has at least one article on one or all of these subjects. Self-styled experts on family problems write syndicated columns and appear on talk shows like Oprah, Leeza, and Montel Williams, and even a number of government agencies will furnish anxious wives and mothers with authoritative literature on these matters at nominal cost.

The anxieties of parents in the area of child-rearing and education are heightened by their desire to provide their children with better opportunities for success than they had. This desire to see that one's children have advantages that were not available to oneself is part of the American faith in progress. It has often been pointed out by students of American culture that the constant pursuit of material wealth is not so much a desire to have things for their own value but rather an attempt to provide evidence for one's friends and neighbors that one is succeeding and getting ahead. Therefore, the $200,000 home or the Mercedes is not valued because it represents, in the first case, additional living space or increased comfort, or in the case of the car, better engineering or better transportation. These material possessions are valued as symbols of hard work, ability, and achievement.

It is inconceivable for a person who identifies with the American middle class ever to refuse to accept a better position with his/her firm whether it means taking on added responsibility, working longer hours, or even selling the house and moving to another community. The prospect of hard work is no obstacle to this average American if there is any opportunity at all to succeed. Hard work is, for Americans, not only a means to an end but to a great extent an end in itself. A survival of puritan philosophy is the association of idleness with sin and industry with virtue. In commenting on this principle, Margaret Mead stated, "Within traditional American culture, leisure is something that has to be earned and reearned, except for the very old . . . . Unearned leisure is something which will have to be paid for later" (1957: 11).

The hard work ethic appears as operative for the younger generation as it was for their parents, despite a temporary lapse during the late 1960s and early 1970s when young people raised in comfortable middle-class homes rejected the ideas of striving for material wealth in favor of promoting such noble causes as the eradication of war, poverty, and bigotry. While these high ideals have not been completely abandoned, a survey of college freshmen in 1976 found 61 percent of men and 45 percent of women maintained that they were seeking the goal of "being well-off financially" while five years earlier only 50 percent of freshman men and 28 percent of women claimed pursuit of such an ambition (Mann and Astin 1977). Two decades later, a report in the *Washington Post* indicated that large numbers of high school students were working 10 or even more hours a week, often to the detriment of their grades. While some claimed to be planning ahead for college, many were using earnings to buy extras and for entertainment (Salmon 1998).

Americans traditionally are content with simple answers to complex questions, and an example is the belief that there is a positive correlation between hard work and success. Although a commonly heard statement is "It isn't what you know, it's who you know," the behavior of most Americans would indicate that the real axiom that motivates their behavior is "It isn't who you know, it's how hard you work." The failure in business is viewed by the mainstream American as an object of contempt rather than of sympathy. America has always liked winners and has believed that everyone is a potential winner if he puts forward sufficient effort.

Still another facet of this work-success belief is the idea of the "self-made man or woman" and the idea of "pulling oneself up by the bootstraps." A large portion of Americans thoroughly believe that anyone can pull off the bootstrap stunt if he really wants to and they refuse to admit that racial type, lack of educational opportunities, socioeconomic background, or sex are obstacles for the really motivated individual. Fortunately, there aren't many self-made people around these days. The concept is, of course, ridiculous. The self-made man is really the egocentric one with the short memory in regard to all the people who have helped him along the way. The bootstrap concept of self-help is still with us, however. The great popularity of charm schools, positive thinking and assertiveness training, manuals of how to succeed in business, and executive leadership courses testify to the strength of the belief in some circles that people can become more popular and more successful with a minimum of direction and instruction. With a little know-how they are prepared to take it from there.

It was pointed out earlier that while America values youth and welcomes change, both are looked upon with a certain amount of suspicion. While the generation gap has been around for a long time, there was probably no time in history when the average parent and his adolescent or young adult offspring have been farther apart in the basic ideological frames of reference than in the late 1960s and early 1970s. Representative of this communication chasm is the exchange quoted by Margaret Mead in *Culture and Commitment: The New Relationships Between the Generations in the 1970s.* She records a typical elder's remark: "You know, I have been young and you never have been old." But then she quotes an equally typical young person who counters, "You never have been young in the world I am young in, and you never can be" (1978: 33). The world that the youth is referring to is, of course, very different from the one in which his father and mother gained their experience for living. It is a world of hydrogen bombs, space exploration, world-wide satellite communication, air and water pollution and energy crises.

During the 1960s this existential awareness prompted the emergence of a set of values and a configuration of behavior which social scientists labeled the "counter-culture." Theodore Roszak described it as a "cultural constellation that radically diverges from the values and assumptions that have been in the mainstream of our society at least since the scientific revolution of the seventeenth century" (1969: xii).

Symptomatic of this new cultural perspective were the civil rights movements (involving demonstrations, boycotts, and civil disobedience) of the early 1960s, the student revolts which began in the mid sixties, and the anti-war sentiments and demonstrations which continued up until the American withdrawal from Vietnam in 1975, although the Nixon White House had announced in 1970 that nothing the young could do or say would influence public policy in any way.

The avant-garde of this movement for cultural revision had been a small minority of college and high school young people who were the sons and daughters of those middle-class parents whose traditional value system and behavioral patterns are the subject of this article on the American cultural configuration. Margaret Mead referred to this group as the "children of electricity and electronics who believed they could make the world new overnight." They were accustomed to pushing buttons "so there would be light" (1978: 95).

A major reason why this configuration of values and behavior developed is explained by Mead as being associated with the creation of a massive generation gap between those born and raised before the advent of the atomic bomb and those who grew up under the shadow of its holocaustic potential. Wars had now become for the first time in the history of mankind a proposition where everyone stood to lose everything. Mead explains,

> As the world became one inter-communicating whole, the experience of all those, every-where on earth, reared in the post-World War II world, became a shared experience and differentiated them from all their elders. The colleges and universities had exploded under the pressure of their fresh vision. Empowered by this freshness and by the new ethics of shared responsibility, sufficiently alienated from the Establishment—from all establish-ments—the post war generation demanded a changed world. (1978: 100)

But what has happened to the counterculture today? The end of the Vietnam War in the spring of 1975 brought an end to the draft and to anti-war demonstrations, but then there were financial problems associated with a deepening economic reces-sion. Jobs became scarce and so did the quotas for law and medical schools. Now the children of the upper middle class were faced for the first time with a very per-sonal problem—how to make a living. Students on college campuses gave up the luxury of philosophy, English literature, and art appreciation courses and began to take accounting, industrial education, and business administration. No longer was there outspoken opposition to out-outmoded methods and undemocratic university procedures. Mead describes that university environment, an environment drastically different from that surrounding the dissenting countercultures:

> Activists are almost as rare as they have traditionally been on American campuses. Undergraduate life is again seen as a perpetuation of adolescence, a postponement of choice, or where a professional choice has been made, for a determined pursuit of its aca-demic requirements. Saving the world, like earning a living, can be postponed until later—when once out of law school, one can take up advocacy or out of medical school,

one can work for free clinics. . . . The new graduates will not retire to the suburbs any more than their predecessors did. The campuses look more like the 1950s but the questioning on the campuses of the 1960s is still with us. (1978: 107)

While the end of the Vietnam War brought changes to the college campus, a survey taken just two years after the end of the war indicated that although undergraduates had a greater tendency to think of themselves as "middle-of-the-road" rather than liberal, 78–80 percent supported "liberal" positions on energy, pollution, consumer protection, women's rights, student autonomy, and legalization of marijuana (Mann and Astin 1977).

A number of observers of the American cultural scene today believe that the ferment of the 60s is lying dormant and could be revived again given the right set of circumstances—perhaps over an issue such as nuclear power, environmental pollution, intervention in foreign military conflicts, or administration policy on affirmative action or civil rights.

THE PARADOX OF EDUCATION

One of the simple answers that Americans have singled out to solve complex problems is that almost any social problem can be solved through education; and most Americans value the type of education that most directly deals with practical problems. Parents often object to their children majoring in philosophy, history, or anthropology because, after all, "What can you do with the kind of an education?" Training in medicine, law, engineering, computer science, or business administration can clearly be seen as avenues leading to good jobs and the material wealth that symbolizes success. There is less emphasis on what one learns in college than on what one can do professionally with a college diploma. There have even been those who were "smart" enough to short-cut the whole process by purchasing a sheepskin from a "diploma mill" and therefore have not had to waste all that time being educated. Much is made also of the monetary value of a college degree. In 1996, the median annual income of a college graduate was $55,137; for a high school graduate, $32,295 (U.S. Bureau of the Census 1998).

Although there is great faith in the necessity for education in America, it can hardly be said that we have a nation of scholars. People in this country read book reviews and digests of articles, rather than spending the time with the original. While every English and French hamlet has at least one book store, it is almost impossible to find such an establishment in most of the small towns of America unless it's a college town. A poll taken several years ago of international reading habits sought to discover how many people were currently reading a book. In England the figure was 55 percent; in Germany 34 percent; in Australia 33 percent; and in the United States the figure was a pathetic 17 percent.

Intellectuals have been much publicized in this country as "egg-heads," impractical dreamers, or just plain eccentrics, and they are frequently suspected of being subversives. Many states insist that educators at all levels take loyalty oaths to state or national constitutions while the same demands are not made of ministers, lawyers, doctors, or business people. College professors are generally pictured in movies and on television series as absent-minded, cloistered, and terribly impractical. Parents of college students are often resentful of the fact that professors engage in research rather than just parroting the findings of others to their students.

A number of churches look upon colleges and college professors as corrupters of young people's faith and morality, and in the state of Kansas in 1999 the State Board of Education came out against teaching evolution at all public schools. Jules Henry believes "there is no more vulnerable white collar group than educators. For the most part without unions—subject to the whims of principals, superintendents, boards of education, and local parent organizations—elementary and high-school teachers stand unprotected at the bottom of one of the most extended pyramids of power in the country" (1971: 160).

Although there is faith in what education can do to increase the prospects for success for one's children, there is also a reluctance to pay for education. Teachers as a group are the lowest paid professional people in America, and the defeat of school bond issues at the polls has become more the rule than the exception. While many citizens find no difficulty in purchasing a new car every year, they think that the cost of a college education for their son or daughter is nothing less than bankrupting.

TECHNOLOGY — THE SACRED COW

America is a machine-and-computer culture. It is a culture where machines think, talk, teach our children, put people out of work, inform on us when we are lying, predict the outcome of elections from 2 percent of the returns, and carry us through space on missions to the moon at 18,000 miles an hour. This is a country where improving education means buying more overhead projectors, video equipment, tape recorders, and computers. And at home the students' families have three times as many motor vehicles, VCRs, and television sets, and twice as many telephones as any single country in Europe, including England.

Technology influences our national policy, our motor behavior, our ideas of cleanliness and punctuality, and it influences our whole philosophy of life and our world view. Howard Stein contends that technology is our "impersonal animism and personal deity. Our love (and love-hate) affair with our machines and computers resembles the so-called 'primitives' love affair with Nature, Fate and the Cosmos" (1985: 8).

Of all the cherished technological artifacts in the United States, none is more loved than the automobile. Berger suggests that "the automobile dominates us economically as well as physically, and has affected the pattern of our housing (the suburb), consumption (the shopping center), and even our sense of who we are in the world—and where we are going" (1973: 166). He further submits,

> There may be an inverse correlation between a person's sense of "self" and the size of the engine in his car. People who feel petty and insignificant, for whatever reason, may need gigantic V-8s, and people who feel weak may need "muscle" cars. Choosing options for cars may be one of the few ways left in which individuals can make decisions that count, and for many it is the only means at their disposal for displaying creativity, as well as status. (1973: 168)

Ours is a nation that places high value on energy, efficiency, orderliness, and precise measurement, and much of this can be directly attributed to the machines that we control and the machines that control us. Marshall McLuhan (1951) once suggested that our answer to a machine world was to become one, and Howard Stein maintains, "Believing ourselves to be machine-like, we create machines to be replicas of ourselves, only to conclude that the human mind is a computer and the body is a sublimely engineered specimen of machinery." (1985: 8).

It is interesting to note how when seven astronauts reached out for technological progress and failed in our worst space disaster, the values of the "common man" and the "work ethic" were called upon in the creation of a moving eulogy. *Time* reporter Paul Gray (1986) wrote about the Challenger tragedy:

> They would not have seemed out of place at a supermarket check-out or standing in line to see a movie. They could have come together by chance just about anywhere in the United States. Nothing odd here, in this assemblage of sexes and ethnic strains and religions, except maybe the extraordinary American experiment in equality inching forward for the nation and the world to see, and being taken largely for granted.
>
> They were, all of them, human like us. Their courage and ambition took root in the familiar, sustained by circumstances and routines that everyone can recognize. On that last morning they were in pre-flight isolation but still a part of us. They got up and dressed, had breakfast and went to work. (1986: 32).

When the authors of this chapter were doing anthropological research in the Samoan Islands they became aware of two kinds of time—*"fa'asamoa* time" and "white man's time." *"Fa'asamoa,"* or "the Samoan way" time was far from being precise, because it tended to be calculated by the position of the sun or the length of shadows. Whether a Samoan's calculations were a half hour or so in error didn't make too much difference, because the nature of the culture was such that there was little need for keeping appointments at a precise time. On Sunday morning, church services were supposed to start at eight o'clock, but no one really minded if the church bell rang at seven o'clock or at nine. There was not a single thing in the culture that had to be done exactly at an appointed hour.

The same lack of precision was also found in lineal measurement. The length of a man's forearm or the length of a man's outstretched arms (the fathom) were sufficient standards of measurement. Houses varied a bit in size because of the various sizes of carpenters' forearms, but no one got very upset over this. Measurement in the production of a finely balanced machine must, on the other hand, be accurate to the thousandth of an inch. One would hate to ride in a commercial airliner, for example, that had been built on the basis of forearm measurements. Mass production of complex products with interchangeable parts must feature precision and accuracy.

It is interesting to see how this necessity for precision has been transferred to American culture in general. The batting ability of baseball players is measured quantitatively down to the third place past the decimal point. Weather forecasters tell us that there is a 65 percent chance of rain within the next 24 hours. Each of us has been assigned a social security number, a car registration number, a driver's license number, a zip code number, an area code number, and a dozen or more credit-card numbers.

Many American mothers believe that the feeding of infants must be by strict schedule even if it means waking the baby at a definite time during the night. People do not sleep until they are rested; they attempt to get eight hours of sleep as though that were a magic number. And for years the bottlers of Dr. Pepper specified on the bottle and in all their advertisements that the soft drink should be consumed precisely at 10, 2, and 4.

Our educational system also bows to technology. To begin with we have gotten into the habit of referring to college graduates as "products" of their *alma mater*, and to a large extent the university is a large assembly line wherein individual professors are expected to perform their specialized function on the student and send him down the line to the next specialist. In most schools letter grades have a corresponding numerical equivalent. As are worth four points, Bs three points, etc. Upon graduation a grade-point average such as 3.548 is recorded in the student's record. Far too often a student may lose a valuable scholarship to graduate school because some other student surpassed him in his grade-point average by two or three thousandths of a point. The giving of grades is a most subjective task, to say the least, but once the grades are recorded and averaged, the result becomes an infallible, precise "measurement" of the student's academic and intellectual ability.

The wealth of American technical knowledge has without doubt created a more comfortable existence for its citizens—that is, up to now. But it has made America into a "throw-away" culture, notorious for its capacity for waste. Marya Mannes (1962) asks what future archeologists some hundreds of years hence may find as the monuments of our civilization. She writes,

> And what will we leave behind when we are long dead? Temples? Amphora? Sunken treasure? Or mountains of twisted, rusted steel, canyons of plastic containers, and a million miles of shores garlanded, not with the lovely wrack of the sea, but with the cans and bottles and light bulbs and boxes of a people who conserved their convenience at the expense of their heritage, and whose ephemeral prosperity was built on waste. (1962: 167)

THE INDIVIDUAL VERSUS THE FAMILY

Eighty years ago the American had a much greater sense of family than he does today. In the 1920s more than half of our households had an additional adult relative in residence. Today only 5 percent of homes have a grandmother, uncle, unmarried sister or some such kinsman living in. Many Americans have never even met all of their cousins and aren't particularly upset about it. The family reunions of yesterday are now rare, and when they occur they are often a source of stress. In the old days, families tended to be localized, and reunions were occasions when relatives could get together and compare crop successes and failures. With the geographical mobility of people today, when such get-togethers occur the various family members are so different in their interests and occupations that there is little to talk about.

In his book *Clan, Caste and Club* anthropologist Francis Hsu (1963) pointed out that the American family is definitely individual centered and that personal happiness is stressed over family welfare or family solidarity. Recent evidence documents an even greater emphasis on individuality at the expense of family structure. According to Bronfenbrenner, "Although family is a core institution the world over, for most Americans it takes a back seat to the 'individual.' We talk about disadvantaged *individuals*, *individual* achievement, discovering ourselves as *individuals*, and 'the *individual* vs. the state'" (1977: 39).

In America, marriages are contracted to make two individuals happy; not for economic, political, social, or procreative reasons as in other societies. Based largely on the principle of romantic love, marriage is in effect a continuation of courtship.

There is a constant need for the marriage partners to keep reassuring their spouses that they still care. One of the worst crimes in domestic life is to take one's husband or wife for granted. Wives become upset when their husbands forget anniversaries or birthdays, and husbands believe that their wives should "fix themselves up" in preparation for the husband's arrival home from work. Going out now and then to eat in a restaurant and perhaps also to take in a show is very much like the couple's courtship and is considered vital to the happiness of the wife.

The "happiness marriage," based as it is on a fragile foundation of romantic love and personal independence, could become an endangered species. Not only are divorces three times as frequent today as 30 years ago, with nearly half of modern marriages destined to dissolve, but interest and attention devoted to care of children has been greatly curtailed. Less and less affection is forthcoming from parents.

Our lack of interest in children is also reflected in national policy, in spite of Congressional pronouncements that it is pro-family. The United States is the only industrialized nation in the world whose government does not ensure health care or a minimum income for every family with young children and the only one that has not established a program of childcare services for working mothers.

Indeed, the members of the American family see that social unit as a source for obtaining personal happiness. The partners marry for happiness, refrain from or have children for happiness, and have little concern for family tradition or continuity. The family is something to be exploited rather than sacrificed for. Why are we like this? Alexis de Tocqueville once said that our zeal for democracy and personal freedom made us so. In *Democracy in America* he wrote,

> Among democratic nations new families are constantly springing up, others are constantly falling away, and all that remain change their condition; the woof of time is every instant broken, and the track of generations effaced. . . . As social conditions become more equal, the number of persons increases who, although they are neither rich nor powerful enough to exercise any great influence over their fellows, have nevertheless acquired or retained sufficient education and fortune to satisfy their own wants. They owe nothing to any man, they expect nothing from any man; they acquire the habit of always considering themselves as standing alone, and they are apt to imagine that their whole destiny is in their own hands.
>
> Thus not only does democracy make every man forget his ancestors but it hides his descendants and separates his contemporaries from him; it throws him back forever upon himself alone and threatens in the end to confine him entirely within the solitude of his own heart. (1899, Vol. 2: 105–6)

RELIGION IN AMERICA

America is primarily a Protestant Christian nation with roots well planted in a Puritan tradition. Census data from 1997 indicated American religious preferences as being 58 percent Protestant, 26 percent Roman Catholic, and 2 percent Jewish (U.S. Bureau of the Census 1998). It took 184 years for the people of this country to bring themselves to elect a Roman Catholic president, John F. Kennedy, and then there were grave misgivings, particularly among Protestant clergy. Over 80 percent of directorships of banks, insurance companies, and colleges are held by Protestants. America has a long history of Protestant denominations because the value system of its people find Protestantism more acceptable than Roman Catholicism. Americans have never been much for ceremony or ritual, they tend to reject authority and rigid, absolute doctrine, and they will not tolerate an institution that is controlled in part by foreigners. There are in America more than 75 distinct religious bodies. Free to interpret the Bible as they see fit, each of these groups has placed special attention on certain interpretations. Many represent splinter groups from the major denominations or, in some cases, entirely new denominations. The demand for doctrinal freedom appears to be basic in America. Bellah et al. note its presence even in the eighteenth century:

> Thomas Jefferson said, 'I am a sect myself,' and Thomas Paine, 'My mind is my church.' Many of the most influential figures in the nineteenth century American culture could find a home in none of the existing religious bodies, though they were attracted to the religious teaching of several traditions. One thinks of Ralph Waldo Emerson, Henry David Thoreau, and Walt Whitman. (1985: 233)

The independent spirit of Americans is seen in many other aspects of religion. There is relatively complete separation of church and state, and a lack of an established church such as the Church of England in the British Isles, the Lutheran church in Sweden, or the Roman Catholic church in Spain. Furthermore, even among the major denominations, seldom is there any central authority or control. In nearly all American churches (including the Catholic) there is a great deal of district and church autonomy. Most churches are quite democratic and often give lay officials as much or more power than the ministers. Still another aspect of the opposition to authority is the tendency in many churches not to require theological training for religious leaders. People without any formal religious training establish churches of their own or declare themselves evangelists.

Being great advocates of tolerance and fair play, Americans generally believe in religious freedom. People tend to respect the rights of others to worship as they wish, although they may disagree violently with their beliefs. Whether or not they want an individual of a certain denomination in a position of authority or government is another matter.

In spite of frequent references to America being a Christian nation, and in spite of the high proportion (67 percent) of adults claiming church or synagogue membership, students of American culture agree that America is not a particularly religious nation. In 1997 only 40 percent indicated attendance at religious services (U.S. Bureau of the Census 1998). With the exception of certain rural areas, where the church continues to influence the social and moral aspect of life, religion tends to be a Sunday-morning phenomenon. Generally, religious precepts have little influence on business ethics or social issues. The organized church all too frequently stays aloof from political struggle and tends to support public opinion. Some of the basic principles of Christianity—the brotherhood of man, the renunciation of struggles for riches and worldly goods—are not popular causes in America, and therefore very little is said about these things from the average pulpit.

A 1976 national survey conducted by the Knight-Ridder newspaper syndicate found that those who identified themselves as having "strong religious convictions"

1. Did not consider themselves "liberals."
2. Felt civil rights progress was proceeding too fast.

3. Favored laws against abortion.
4. Believed that jobs were available for those who wanted them.
5. Were for restricting free speech when its content is obscene.
6. Believed that the solution to crime is more severe penalties.
7. Were against reducing marijuana penalties.

Many churches go out of their way to cultivate a wealthy membership. Those white pastors who have taken strong stands against segregation or other forms of social injustice are in the minority, and they find little support in their congregations.

Generally churches provide a comfortable atmosphere with emphasis on maintaining the status quo. Local religious leaders don't take stands on certain moral issues for fear it will offend members of the congregation who will then sever their membership connections. One major denomination recently reported a loss of more than 250 ministers in a two-year period. When asked why they left the ministry, a large share of them listed dissatisfaction or disillusionment with the organized institutional church. Individual ministers commented on their congregation's "greater interest in building, real estate, and statistics than in people" or on the "smallness, insincerity, and untruthfulness of church people."

Demands for change in religious attitudes and practices have become vital issues among a new breed of theological students and young clergymen who have become critical of the failure of the organized church to address itself to the urban and racial crises and to the moral question of American military involvement.

Critics of the organized church in America claim that too much time is spent on social activities and group fellowship. Men's clubs, ladies' aid societies, scout troops, bowling teams, young people's recreation groups, athletic programs, and fellowship dinners have come to be recognized as essential parts of any church program, although they may be quite unrelated to the spiritual activities of the church. In regard to the fellowship aspect of American religion, Harry Golden wrote, "The first part of a church they build nowadays is the kitchen. Five hundred years from now people will dig up these churches, find the steam tables and wonder what kind of sacrifices we performed" (1955: 295).

An editorial in *The Economist* following the James Jones flock tragedy at Jonestown, Guyana, speculated on the meteoric rise of religious cults in recent years. It explained,

> The last third of the twentieth century is a period in which the familiar forms of organized religion have lost their hold on most . . . members of the educated middle class. . . . This is probably the first time in history in which . . . to be intelligent and educated is also to be without religious belief.
>
>   The disintegration of the old religious institutions has not produced a world in which everybody is contented to live in the confines of an existence without gods. . . . The market place of religious innovation is one of the last and best examples of free enterprise in the world today. (1978: 11)

Demands for new forms of spiritual experience have spawned a startling number and variety of cults, some of which recruit and hold their membership through disturbing techniques of social conditioning and mind control. When orthodox religion decays, those who most hunger for the certainty of faith often find it in groups like the Unification Church, The Way, Hare Krishna, or the Branch Dividians of Waco, Texas. *The Economist* reported that when seeking God in a secular world "it is all too easy to blunder into the arms of Satan instead" (1978: 11).

Americans generally do not think deeply about religion. With the exception of a few professors and students of theology, there is little searching or questioning of religious beliefs. Most Americans are content to accept the interpretation and traditions of their denomination. Like swallowing a capsule, no chewing is required. A great number of Americans are quite ignorant, however, of the doctrine of their own denomination, although they are quite sure that it is better than the others.

While most social scientists agree that Americans are not particularly religious, they also feel that they are not anti-religious. Our country has never experienced any anti-clerical movements. Our pastors and priests, although poorly paid, are usually treated with respect. Those who do not participate in the activities of a church tend to do so out of indifference rather than opposition to religion.

RESOLVING THE PARADOXES

At the beginning of this chapter a number of cultural contradictions was cited. Although social scientists have long recognized and discussed these apparent paradoxes, few have provided any explanation of how or why they exist. This very perplexing matter is, however, discussed in articles (1961, 1966) and in a book (1953) by Francis Hsu, an anthropologist of Chinese extraction, who in his many articles and books on American character has proved to be a very competent observer and theorist.

Hsu maintains that many of our cultural contradictions can be understood in terms of a single important core value, *self-reliance,* which is primarily manifested in a fear of dependency. Self-reliance is considered the key to all individual freedom, and it is the ruler by which Americans measure all mankind. Self-reliant people consider themselves their own masters, controlling their own destinies through their own hard work and planning. Since the American seems to adhere to the "bootstrap" theory, people who are forced to collect welfare money or the dependent aged are viewed with hostility and are considered misfits. Absolute self-reliance denies the importance of others and explains the rather unique phenomenon of the "self-made man." This denial of the value of others has a tendency to produce instability in ascribed relationships within the family and in achieved relationships such as between business partners or between husbands and wives.

American self-reliance prompts people to compete and to value individualism on the one hand but demands conformity on the other. In order to be deemed a success, a person must belong to the right status-conferring organizations, but to do so one must conform to their standards and involve him- or herself in their time- and energy-consuming organizational activities.

Self-reliance is also indirectly responsible for the coupling of such laudable values as Christian love, equality, and democracy with the less desirable values of religious bigotry and racism. This is because religious affiliation in the United States and in the West generally has become mostly a matter of associational affiliation. The successful person is drawn to the successful church that others of similar social position attend. Hsu believes that the church is most frequently valued because of its social importance and this consideration greatly overshadows its doctrinal position or spiritual qualities.

The history of Western religion is believed to have always been marked by a search for original purity in both ritual and belief, and this has led to the Reformation, the rise of multiple denominations, and even the Holy Inquisition. Dr. Hsu asserts that:

> This fervent search for and jealous guard over purity expresses itself in the racial scene as the fear of genetic mixing of races which feeds the segregationist power in the North as well as in the South. . . . When religious affiliations have become largely social affiliations, this fear of impurity makes religious and racial prejudices undistinguishable. (1961: 222–223)

In an open society like America there are no fixed or permanent places in the social structure. People have an opportunity to climb, but so do others who are below them socially or economically. Thus, self-reliant persons are afraid of being contaminated by those considered inferiors. They can be accepted as long as their upward mobility is prevented, but when they have the opportunity to share desks in their child's school, live in their neighborhood, or share the pews in their church as equals, insecurity mounts. Since discrimination against particular racial or socio-economic groups runs contrary to both democracy and Christian theology, the self-reliant American must disguise their objections. In the South they have evaded the real issue by stressing states' rights and in the North by stressing property values.

The only security in a society stressing self-reliance is in personal success, superiority, and personal triumph, but unfortunately these achievements must of necessity be based upon failure or defeat of others, for there can be only one winner in every race. People are not valued for their mere participation.

In spite of its several shortcomings self-reliance is the key to progress. Because of this emphasis, the United States and the West generally have prospered and developed a great technological and industrial civilization. Leaders of developing nations are beginning to realize that if they wish to compete for recognition with Western nations they will have to develop the value of self-reliance in their people. Thus we have the final paradox—that the core value of American culture, self-reliance, is parent to both the best and the worst that are in us.

REFERENCES

Bellah, Robert, Richard Madsen, William M. Sullivan, Ann Swidler, and Steven M. Tipton. 1985. *Habits of the Heart.* Berkeley, CA: University of California Press.

Berger, Asa. 1973. *The Comic Stripped American: What Dick Tracy, Blondie, Daddy Warbucks and Charlie Brown Tell Us about Ourselves.* New York: Walker.

Bronfenbrenner, Urie. 1977. The American Family in Decline. *Current* (January): 39–47.

de Tocqueville, Alexis. 1899. *Democracy in America,* Vol. II. New York: Knopf. (Vintage ed. 1954).

Economist, The. 1978. The Role of Religious Cults. (November 25): 11–13.

Golden, Harry. 1955. Personal Journal. *The Carolina Israelite* (May).

Gray, Paul. 1986. Seven Who Flew for All of Us. *Time* (February 10): 32.

Heilbroner, Robert. 1976. Middle-class Myths, Middle-class Realities. *Atlantic Monthly* (October): 37–42.

Henry, Jules. 1971. Is Education Possible? In *Anthropological Perspectives in Education.* Murray Wax, S. Diamond, and F. Gearing, eds. New York: Basic Books.

Hsu, Francis L. K. 1953. *Americans and Chinese: Two Ways of Life*. New York: Schuman.

___.1961. American Core Value and National Characters. In *Psychological Anthropology*. Hsu, F. L. K., ed. Homewood, IL: Dorsey Press.

___.1963. *Clan, Caste and Club*. Princeton, NJ: Van Nostrand Company.

___. 1966. The United States and China: Psychological Factors for Mutual Isolation. *Northwestern Review* 2 (Fall): 2–10.

Kinsella, K., and C. M. Taeuber. 1992. *An Aging World II* (U.S. Bureau of the Census, International Population Reports, P-25, 92–93). Washington, DC: Government Printing Office.

Lerner, Max. 1957. *America as a Civilization*. New York: Simon and Schuster.

Mann, James, and Alexander Astin. 1977. The End of the Youth Culture. *Current* (November): 3–7.

Mannes, Marya. 1962. Wasteland. In *Man Alone: Alienation in Modern Society*. Eric and Mary Josephson, eds. New York: Dell Publishing Co.

McLuhan, H. Marshall. 1951. *The Mechanical Bride*. New York: Vanguard Press.

Mead, Margaret. 1957. The Pattern of Leisure in Contemporary American Culture. In *The Annals of the American Academy of Political Science: Recreation in the Age of Automation*. Paul Douglas, John Hutchinson, and Willard Sutherland, eds. Philadelphia: American Academy of Political Science.

___. 1978. *Culture and Commitment: The New Relationships between the Generations in the 1970s*. New York: Doubleday Anchor.

Montagu, Ashley. 1967. *The American Way of Life*. New York: Putnam.

Potter, David. 1964. Individuality and Conformity. In *The Character of Americans*. Michael McGriffert, ed. Homewood, IL: Dorsey Press.

Riesman, David, N. Glazer, and R. Denny. 1950. *The Lonely Crowd*. New Haven: Yale University Press.

Roszak, Theodore. 1969. *The Making of a Counter Culture*. Garden City, NY: Doubleday.

Salmon, Jacqueline. 1998. Their Money or Their Life. *The Washington Post National Weekly Edition* (August 27): 19.

Stein, Howard. 1985. *Psychoanthropology of American Culture*. New York: Psychohistory Press.

U.S. Bureau of the Census. 1998. *Statistical Abstract of the United States* (118th ed.). Washington, DC: Government Printing Office.

Weatherford, J. McIver. 1981. *Tribes on the Hill*. New York: Rawson, Wade Publishing Co.

Wolfe, Alan. 1998. *One Nation, After All*. New York: Viking.

STUDY QUESTIONS

1. What are some of your own cultural behavior patterns that might appear strange or exotic to someone from a foreign culture who is studying American behavior?

2. Can you envision any of your own cultural beliefs and actions that might be considered paradoxical?

3. What is an "average" American? Do you consider yourself to be an average American with middle-class values?

4. Do you agree with Max Lerner's assessment that Americans conform to the degree that thinking for oneself is greatly reduced?

5. How are your own personal liberties and freedoms restricted by federal, state, or local laws?

6. Can you think of any public figures whom you respect for having the qualities of the common man or woman? Have there been, in your own experiences, authority figures whom you respected?

7. How do you feel about the road to success being not due to hard work or what you know but due to who you might know?

8. Do you believe that machines are controlling your life and are rapidly changing the traditional cultural values?

9. How do you explain the fact that over 50 percent of American marriages end up in divorce?

10. Why can't we generally consider the United States to be a particularly religious nation?

11. In which ways, according to Francis Hsu, can we understand many of our own cultural contradictions in terms of the single core value of self-reliance? Do you agree with the authors that self-reliance "is parent to both the best and the worst that are in us"?

THREE

Body Ritual
Among the Nacirema

HORACE MINER

Professor Horace Miner discovers a culture bound by many strange beliefs and habits. Where else in the world do we find a culture, believing that the human body is ugly, totally devoted to shrines and rituals to overcome this predominant configuration? The conduct of these peoples' exotic behaviors, in many ways both sadistic and masochistic, is investigated by a highly respected anthropologist. The findings were published in the prestigious American Anthropologist.

Horace Miner (1912–1993) received his A.B. from the University of Kentucky and his Ph.D. from the University of Chicago in 1939. Miner began his training as an archaeologist, but shifted to cultural anthropology during his graduate training. He began his teaching career at Wayne University in 1939. His academic career was interrupted by the Second World War, in which he served with distinction. In 1946 he became an assistant professor of sociology at the University of Michigan. Subsequently, he received an appointment at the Museum of Anthropology at Michigan. Miner is best known for his work in Africa, but also did significant research in Canada and Iowa. Among his best known publications are St. Denis: A French Canadian Parish *(1939),* Culture and Agriculture *(1949),* The Primitive City of Timbuktu *(1953), and* Oasis and Casbah: Algerian Culture and Personality and Change *(1960). Although he made notable contributions to applied and psychological anthropology, he is probably best known for the article included in this collection.*

The anthropologist has become so familiar with the diversity of ways in which different peoples behave in similar situations that he is not apt to be surprised by even the most exotic customs. In fact, if all of the logically possible combinations of behavior have not been found somewhere in the world, he is apt to suspect that they must be present in some yet undescribed tribe. This point has, in fact, been expressed with respect to clan organization by Murdock (1949: 71). In this light, the magical beliefs and practices of the Nacirema present such unusual aspects that it seems desirable to describe them as an example of the extremes to which human behavior can go.

Professor Linton first brought the ritual of the Nacirema to the attention of anthropologists twenty years ago (1936: 326), but the culture of this people is still very poorly understood. They are a North American group living in the territory between the Canadian Cree, the Yaqui and Tarahumare of Mexico, and the Carib and Arawak of the Antilles. Little is known of their origin, though tradition states that they came from the east. According to Nacirema mythology, their nation was originated by a culture hero, Notgnishaw, who is otherwise known for two great feats of strength—the throwing of a piece of wampum across the river Pa-To-Mac and the chopping down of a cherry tree in which the Spirit of Truth resided.

Nacirema culture is characterized by a highly developed market economy which has evolved in a rich natural habitat. While much of the people's time is devoted to economic pursuits, a large part of the fruits of these labors and a considerable portion of the day are spent in ritual activity. The focus of this activity is the human body, the appearance and health of which loom as a dominant concern in the ethos of the people. While such a concern is certainly not unusual, its ceremonial aspects and associated philosophy are unique.

The fundamental belief underlying the whole system appears to be that the human body is ugly and that its natural tendency is to debility and disease. Incarcerated in such a body, man's only hope is to avert these characteristics through the use of the powerful influences of ritual and ceremony. Every household has one or more shrines devoted to this purpose. The more powerful individuals in the society have several shrines in their houses and, in fact, the opulence of a house is often referred to in terms of the number of such ritual centers it possesses. Most houses are of wattle and daub construction, but the shrine rooms of the more wealthy are walled with stone. Poorer families imitate the rich by applying pottery plaques to their shrine walls.

While each family has at least one such shrine, the rituals associated with it are not family ceremonies but are private and secret. The rites are normally only discussed with children, and then only during the period when they are being initiated into these mysteries. I was able, however, to establish sufficient rapport with the natives to examine these shrines and to have the rituals described to me.

The focal point of the shrine is a box or chest which is built into the wall. In this chest are kept the many charms and magical potions without which no native believes he could live. These preparations are secured from a variety of specialized practitioners. The most powerful of these are the medicine men, whose assistance must be rewarded with substantial gifts. However, the medicine men do not provide the curative potions for their clients, but decide what the ingredients should be and then write them down in an ancient and secret language. This writing is understood only by the medicine men and by the herbalists who, for another gift, provide the required charm.

The charm is not disposed of after it has served its purpose, but is placed in the charm-box of the household shrine. As these magical materials are specific for certain ills, and the real or imagined maladies of the people are many, the charm-box is usually full to overflowing. The magical packets are so numerous that people forget what their purposes were and fear to use them again. While the natives are very vague on this point, we can only assume that the idea in retaining all the old magical materials is that their presence in the charm-box, before which the body rituals are conducted, will in some way protect the worshipper.

Beneath the charm-box is a small font. Each day every member of the family, in succession, enters the shrine room, bows his head before the charm-box, mingles different sorts of holy water in the font, and proceeds with a brief rite of ablution. The holy waters are secured from the Water Temple of the community, where the priests conduct elaborate ceremonies to make the liquid ritually pure.

In the hierarchy of magical practitioners, and below the medicine men in prestige, are specialists whose designation is best translated "holy-mouth-men." The Nacirema have an almost pathological horror and fascination with the mouth, the condition of which is believed to have a supernatural influence on all social relationships. Were it not for the rituals of the mouth, they believe that their teeth would fall out, their gums bleed, their jaws shrink, their friends desert them, and their lovers reject them. (They also believe that a strong relationship exists between oral and moral characteristics. For example, there is a ritual ablution of the mouth for children which is supposed to improve their moral fiber.)

The daily body ritual performed by everyone includes a mouth-rite. Despite the fact that these people are so punctilious about care of the mouth, this rite involves a practice which strikes the uninitiated stranger as revolting. It was reported to me that the ritual consists of inserting a small bundle of hog hairs into the mouth, along with certain magical powders, and then moving the bundle in a highly formalized series of gestures.

In addition to the private mouth-rite, the people seek out a holy-mouth-man once or twice a year. These practitioners have an impressive set of paraphernalia, consisting of a variety of augers, awls, probes, and prods. The use of these objects in the exorcism of the evils of the mouth involves almost unbelievable ritual torture of the client. The holy-mouth-man opens the client's mouth and, using the above mentioned tools, enlarges any holes which decay may have created in the teeth. Magical materials are put into these holes. If there are no naturally occurring holes in the teeth, large sections of one or more teeth are gouged out so that the supernatural substance can be applied. In the client's view, the purpose of these ministrations is to arrest decay and to draw friends. The extremely sacred and traditional character of the rite is evident in the fact that the natives return to the holy-mouth-men year after year, despite the fact that their teeth continue to decay.

It is to be hoped that, when a thorough study of the Nacirema is made, there will be a careful inquiry into the personality structure of these people. One has but to watch the gleam in the eye of a holy-mouth-man, as he jabs an awl into an exposed nerve, to suspect that a certain amount of sadism is involved. If this can be established, a very interesting pattern emerges, for most of the population shows definite masochistic tendencies. It was to these that Professor Linton referred in discussing a distinctive part of the daily body ritual which is performed only by men. This part of the rite involves scraping and lacerating the surface of the face with a sharp instrument. Special women's rites are performed only four times during each lunar month, but what they lack in frequency is made up in barbarity. As part of this ceremony, women bake their heads in small ovens for about an hour. The theoretically interesting point is that what seems to be a preponderantly masochistic people have developed sadistic specialists.

The medicine men have an imposing temple, or *latipso*, in every community of any size. The more elaborate ceremonies required to treat very sick patients can only be performed at this temple. These ceremonies involve not only the thaumaturge but a permanent group of vestal maidens who move sedately about the temple chambers in distinctive costume and headdress.

The *latipso* ceremonies are so harsh that it is phenomenal that a fair proportion of the really sick natives who enter the temple ever recover. Small children whose indoctrination is still incomplete have been known to resist attempts to take them to the temple because "that is where you go to die." Despite this fact, sick adults are not only willing but eager to undergo the protracted ritual purification, if they can afford to do so. No matter how ill the supplicant or how grave the emergency, the guardians of many temples will not admit a client if he cannot give a rich gift to the custodian. Even after one has gained admission and survived the ceremonies, the guardians will not permit the neophyte to leave until he makes still another gift.

The supplicant entering the temple is first stripped of all his or her clothes. In every-day life the Nacirema avoids exposure of his body and its natural functions. Bathing and excretory acts are performed only in the secrecy of the household shrine, where they are ritualized as part of the body-rites. Psychological shock results from the fact that body secrecy is suddenly lost upon entry into the *latipso*. A man, whose own wife has never seen him in an excretory act, suddenly finds himself naked and assisted by a vestal maiden while he performs his natural functions into a sacred vessel. This sort of ceremonial treatment is necessitated by the fact that the excreta are used by a diviner to ascertain the course and nature of the client's sickness. Female clients, on the other hand, find their naked bodies are subjected to the scrutiny, manipulation and prodding of the medicine men.

Few supplicants in the temple are well enough to do anything but lie on their hard beds. The daily ceremonies, like the rites of the holy-mouth-men, involve discomfort and torture. With ritual precision, the vestals awaken their miserable charges each dawn and roll them about on their beds of pain while performing ablutions, in the formal movements of which the maidens are highly trained. At other times they insert magic wands in the supplicant's mouth or force him to eat substances which are supposed to be healing. From time to time the medicine men come to their clients and jab magically treated needles into their flesh. The fact that these temple ceremonies may not cure, and may even kill the neophyte, in no way decreases the people's faith in the medicine men.

There remains one other kind of practioner, known as a "listener." This witch-doctor has the power to exorcise the devils that lodge in the heads of people who have been bewitched. The Nacirema believe that parents bewitch their own children. Mothers are particularly suspected of putting a curse on children while teaching them the secret body rituals. The counter-magic of the witch-doctor is unusual in its lack of ritual. The patient simply tells the "listener" all his troubles and fears, beginning with the earliest difficulties he can remember. The memory displayed by the Nacirema in these exorcism sessions is truly remarkable. It is not uncommon for the patient to bemoan the rejection he felt upon being weaned as a babe, and a few individuals even see their troubles going back to the traumatic effects of their own birth.

In conclusion, mention must be made of certain practices which have their base in native esthetics but which depend upon the pervasive aversion to the natural body and its functions. There are ritual fasts to make fat people thin and ceremonial feasts to make thin people fat. Still other rites are used to make women's breasts large if they are small, and smaller if they are large. General dissatisfaction with breast shape is symbolized in the fact that the ideal form is virtually outside the range of human variation. A few women afflicted with almost inhuman hypermammary development are so idolized that they make a handsome living by simply going from village to village and permitting the natives to stare at them for a fee.

Reference has already been made to the fact that excretory functions are ritualized, routinized, and relegated to secrecy. Natural reproductive functions are similarly distorted. Intercourse is taboo as a topic and scheduled as an act. Efforts are made to avoid pregnancy by the use of magical materials or by limiting intercourse to certain phases of the moon. Conception is actually very infrequent. When pregnant, women dress so as to hide their condition. Parturition takes place in secret, without friends or relatives to assist, and the majority of women do not nurse their infants.

Our review of the ritual life of the Nacirema has certainly shown them to be a magic-ridden people. It is hard to understand how they have managed to exist so long under the burdens which they have imposed upon themselves. But even such exotic customs as these take on real meaning when they are viewed with the insight provided by Malinowski when he wrote (1948: 70):

> Looking from far and above, from our high places of safety in the developed civilization, it is easy to see all the crudity and irrelevance of magic. But without its power and guidance early man could not have mastered his practical difficulties as he has done, nor could man have advanced to the higher stages of civilization.

REFERENCES

Linton, Ralph. 1936. *The Study of Man.* New York: D. Appleton-Century Co.
Malinowski, Bronislaw. 1948. *Magic, Science, and Religion.* Glencoe: The Free Press.
Murdock, George P. 1949. *Social Structure.* New York: The Macmillan Co.

STUDY QUESTIONS

1. What is the precise geographical location of this strange tribe, the Nacirema?
2. What are the private and secret shrines of the Nacirema?
3. Who are the Nacirema's holy-mouth-men?
4. What is the *latipso* used by Nacireman medicine men?
5. Who is the witch-doctor "listener" who is able to cure bewitched people?
6. Is Miner's interpretation of Nacirema body rituals ethnocentric? Why or why not?

FOUR

Professor Widjojo Goes to a Koktel Parti

WESTON LABARRE

An eminent African anthropologist analyzes the apparently strange customs at American rituals that he has an opportunity to directly observe. Of course, his only reference points are those from his own cultural background. In observing others, we tend to contrast their behavior to our own value systems. Thus, the visiting scholar's efforts at understanding the rituals of the American "drinking season" may be lacking in culturally relativistic clarity. One would wonder how the visitor to America would view other customs or perhaps interpret the drinking habits of Usan college students and dating rituals.

Weston LaBarre (1911–1996) *received his A.B. from Princeton and his Ph.D. from Yale in 1937. LaBarre taught at Rutgers University and at Duke University, where he was the James B. Duke Professor of Anthropology for many years. He was a prolific writer and had exceptionally broad interests and research experiences. He considered himself to be a psychiatrically oriented anthropologist, but is equally well known for his work on religion. LaBarre's major publications are* The Peyote Cult *(1938),* The Ayamara Indians of Lake Titicaca Plateau, Bolivia *(1948),* The Human Animal *(1954),* They Shall Take Up Serpents *(1962),* The Ghost Dance: Origins of Religion *(1970),* Muelos: A Stone Age Superstition about Sexuality *(1984), and* Shadow of Childhood: Neoteny and the Biology of Religion *(1991).*

"Of course," mused Professor Widjojo, the eminent anthropologist of the University of Nyabonga, "the natives of the U.S.A. have many strange and outlandish customs; but I must say the drinking rituals of the Usans impressed me the most. These rituals occur yearly during an extended period in the calendricai round, beginning at the time of the harvest rites of Thanks-for-Blessings and ending largely at the drinking bouts at the New Year. This is called The Season, after which those who can afford it usually leave their homes entirely and flee southward into retirement for recuperation."

"Rather like our Nyabongan puberty ordeals?" asked a brilliantly dark matron dressed in a handsome apron of tiki feathers and little else.

"Well, no, not exactly," said Professor Widjojo, fingering his nosestick politely before replying. "Perhaps I could describe it best by telling you of the Usan *koktel parti,* as they call it. You know. of course, that the Usan women, despite their rigid tribal clothing taboos, in general take off more clothes at their gatherings, depending upon the time of day. The neckline drops more and more, both in front and in back, as the *parti* is held later and later in the evening. They are entirely covered in the day-time, but this night-time disrobing is considered to be more formal. At the same time the length of the skirt increases, until it reaches the ground or even drags on it.

"On the other hand, men put on more and more clothes as the formality of the occasion increases. The interesting point, however, is that the men, at *koktel partis,* do not ordinarily wear the beetle coats and white cloth neck-chokers of their most formal rituals, but dress rather more moderately as for church; furthermore, the women keep their hats on at *koktel partis,* thus clearly establishing the ritual significance of the *koktel partis.*

"Social status is indicated by the number of *partis* that a couple is invited to attend—and, of course, wealth, since a woman cannot wear the same dress and hat to more than one *parti.* People complain bitterly at the number they have to go to—sometimes even during the *parti* they are attending—but it is nevertheless plain that they are proud of their ability to sustain many ordeals, and this is a form of polite boasting. This point comes out most clearly in the *aignawg partis* when they are heard to boast, after they have stayed long enough at one to save face, that they must 'get on' to a number of other New Year *partis* before midnight. They always say they 'hate to go' though it is plain that they would really hate to stay.

"Not that these other rituals are any different, or that they provide escape from the ordeal," continued Professor Widjojo, "for at all of them the natives receive the same ritualized drink called *aignawg.* Everybody hates it, and freely says so in private, but they must drink some of it so as not to offend their hostess. Despite the superficial phonetic resemblance, *aignawg* has no connection whatever with eggs. It is really skimmed milk, made commercially and thickened with seaweed jelly; and the cream, if any, is whipped and placed on top of the handled cup they must drink it in.

"The ordeal aspect of the ritual is indicated in the fact that the hostess presses more and more cups upon her guests, who must pretend to praise the virtues of the drink—but even more so in the fact that they sprinkle *nutmaig* powder on top which, in larger quantities, of course is a violent poison inducing fainting, convulsions and death. But this *aignawg* has only enough *nutmaig* on it to make the people ill for several days. The Usan natives pride themselves on 'holding their liquor' so that this ceremony is plainly a contest between a hostess and her guests.

"But I am getting ahead of my chronology. Really, the drinking season of the Usans begins in the fall of the year, after a wholesome summer vacation, at the time of the *futbol* games. The purpose of the Usan colleges is to collect young men by competitive subsidies to engage in these mock battles, during which they rush ferociously at one another wearing padded armor and ritually kill one another. It seems to be some sort of contest over a sacred pigskin, and everyone gets up alive after each act in the ceremony. Rarely is a young man killed. However, the warriors are often 'punch-drunk' (an odd phrase because they are not allowed to drink, in contrast with spectators) and they may suffer broken legs, or faces mutilated by the nailed shoes of their opponents.

"Colleges seem once to have been trade schools where tribal lore was taught, but this was long ago and is now hardly remembered. The importance of a college nowadays is rated by the number of *futbol* games its team wins, and this in turn attracts further desirable young warriors to that college. The watchers urge on the warriors with blood-curdling chants, and between acts there are military maneuvers of a more rigorous form than in the battle itself. Afterward, they either celebrate their victory or 'drown their sorrows' in mourning if the warriors have sustained too many broken bones to win.

"These *futbol* ceremonies seem to be totemistic celebrations mainly, for each side has an animal totem—such as a bulldog, a tiger or a goat—which symbolizes the mystical unity of each side in their oddly named *alma mater*, or 'protective mother,' probably so called because she is the patron mother goddess of the young warriors frequently invoked in the battle hymns at these war games. Strangely, however, these totems do not govern marriage rules either inside or outside the *alma mater* group. I collected figures on this critical matter and found it is about as common to marry outside one's totem as within. In fact, *futbol* games are a recognized way to meet young people belonging to another totem."

"Are there totems governing marriage in the *koktel* gatherings you mentioned earlier?" asked a young girl just past her puberty ceremonial.

"No, I would think not," replied Professor Widjojo, thoughtfully. "On the contrary, the *koktel partis*, more resembles a primitive orgy, with no reference to marriage bonds whatever. You see, as a point of etiquette husbands and wives do not remain near one another at *koktel partis*, but circulate around making conquests. After a few drinks, the males display their 'lines,' which are ritualized ways of approaching the brightly decorated and painted females—a strange custom, incidentally, since it is the males naturally who ought to be painted, as among us Nyabongans.

"The sexual nature of these ceremonies is shown in the magic plants called *mislto* which they hang up at these winter rituals in particular. These are parasitic plants with white berries that grow on oak trees—both of which have symbolical significance—but they are by no means necessary as a sanction or encouragement for pawing and kissing, especially at a New Year's *koktel parti* in full swing. The idea seems to be to crowd as many people together as possible, to increase inescapable physical contacts. Many times people moving restlessly about in search of new partners spill drinks on one another's fine clothes, and then the person who does this is allowed to rub the other ritually with a pocket-cloth, pretending to be much distressed at the accident."

"Are these **koktel partis** always orgies?" inquired a plump, middle-aged Nyabongan man.

"Not entirely, perhaps," replied Professor Widjojo. "There is one which is called a *literari koktel*, the ostensible reason for which is to celebrate the birth of a new book. Naturally, no one ever discusses the book being celebrated, since no one has read it, although everybody expresses a readiness to analyze it critically. Mostly, the people talk about their own books, past, projected or purely conjectural. They allude meaningfully to the amount of their royalties, complain about editors and publishers, mention their translation into Japanese and other languages, including the Scandinavian, and make the most they can of some tenuous dickering for movie rights or 'coming out in paperbacks.' *Literari koktel partis* are mainly an opportunity to advertise books other than the one by the publisher giving the *parti*. At these there is much *karakter-as-asination*, or verbal witchcraft, designed to decrease the sales of rival authors and to increase one's own reputation for cleverness of expression and literary insight."

"Do the same people always go to one another's *partis?*" asked the tiki-attired matron.

"Well, this is largely the case," said the distinguished Nyabongan anthropologist. "However, hostesses complain proudly of the number of 'people we hardly know' whom they invite to their *partis*. The reason for this is probably owing to the fact that both host and hostess are too busy seeing that drinks are replenished to have more than a few words with any one person. But it is a matter of prestige, as guests, to meet the same people briefly at two successive rituals on one evening, and in this manner they can gather more people they hardly know for their own next gathering.

"Hostesses also compete with one another in exotic foodstuffs. Smoked oysters, fish pastes, rare fish eggs, sea-spider and shrimp purées are commonplaces, as are foreign cheeses; the successful hostess is one who uses something like *kashu-nut* butter on new and unfamiliar wafers before these in turn become commonplace. Some like to present new drink mixtures with names like Rag-Pickers' Toddy or Purple Nose or Longshoreman Slugger, but mostly *koktels* are of the same few types, like Manhattans (named after an island off the Usan mainland to the east), poured into an inverted conical or hemispherical stemmed glass—quite unlike the *aignawg* cup—with an onion or a stuffed olive or a cherry, which of course no one is required to eat, this being a sign of naiveté. Sometimes there are 'tall ones,' so called because of the long glass cylinders they are served in. But all these drinks contain some sort of drug that makes the people fatuous, foolish, talkative, tearful or amorous."

"Where does this word *koktel* come from?" another interested Nyabongan listener inquired.

"Well, literally, the word means the hind feathers of a male chicken or cock," replied the professor. "But, though Usan natives readily admit this derivation upon questioning, no one seems to know why they are called this. They claim that *koktels* began only as late as the Nineteen Twenties when they were forbidden and had to be obtained in secret ritual underground chambers called *speekeezies* or from *butlaigers*."

"But don't the Usans get exhausted running from one *koktel parti* to another, especially in this restricted season?"

"Oh, yes, and they frequently say as much," answered the Nyabongan savant. "There is another institution, though, that is protectively exploited in these circumstances. This is the *baybisitter*. The Usans do not have the extended family that we Nyabongans do, but live in one-family units called houses or apartments. For this reason they have to hire a *baybisitter* to take care of the children in their absence; of course, they couldn't bring the children to these ceremonies, because they would be trampled underfoot in their crowded ritual chambers.

"The word does not mean, despite its form, that they hire a *baybi* or infant to sit, for these persons are often someone else's grandmother. It seems, rather, that they hire someone to sit on the *baybi*, to prevent its destroying the furniture while they are gone. *Koktel*-goers are able to invent the most fantastic and transparent excuses involving these *baybisitters* which require the imminent presence of the parents back home. Other parents at the *parti* commiserate, though disbelieving these excuses, and the couple is allowed to leave without losing face."

"Strange people, these Usan natives," said the fat, middle-aged Nyabongan.

"That they are, that they are!" echoed Professor Widjojo, touching his nosestick thoughtfully.

STUDY QUESTION

1. What other Usan rituals in which you participate would a foreign visitor interpret as Professor Widjojo did?

FIVE

An Outsider's View
of American Culture

JANUSZ L. MUCHA
Nicolaus Copernicus University, Torun, Poland

A frequent visitor to America, Professor Mucha compares his European idea of the "city" to what he discovered in the United States. The immediate and informal cordiality of Americans is also discussed, as is urban anonymity, the profane naturalness of violence, patriotism, education, ethnocentrism, and the American potluck dinner.

Janusz L. Mucha is a professor of Sociology at Nicolaus Copernicus University, in Torun, Poland. He received an M.A. in Sociology, an M.A. in Philosophy, a Ph.D. in Humanities, and a Habilitation Degree from the Jagiellonian University of Cracow, Poland. He also studied as a postdoctoral fellow at the Johns Hopkins University; the Bologna Center in Italy; the Taras Shevchenko University in Kiev, Ukraine; the University of Wisconsin; and the University of Chicago. His primary fields of interest are urban communities of Native Americans and Polish-Americans and the symbolic anthropology of Polish society.

It is quite difficult to look at American culture with a fresh eye. One can easily become bewildered or upset, especially if one comes from a country where America has been treated as something special. And, in my case, having an education based on American sociology, cultural anthropology, and social psychology, having read all the classics of American literature, and having watched many movies, both classic and modern, directed by both foreigners and Americans, confusion about the culture persists. Further, this being my fifth time in the United States, having lived for months in big cities like Chicago and New York, in small towns like Stevens Point, Wisconsin, and South Bend, Indiana, I have had an opportunity to view, firsthand, the diversity of American culture.

Having the experience mentioned, liking America, and being rather flexible, I see how one can easily lose the sense of novelty of first contact and view this initial contact through later experiences. Ultimately, one too easily begins to treat everything as normal; one attempts to understand everything, perceive the causes of everything that is going on, and frame one's observations and experiences into some structural and functional context.

Nothing bewilders or upsets me in America. After all these years I still see things that are different here than they are in both my native Poland and the many other countries that I have visited. Unfortunately, these observations are neither novel nor original: They are, or at least should be, obvious to many people, foreigners and Americans alike.

I love nature, but I am a city boy. I was born and raised and had lived for forty years in Cracow, a medieval university town of a half million inhabitants in southern Poland. An urban environment is very important to me. This is something I miss in America. The idea of the "city," as I conceive it, hardly exists in America. My idea of "city" can be found in parts of three American cities: San Francisco, New York, and New Orleans. There is a noticeable lack of an urban environment in America. I do not refer here to the fact of the deserted, burned-out, or depopulated parts of cities. I have noticed many empty, run-down apartment houses that would be put to good use in Poland. What I refer to is the physical and social structure of the towns and cities of America. It is the exception in America to have the excellent public transportation found in Vienna, Paris, London, and even Warsaw. In many American cities there are not even sidewalks: The people rarely walk, so why invest in sidewalks? If one jogs, one can use the street or roadway. American drivers understand the use of the roads for exercise and, unless a driver is drunk, there's not much risk.

Not only are there no sidewalks, there are no squares where people can safely gather, meet other people, talk, or buy flowers. There are no coffee shops like in Vienna, Rome, or Budapest. If you want coffee, you must drive to McDonald's or go to a restaurant. If you walk beyond the environs of "downtown," or the shopping mall, you will most likely be stopped by a police officer who will, if you are white, offer to assist you. But how can the officer be of assistance? Can he or she give you a ride to a real café? Can he or she return you to the "downtown" that, after dark, is most often both unsafe and deserted? There is no such thing as a real theater, and the movie theaters are back at the shopping mall, far removed from the empty downtowns of America.

Numerous sociologists and cultural anthropologists tend to identify American urban life with anonymity, the lack of primary groups and face-to-face contact, with only superficial and formal relationships. How do I see America? I have experienced a lot of friendliness and kindness in America. Everyone wants to help me, to thank me for calling or for stopping by. Everyone seems to care about me. When I make new acquaintances, including the dental hygienist, everyone addresses me by my first name, and I can be certain that he or she will make every effort to pronounce it as correctly as possible. Very soon, I discover that I am learning many intimate details of the personal lives of the people I have just met. I find myself a bit embarrassed, but I doubt that they are. They become my friends so quickly, and as quickly they begin to share their problems with me. There are, in the English language, the nouns *colleague,* and *acquaintance,* but I do not discover them to be in popular use. In America, when one meets someone, he or she immediately becomes a *friend.* Does this mean, for instance, that you can expect to be invited to his or her home for dinner or to just sit and talk? Absolutely not. I have often been invited to dinner, but perhaps I have been fortunate in meeting a different type of American. My brother, who teaches Russian and Polish at a Texas university, had not been invited to anyone's house for dinner during the entire academic year. My American friend, who teaches history in a New England college, had not been invited to anyone's home during her first year in the small college town. Therefore, I am forced to conclude that quality friendships in the sense of lasting, intimate, emotionally involving relationships are more difficult to develop.

In reference to the anonymity of urban life, as I have mentioned earlier, urban "life" hardly exists. There are neighborhoods, however, and "urban villagers" reside therein. Is this anonymity a feature of these neighborhoods? I do know, at least by the faces, everyone who lives in my own neighborhood in South Bend. If I do not recognize someone, I can tell whether that person "belongs" to my neighborhood. If a nonresident is in the neighborhood, he or she will be singled out immediately. It is possible that a patrol car will stop and a police officer will kindly ask the stranger to produce identification. A black person obviously cannot rely on anonymity in a predominantly white neighborhood. Neighborhoods do not want anonymity. The neighbors, in this instance, want to know everyone, to be able to address everyone by his or her first name, to be able to say "hello," and to ask how one is doing. And, as I've learned, they prefer the answer to be brief and positive: "I am fine, thank you."

An obvious reason for this fear of urban anonymity is the problem of security. However, the lack of anonymity does not imply that the relationships are truly friendly in the deeper sense of the word. The neighbors know each other, but they do not visit each other's homes to sit and talk, to exchange recipes, to borrow household tools, or to help if the automobile is not running. In this age of telephones, neighbors do not ordinarily just stop by unexpectedly.

American society is famous for the brutality of social life. The high rate of violent crime is incomprehensible. Rapes, female battering, child abuse, and molestation are the lead stories for local television and the print media. This information about violence has many positive consequences. If we wish to fight something, if we want to prevent crime, we must be aware of it. However, the constant forced awareness—the information on why and how someone was killed or raped—accustoms Americans to violence. They treat it as something natural, as just another case of a person killing or being killed. Violent death or abuse belongs to the profane, ordinary world of America. There is nothing sacred about it, unless it is the residual fear that it can also happen to you. On the other hand, death of natural causes is almost completely removed from everyday lives. Old people die in nursing homes or hospitals, and even this type of death, in being generally ignored, does not belong to the sphere of the sacred.

The fact of violence in everyday American life has numerous social consequences. One consequence is the decline of urban life. Americans have now accepted the fact that downtown areas, after dark, belong to the criminals or misfits. Americans accept the fact that strangers may be dangerous. Americans, thus, try to avoid downtown areas and strangers, especially at night.

Patriotism is another feature of American life that appears to differ from many European countries. I have been exposed to patriotism for the greatest part of my life. However, Polish patriotism, or nationalism, is different. Poland was, for forty-five years, under Communist rule, which was, to some extent, accepted, although the majority of Polish society treated it as alien domination. The Communists monopolized the use of national symbols. In the mid-1970s, the ruling party made it illegal to use these symbols without special permission by the state authorities. I can recall the unauthorized use of national symbols only within the religious context. I have never seen a Polish national flag in a private residence. Only once in my life did I see an eagle, the Polish national symbol, in a private residence. From my interpretation, the old national symbols became identified with a state that was not treated as the true embodiment of the national institutions. In America, state and nation are symbolically identified, and, moreover, nearly everyone feels the necessity to emphasize his or her identification with nation or state. I will not elaborate on the yellow ribbons in evidence during the Persian Gulf War, but it seems to me necessary to mention the presence of the American flag in most residences, offices, and clubs I have visited. Further, Lions Club lunches, university graduations, basketball games, and so on all begin with the singing of the national anthem.

Is there anything wrong with these public displays of patriotism? I do not believe so. However, the use of national symbols on an everyday basis has, in my opinion, two questionable consequences. First, the meanings of these symbols are shifting from the sacred to the profane, ordinary, everyday sphere of life. Second, the public display may indicate a strong degree of ethnocentrism. Excessive patriotism, pride in country and its achievements, may signify—and I am convinced that this is true in America—a very strong and blinding conviction that the American ways are much better than the ways of other countries and peoples. After all these years, after all these arrivals and departures, and after all these meetings with many Americans in Poland and in other countries of Europe, my impression is that American people, especially as visitors to foreign areas, are friendly but arrogant. They are arrogant in the sense that they do not understand non-American customs and habits, they do not even try to understand, and they are convinced that other customs "must" be much worse simply because they are not American. Americans are friendly in the sense that they would sympathize with other people; they would pity them and give them advice on how they should elevate themselves . . . to become more American.

What are the reasons for this general behavior and attitude? One reason is that the American educational system does not promote general knowledge about the United States and other countries. Personally, I am not of the opinion that education is the best solution to *all* social problems. Moreover, I believe that the significance of education is often exaggerated by politicians and mass media. However, American students at the grade school, middle school, and high school levels do know *much* less than students their ages outside of the United States. How can students learn more if no one demands that they learn more? I used to participate in monthly faculty meetings of the College of Liberal Arts and Sciences at a state university. Each month, a part of the agenda was a discussion of the admission policy. Should we accept candidates who cannot read, write, and calculate? Eventually, we continued to accept these deficient students . . . to a university! Their knowledge of their own country is minimal and inadequate. Their knowledge of other parts of the world is practically nonexistent. This may be the foundation for Americans' deep convictions that their ways are superior. They know little of their own country and less about other countries. What little they know is evidently the basis for their unquestioned views.

Another reason for the "friendly arrogance" of Americans may be their relative parochialism. The United States is so large and diverse that it is very difficult to learn much more than something of one's own state and, perhaps, neighboring states. Geographically and culturally (regions, ethnic groups), the United States is indeed so diverse that one can travel and study it for years, always learning something new and interesting. But, from my point of view of the whole of humankind, this big and diverse nation is only one relatively homogeneous spot on a map, a spot in which nearly everyone speaks the same language, can stay at the same type of hotel or motel, eat in the same type of restaurant, and shop at the same kind of supermarket. People living in Europe have a much better opportunity to appreciate the world's cultural diversity and to become much more relativistic than Americans. Europe remains a continent of natural cultural diversity, and the differences in the European educational system help in developing a relativistic attitude toward other peoples and customs. Naturally, not all Europeans take advantage of their educational opportunities, and they too often remain as rigidly ethnocentric as many educated Americans.

A third reason why the American is generally more ethnocentric than the average European is the nature of mass media. Reading American dailies (with perhaps the exception of the *New York Times, Chicago Tribune, Washington Post, USA Today,* and a few others), we get an impression that the entire world consists of some extension of the United States. In weekday editions, we rarely learn of the world beyond the Atlantic and Pacific Oceans, or even north and south of the nation's borders. In the case of an assassination of a public figure, a revolution, a minor war, or a significant natural catastrophe, we may learn something of the world beyond the borders. On a regular basis, we learn very little of other countries. I have discovered that educated people are not certain if Poles use the Latin or Cyrillic alphabet, if the Polish language is distinct from Russian, or if the Poles had their own army during the Communist regime. Even interested people are often of the opinion that Hungarians are Slavs and that Lithuanians and Latvians speak Polish or Russian. These facts are common knowledge to the people of Europe, but how could Americans know these things? Schools do not teach them, and the newspapers are more interested in a recent rape in Florida than in the economic, political, and cultural situations of their neighbors in Mexico or Canada.

American television does not help much. "Headline News" and "CNN" provide information about the rest of the world on a regular basis, but the major networks do not, unless, as we discover in the print media, there is news of a sensational nature. Local television stations inform mostly on local crimes or local economic and political happenings, such as the daily whereabouts of the president or governor. For local television, the world is further restricted, ending at the borders of the county.

Every teacher can provide many examples of the blatantly inadequate knowledge of many Americans about the world beyond the county. I offer two examples. An intelligent female student in a course, Principles of Sociology, was very active during the discussions and once volunteered to present a report based on a selection from Emile Durkheim. She came to me before the presentation and complained that it was too difficult. She had happened on a foreign word, *solidarity*. She was even unable to pronounce the word correctly. She did not understand and was curious to know why Durkheim had used the word, which was coined much later, somewhere in Eastern Europe, to describe a political movement. She could not recall the context in which she first learned of the word and, further, in her own town, there was no such thing as "solidarity."

A second example is about another intelligent female, a minority student enrolled in my course, Race and Ethnic Relations. After two weeks of the semester she came to me with a problem: How is it possible that some other students are able to answer some of my questions about racial and ethnic situations in the United States if these particular issues were not presented in the textbook? She was very sad because she knew everything about her town and actually believed that nothing was different than it was in her own social milieu.

During my current visit to the United States, I have, in addition to teaching at the university, been studying a Polish community in a relatively small town. Both as a university professor and as a researcher, I participated in many parties of a more-or-less formal nature that were organized by individuals and various institutions. Nearly always, I went to these parties with my wife. Two things stand out from these gatherings. One was the way people greeted us. Sometimes we simply said hello, but most of the time we shook hands. But, by "we," I mean only myself and the host. Never that I recall, during the entire year, was my wife offered a hand in greeting or farewell. At the beginning, she was quite offended but then began to accept it as a local custom. I am certain that no one intended to offend her. Everyone was friendly to both of us. Why was she treated differently? Was it sexism? I inquired to learn if someone could explain and was told that this was a kind of custom. We do have different customs in Poland.

Another thing that surprised me was that private parties, but not formal dinner parties, were nearly always of the potluck character. The guests were expected to bring their own beverages and specialties. This does not happen in Poland. One may bring flowers (in the United States, women seemed to be deeply embarrassed when I brought them flowers) and/or a bottle of wine, vodka, or brandy. *No one* brings food. The host would be offended. But in America, not only do people bring food but they can take the leftovers home. Many years ago, the first time I experienced this custom, I did not know what to say. I had brought a bottle of very good Polish vodka to an American friend, but it was too strong for the participants of the party. The people tasted it, perhaps out of courtesy. When I departed, the host gave me the bottle, nearly full, to take with me. For a long time I did not know if I was given a message that I had brought something bad or improper. The next time, I brought a six-pack of beer and we drank all of it.

There was an additional surprise in store for me. My wife and I organized a potluck party for my departmental colleagues. One couple brought a homemade cake. Because they had to leave earlier than the other guests, they asked my wife to give them what remained of their cake. My wife was shocked. The fault was clearly mine. I forgot to tell her what to expect.

When I studied the Polish-American community, I participated in more formal dinners, as well. Some dinners were held by upper-middle-class associations of men and women. Sometimes, but rarely, these dinners were organized in restaurants. Mostly, however, dinners were served in large Polish-American clubs. Participants were dressed up: Men, mostly professionals or from the business community, were in suits; the women wore elegant dresses. The "equipment" was of a different nature. The tables were simple, the table cloths were of paper, and the plates were paper or plastic, as were the glasses. There were no separate plates for dessert. Dessert was thrown on next to the roast beef and potatoes. After dinner, the disposable plates and glasses were rolled into the table cloth and discarded. After dinner, coffee was drunk sitting at a formica table.

This is obviously an example of American efficiency and convenience. Paper table coverings and plastic plates, knives, forks, spoons, and glasses are always in evidence. Now, here in America, we have potluck lunches at work, and now my wife and I also use the products of American chemical expertise when we throw a party.

The difference is that, for us, the use of the fake stuff is a problem, especially when the real stuff is so readily available. And, having noticed the dish-washing machines in most of the private houses, we are further confused.

I am led to wonder. American ingenuity, from all quarters addressed to labor-saving devices, serves to free its citizens from the tedious and time-consuming labors of everyday life. This provides free time, perhaps more free time than available in any complex, industrialized society. Why don't Americans devote a portion of this free time to learning something more about the world within and without their own provincial borders?

NOTE

I would like to thank my wife, Maria Nawojczyk, and my brother, Waclaw Mucha, for their helpful comments with this paper.

STUDY QUESTIONS

1. What are the major human and structural differences that Professor Mucha discovered between American cities and cities in Europe?
2. How does the author justify the contention that "urban 'life' hardly exists"?
3. What may be an interpretation of American public displays of patriotism?
4. What is implied as the consequences of "friendly arrogance"?
5. What are some of the reasons why the author found Americans to be ethnocentric?
6. How does the potluck dinner differ from European dinner party customs?

SIX

Growing Up American: Doing the Right Thing

AMPARO B. OJEDA
Loyola University, Chicago

As a young student on her first visit to America, Professor Ojeda, a Fulbright scholar, was reassured that her adjustment to American life and culture would be easy. The orientation survival kit was of minimal help in adjusting to some American customs, especially those involving childrearing. Years later, in returning to the United States with a daughter, Professor Ojeda was faced with a crucial conflict of values—American values versus the more familiar values of her own Philippine traditions.

Amparo B. Ojeda *was born and raised in the Philippines. She completed her undergraduate degree and an M.A. in English Literature from the University of San Carlos, Philippines, and an M.S. in Linguistics from Georgetown University under the Fulbright program. Rudolf R. Rahmann, a Divine Word Missionary (SVD) and an anthropologist, encouraged her to pursue anthropology with a special emphasis in Southeast Asian anthropology and linguistics. She earned her doctorate at the University of San Carlos. Professor Ojeda has conducted fieldwork in the Philippines and is involved in ongoing research on the adjustment of Filipino immigrants in Metropolitan Chicago. She is retired from the Anthropology and Linguistics Departments at Loyola University, Chicago.*

The earliest and closest encounter that I had with Americans, and a most superficial brush with their culture, goes back to my childhood days when an American family moved into our neighborhood. I used to gaze at the children, a boy and a girl, who were always neatly dressed and who would romp around their fenced front yard. Not knowing their names, I, together with a cousin, used to call them, *"Hoy, Americano!"* (Hey, American!), and they themselves soon learned to greet us with "Hey, Filipino!" That was as far as our "acquaintance" went because in no time at all they were gone, and we never again heard about them.

That brief encounter aroused my curiosity. I wanted to know something more about the "Americanos." What kind of people are they? What food do they eat? Where is America? As time passed, I learned about America—about the people and about some aspects of their lifestyle—but my knowledge was indirect. The opportunity to experience the world of the "Americano" directly was long in coming, and when it did I was gripped with a sense of ambivalence. How would I fare in a strange and foreign land with an unfamiliar culture? That was how I finally found myself on the plane that would bring me on the first leg of my cultural sojourn to Hawaii.

Excited as I was, I could hear my heart thumping, and apprehension came over me. Suddenly, the thought hit me: I have journeyed far from home, away from the comforts and familiarity of my culture. You see, in this trip, my first outside of my homeland, I did not come as an anthropologist to do fieldwork. I came as a graduate student to study linguistics. Seven years later I would be an anthropologist. But I am getting ahead of myself.

My host family during my brief two-week stay in Honolulu was waiting at the airport. The whole family was there! The children's beaming faces and the family's warm and gracious greetings gave me a sense of assurance that everything was going to be fine. "There's nothing to it," we Fulbright scholars were reassured during a briefing on aspects of adjustment to American life and culture. So there I was in Hawaii, the first leg of my cultural sojourn (I stayed in the Midwest for another four weeks of orientation, before proceeding east to do graduate work), equipped with a theoretical survival kit designed and guaranteed to work. I would later discover that there were discrepancies between the ideal procedures and techniques and day-to-day behavior.

The differences between my culture and American culture became evident in the first few hours after my arrival. On our way out of the air terminal, the children began to fuss: "I'm hungry," "I'm tired," "I'm thirsty," "I want to go to the bathroom!" Over the whining and fidgeting of the children, my hosts and I tried to carry on a conversation but to no avail. Amazingly, despite the constant interruptions, the adults displayed considerable tolerance and patience. No voice was raised, nor harsh words spoken. I vividly recall how, as children, we were reminded never to interrupt while adults were talking, and to avoid annoying behavior, especially when in the company of adults, whether these people were kin, friends, or strangers.

We left the main highway, drove on a country road, and eventually parked by a Howard Johnson restaurant. The children did not need any bidding at all. They ran inside the restaurant in search of a table for us. I was fascinated by their quite independent and assertive behavior (more of this, later). I had originally been feeling dizzy and drowsy from the long plane ride, but I wasn't anymore. My "cultural" curiosity was aroused by the children's youthful showmanship, or so I thought. As soon as we were all seated, a young man came to hand us menus. The children made their own choices. Not feeling hungry at all, but wanting to show appreciation, I settled for a cup of soup. When the food finally came, I was completely shocked by the portions each child had. I wondered if they could eat it all. Just as I feared, they left their portions only partially eaten. What a waste, I thought. I remembered one of my father's gems of thought: "Take only what you can eat, and make sure to eat the last morsel on your plate." I must confess that I felt very bad looking at mounds of uneaten food. How can so much food be wasted? Why were children allowed to order their food themselves instead of Mom and Dad doing it for them? Was it a part of independence training? Or were Mom and Dad simply indulgent of their children's wants? I did not have any answers, but I surmised that it wasn't going to be easy understanding the American way. Neither would it be easy accepting or adjusting to American customs. I realized later that my difficulty was brought about by my cultural bias and naivete. Given the situation, I expected my own familiar behavioral/cultural response. For instance, in the Philippines, as well as in many other Asian countries, children are rarely allowed, if at all, to "do their own thing" without the consent of their parents. Consultation with parents, older siblings, aunts and uncles, or grandparents is always sought. In America, I found out that from an early age, a person is encouraged to be independent, to make up his or her mind, and to stand up for his or her rights. Individualism is encouraged among the American youth, whereas among Asians, including Filipinos, group unity, togetherness, and harmony are valued.

Values such as obedience to authority (older people are vested with authority) and respect for elders are seriously observed and practiced. The young address their elders using terms of respect. Among the Tagalog, the particle *po* (sir, ma'am) or *opo* (yes sir, yes ma'am) is always used. Not to do so is considered rude. Children do not call anybody older by their first names. This deference to age contrasts sharply with the American notions of egalitarianism and informality.

American children, I observe, are allowed to call older people by their first names. I recall two interesting incidents, amusing now but definitely bothersome then. The first incident took place in the university cafeteria. To foster collegiality among the faculty and graduate students, professors and students usually ate lunch together. During one of these occasions, I heard a student greet a teacher, "Hey, Bob! That was a tough exam! You really gave us a hard time, buddy!" I was stunned. I couldn't believe what I heard. All I could say to myself was "My God! How bold and disrespectful!"

Not long afterward, I found myself in a similar scenario. This time, I was with some very young children of new acquaintances. They called to say hello and to ask if I could spend the weekend with the family. At their place, I met more people, young and not so young. Uninhibited, the children took the liberty of introducing me to everybody. Each child who played the role of "introducer" would address each person by his or her first name. No titles such as "Mr.," "Mrs.," or "Miss" were used; we were simply introduced as "Steve, this is Amparo" and "Amparo, this is Paula." Because I was not acquainted with the sociolinguistics of American communicative style, this took me quite by surprise. I was not prepared for the reality of being addressed as the children's equal. In my own experience, it took me some time to muster courage before I could call my senior colleagues by their first names.

A somewhat similar occurrence happened many years later. I had impressed on my little girl the proper and polite way to address older people, that is, for her always to say "Mr." or "Mrs." before mentioning their first names and family names. I used to prod and remind her often that it was the right thing to do. Imagine my surprise and embarrassment when one day I heard her greet our next-door neighbor saying, "Hi, Martha!" I asked her why she greeted her that way. She readily answered, "Mommy, Martha told me not to call her Mrs. _____, just Martha!" What could I say? Since then, she was always called Martha but I had qualms each time I heard my daughter greet her. In the Philippines, older people, regardless of their status in life, whether they are relatives or strangers, are always addressed using respectful terms such as *mang* (title for an elderly man), *iyo* (abbreviated variant for *tiyo,* or uncle, a title for a male relative but also used to address someone who is elderly), *aling* (respectful title for an older or elderly woman), and *manang* (a regional variant for *aling*). However, one gets used to doing things in a certain way after a while. So did I! After all, isn't that what adaptation is all about? But my cultural adventure or misadventure did not end here. This was only a prelude.

I was introduced into American culture from the periphery, which provided me with only a glimpse of the people's lifestyle, their passing moods and attitudes, and their values and ideas. I did not have the time, effort, or desire to take a long hard look at the cultural environment around me. I returned to the Philippines with some notions about American culture. If I have another chance, I told myself, I want to check it out judiciously and with objectivity. Seven years later, an opportunity presented itself. I was back in the "good old U.S.A.," this time to stay. I humored myself with the thought that I was smarter, wiser, and better prepared for challenges. I did not expect any serious problems. If there were problems, they would be inconsequential and therefore less stressful. This was far from the truth, however!

This time I was not alone against a whole new world. I had become a mother and was raising my child while virtually swimming against the current of cultural values that were not my own. True, there are clusters of universal human values to which everybody adheres. But it is likewise true that certain values are distinctive to a culture. Here lay the crux of an important problem that I needed to resolve. How was I going to bring up my child? Did I want her to grow up American, or did I want her to be a reflection and/or extension of myself, culturally speaking? The longer I pondered on these nagging questions, the more I began to realize that they were rather unfair questions. There were no easy answers.

There was, however, one thing of which I was certain: I wanted the best for my child, that is, the best of two worlds, America and my own. To do this, there were choices to be made. Predictably, I found myself straddling between two cultures, my right hand not knowing what my left hand was doing. At times, I found myself engaged in a balancing act in an effort to understand American culture without jeopardizing my cultural ways. Thus, alternatively, I would be strongly assertive and modestly defensive when my peculiar beliefs and actions were questioned.

Two incidents remain fresh in my mind. Briefly, someone made her observations very clearly to me by her remarks: "I see you always walk your daughter to and from school every day. . . . You know, many children in the neighborhood walk to school unaccompanied by adults. Why don't you let your daughter walk with them to school? She will learn to be on her own if you let go."

Another woman, some years later, asked me whether my daughter had started to drive, to which I answered "No." Surprised, she asked how my daughter could get around (to parties, movies, and so on). She remarked, "It would be easy for her and for you if she started taking driving lessons and got her own car." Forthright remarks! Fair criticism?

These two incidents bring into sharp focus the contrast between Filipino culture and American culture in the area of socialization. It is plain to see that in these instances, I am perceived as controlling and reprimanding, whereas the other person (American) is viewed as sociable, egalitarian, and indulgent. Because of the American emphasis on self-reliance and independence, relationships between the children and the (Asian) Filipino mother are often interpreted as overdependent. Mothers are often perceived as overprotective. This observation results from unfamiliarity with the traditional family dynamics of the (Asian) Filipino family. In order to avoid a distorted perception of one culture by another, it is extremely important that the uniqueness and cultural distinctiveness of a culture be explored, recognized, and respected for what it is. Otherwise, that which is not familiar, and therefore not clearly understood, would be viewed as "bizarre," although it is completely meaningful to members of another culture.

Among the Filipinos, life is governed by traditions that do not stress independence and autonomy of the individual. The family surpasses the individual. Hierarchical roles define each member's position in the network of relationships. These relationships are strictly prescribed, such as the relationship between children and parents, between father and children, and between mother and children. For instance, the mother plays a paramount role in the nurturance of the children. The burden of the child's well-being rests on the mother.

Going back to the heart of the problem—that is, the issue of childrearing values—I have made a conscious choice, and in doing so, my values, beliefs, and actions have been brought into question. I have reassured myself that there is no need to worry as long as my child benefits from the quality of life I have prayerfully sought and arduously worked for.

At this point, I come full circle to the question: How am I doing as a parent, as a mother? Did I do the right thing? Is my daughter growing up American? My answer would have to be "It depends. Let's wait and see!"

NOTE

I wrote this article not to discredit or minimize the significance of American childrearing ideas, attitudes, and practices. I simply want to emphasize that there are crosscultural differences in outlook, values, customs, and practices. Certainly, the socialization of the young is no exception.

SUGGESTED READINGS

McGoldrick, Monica, John Pearce, and Joseph Giordano, eds. 1982. *Ethnicity and Family Therapy.* New York: Guilford Press.

Mead, Margaret, and Martha Wolfenstein, eds. 1955. *Childhood in Contemporary Cultures.* Chicago: University of Chicago Press.

Whiting, Beatrice B., and Carolyn P. Edwards. 1988. *Children of Different Worlds.* Cambridge, MA: Harvard University Press.

STUDY QUESTIONS

1. What are some significant differences between child-adult relationships in American and Asian cultures?
2. If you were Professor Ojeda, how would you have raised your child in America? Why?

3. What are the important distinctions between Filipino and American childrearing practices?
4. Can you perceive any problems with American children being raised with emphasis on individuality, self-reliance, and independence?

SEVEN

My American Glasses

FRANCISCO MARTINS RAMOS
University of Évora, Portugal

From a Portuguese perspective, Professor Ramos examines a few American cultural traits, such as informal language use, social life, body ritual, football, and that great American shrine, the bathroom. In the style of Horace Miner, the author offers lucid and critical insights into many of the customs that Americans take for granted.

Francisco Martins Ramos is *Associate Professor of Anthropology at the University of Évora (Portugal). He is presently chair of the Department of Sociology and president of the Scientific Council of Human and Social Sciences of the same university. He was raised in the Alentejo, a southern rural area of Portugal. He lived in Africa and visited the United States several times. He received his B.A. in Anthropology from the Technical University of Lisbon (1978) and earned his doctorate in Anthropology at the University of Évora.*

The following text is a humble reflection on American daily life, resulting from my contact with American society. I must say that a foreigner's careful look is not necessarily more refined, precise, and detailed than that of the indigenous people. As paradigmatic examples I recall the famous articles Ralph Linton (1936) and Horace Miner (1956) wrote on aspects of American cultural reality. Inspired by the brilliant words and original ideas transmitted by these authors, respectively, in "One Hundred Percent American" and "Body Ritual Among the Nacirema," I will present a critical view of some forms of behavior, phenomena, and attitudes within American daily life that raised my interest or shocked me.

Half a dozen visits to the United States (totaling about eight months) allow me some insight, simultaneously close and distant, and have led me to the present reflections. The title I have selected simply reflects a new perspective resulting from a new angle of observation.

These comments do not pretend to reduce or caricature American culture or Americans, and they are not, surely, meant to express any superiority on the part of the author. Thus, the *chiens de garde* (guard dogs) of ethnocentrism will be warned, since this is a perspective that wishes to emphasize the richness of cultural differences and of people's identity and singularity.

When I mention American culture, the idea of diversity and heterogeneity is implicit, which is the consequence of a varied number of cultural inputs from the most diverse origins. American culture is the result of a multicultural amalgam that has been consolidating itself through the years and that is in permanent evolution, with a rhythm and a dynamic that surprises a European point of view.

The ideas expressed in this article correspond not only to my own personal opinions but also to those of many colleagues and friends who gave me help and important information. I assume total responsibility for their contributions.

The United States has always exercised a strange attraction for the spirit of the Portuguese: first, as the land of quick success; second, as the cradle of democracy; third, as an unrestrained jungle of competition; and, finally, as the model to follow. Perhaps for these very reasons there has never existed in Portugal the deep anti-American sentiment that characterizes other well-known European and world situations.

Nowadays, America comes to us, fresh and quickly, at the hour of TV news, ritually and arithmetically. Radio news programs or TV reports give information and news about the American nation every day. But the situation was not always like this.

Thirty or forty years ago, what we knew about America was mythologically overemphasized in the letters of some Azorean relative.

What we knew about America came from cowboy films and documentary movies that filled our eyes with the skyscrapers of New York or the memories of Al Capone's peripeteias.

What we knew about America was part of another world, distant, unreachable, almost abstract.

In Portugal, however, what used to confuse us were the inconceivable episodes of racial segregation. In fact, the Portuguese still had one foot (and its heart) in Africa and did not easily accept this business of ethnic discrimination—we who have mixed ourselves with African, Asian, and Amerindian peoples in the seven corners of the world.

Each Portuguese who learned on school benches that America separated herself from the British Empire had a secret and inexplicable sensation of joy and satisfaction at knowing the English were defeated. Because of an ancient treaty signed in the fourteenth century, we had to bear the British after their help against the French Napoleonic invasions, and this agreement has functioned more to their benefit than to ours. Thus, nations of colonial vocation vibrate with these pretty little joys!

We cried for John Kennedy and Martin Luther King, citizens of humankind, and, still today, we are commonly surprised how Ronald Reagan could become president of the greatest nation in the world.

With the development of modern media technologies, with the increase and improvement of the means of transportation, with the implementation of exchange programs and visits, with the increase of reciprocal tourism, America is today very close to us, and her mythology is no longer incomprehensible. She now generates other myths.

La recherche du temps perdu (the search for the lost time) is for a middle-class American the search for a history and for European roots. For that reason, Europeans are not badly treated in America. As Octavio Paz has said, "The United States drown themselves in the challenges of conceiving a country" (Santos 1989:

2). As Walt Whitman wrote, what has united Americans has not been a common history, which they did not have, but "the will to build a future: a common future where utopia blends with reality" (Santos 1989: 3).

I first visited the United States in 1982. For five months I lived in Madison, Wisconsin, a state with rural characteristics, which I was comfortable with. The Alentejo Province, where I was born and raised, was also rural, as are many of the areas of my country that lack the rapid advances of industrialization.

Later, during other visits, I had the opportunity to visit Milwaukee, Chicago, Washington, D.C., New York, Phoenix, Los Angeles, Dallas, Boston, and San Francisco, areas that offered examples of the rich urban vocation of the American nation.

What surprises us as Europeans is the fact that Americans could have done in less than 150 years what it took centuries for us to do. For better or worse, in this duel of contradictions, the struggle is between the old Puritan morality and a new hedonism. The paradox is the democratic identity of the United States—a collective project—and the constantly growing individualistic trend.

A Portuguese citizen arrives in America, conscious of his or her rural extraction, and the first thing that he or she realizes is that America is not a big megalopolis. We feel perfectly integrated in the rural world of a state such as Wisconsin—with an economy based on the primary sector, with conservative political horizons as in the majority of rural societies.

A less observant visitor can lose himself or herself in the complexity of multiple and contradictory cultural traits. First, we become submersed in the imperialism of material culture, in terms of shape, space, and time. After this comes the invasion of cultural behavior traits.

Unexpectedly, the first thing I found strange, even bizarre, was the use and abuse of the word *nice*, both in formal conversations and in colloquial language. I participated in the following dialogue at a family party on Thanksgiving Day:

"Nice to meet you. What's your name?"
"Francisco."
"Oh, nice! Do you have a family?"
"Yes, I have two children. . . ."
"Very nice! Do you like America?"
"Yes, but . . ."
"That's very nice! Do you like our weather?"
"It's a little cold for me. . . ."
"But today is a nice day! By the way, did you watch the football game last night?"
"I did, but I don't understand American football. . . ."
"Oh, it's a pretty nice sport!"

Some hours later:

"Bye-bye, Francisco. It was nice to meet you. . . . Have a nice stay in the States."

In fact, the abuse of the word *nice* shocks the hearing of an attentive interlocutor and of the visitor who is interested in dominating the meandering of North American language. Either a certain mental laziness exists that generates a simplification of the linguistic process of communication, or the English language does not have the vocabulary and the semantic richness to avoid abusive repetitions. "Pretty nice" and "It's nice to be nice" are expressions that capture the extreme of what I am referring to.

An American woman who has been introduced to us always hesitates in shaking hands and is not prepared to be kissed, even by another woman. I presume that this attitude derives from educational rules or is a self-defense mechanism. The compliment normally is "Hi! Nice to meet you!"

It is interesting to note the practical sense that Americans give to forms of address. They avoid the European or Portuguese formalities of titles: mister doctor, mister engineer, mister architect, and so on. In America, preferential treatment stresses the Christian name, which in Portugal is used only with the passage of time or between kin and friends. There is a difference between the practical meaning of social relations and the world of true formality.

In the States, social life is programmed to arrange a dinner, a party, a picnic, a visit, and so on. These are operations planned far ahead. Sociability is not improvised; it is highly programmatic, predictable, and repetitive.

America has no parallel in the cult of physical exercise: Gymnastics, athletics, and life in the open air are integral parts of the daily life of Americans of all ages. Physical exercise is just one more part of Miner's "body ritual."

American football, in spite of being a game of truly male orientation, also attracts women as spectators, fans, and strong participants in discussions about the game. Up to now, European women have not been attracted by European soccer at any level: participation, attendance at games, or club/team discussions.

Football is characterized by virility, difficulty, and risks and is considered to employ a combination of war and chess strategies. Such a combination of animation and subtlety and the equilibrium of the metaphor appease the American conscience against all those (Europeans) who consider American football an exercise in brutality.

When Portuguese citizens leave their native province and arrive in America, they are confronted with a series of strange situations. Some situations provoke laughter, and others are quite dramatic and embarrassing. Many situations generate stupefaction. As a matter of fact, Horace Miner (1956), who some time ago had already subtlely played with some traits of North American culture, called our attention to the characteristics of the bathroom, the true ceremonial center of body ritual. A Portuguese who visits the bathroom in the home of an American friend faces some puzzling situations. For example, in the bathrooms of more than twenty American couples that time and friendship have allowed me to know, in dozens of hotels, motels, dormitories, bus and train stations, restaurants, and bars, no two water taps are alike. Consequently, I have encountered great difficulties in turning the water on, in adjusting cold and hot water, in regulating the faucet pressure, and in stopping the flow. The problem is that the tap mechanisms can be put into action by the pressure of a forefinger on a generally hidden button, by turning a screw that we wouldn't think to turn, by moving an appurtenance considered to be ornamental, or by using a masked hook, a secondary metal arabesque, or an invisible pedal.

If from the taps we move to showers, baths, and toilets, it is easy to recognize the embarrassment of a common Portuguese who is forced to make a detailed preliminary study of the sanitary equipment, which the circumstances do not always permit. We perfectly understand Americans' exemplary obsession with bad smells, as we can verify through the shape of toilets and the volume of water they consume in restrooms. However, the paraphernalia, mechanisms, and equipment are so different as to constitute a labyrinth for the rural European Portuguese.

In public rest rooms, the Portuguese amateur in urbanities will certainly be quite surprised with a form of cultural behavior never dreamt of: The American who urinates in public initiates conversation with the partner at his side, even if he does not know the latter! Themes of these occasional dialogues are the weather, football, politics, and so on. We can guess at the forced pleasure of the Portuguese, who heretofore has regarded urination as a necessary physical function, not as a social occasion. The public restroom! Is it an extension of the bar room?

Next, I would like to comment on gastronomy. The first consideration is the diversity of American food, rich and varied as many others, as a form of cultural manifestation. In this case, the gastronomic contributions from different and distant cultures make American cuisine a true "melting pot," an opportune expression to describe so-called "ethnic" food. A Portuguese who has not traveled much will be faced with the dilemma of choice in a restaurant or at the supermarket. In fact, there are seemingly endless types of sauces, numerous varieties of bread, an immense number of different kinds of cheese, potatoes cooked in various ways, and so on. Another marvel is the fast-food system, which fits perfectly into the American way of life. Indeed, during weekdays, the fast-food system is oriented to the performance of work, in a real struggle against time.

My discussion of gastronomy would not be complete without reference to table etiquette. Americans normally use the knife very little but use the fork continually. Those of us who have been educated by the French bible of good manners at the table have always been told that it is good etiquette to use a fork and knife simulta-neously: fork in the left hand, knife in the right. Thus, we find it difficult to accept as proper etiquette the use of the fork with the right hand, leaving the left hand under the table as a sign of good manners.

Speaking of manners, if an American cannot avoid belching in public (he burps and naturally apologizes), for a Portuguese this means a lack of good manners. However, the same Portuguese will be positively impressed with the kindness and amiability showed by American pedestrians or drivers, who are always willing to give the correct information any time it is requested. The paradox is that Americans think the same way about the Portuguese.

Whereas some differences amaze and delight us, others are true shocks. One dif-ference is the idea of one's sharing a bedroom with an American woman, without being involved in sex. Indeed, it is normal and current among university students, participants at conferences, and friends to share a bedroom and a bed only for prac-tical reasons. We can imagine how a Portuguese (or a Spaniard or an Italian) would conceive of such partition without generating conflict with his engraved honor as a Latin macho. Something that an American woman does, with the greatest natural-ness, will be more than reason for a Latin man not to sleep a wink all night, if it should happen that he shares the same room only with the intent of having a good sleep and reducing expenses. The Latin caught in this trap will necessarily have his night replete with dreams, his imagination well fed, and a prolonged insomnia. . . .

The United States is a country where everything must be paid for, with two honorable exceptions: the ice vomited up by machines strategically placed in hotels and service stations, and matches, which are publicity tools offered by cigarette machines and free at any hotel or restaurant of any category. However, there is an institutionalized payment that surprises me: the tip. It is a quasi–imposition that I consider contradictory in a society like the United States. In fact, the philosophy that informs American life is one of merit, of success, and of justice. It seems to me that in this society, to give a tip would be to humiliate someone who fulfills his or her duty, renders a service, or performs a task that does not need to be rewarded beyond the normal circuit. Tips pay favors, compensate insufficiencies and not duties, and are the embryo of corruption. They never will be just, even in societies where class differences are clandestine or hidden. Tips in the States are equivocal; they are a form of oblivion and in contradiction to American life and values.

A big country, from a geographical point of view, the United States is a country closed in on itself. Americans know little about the world except when a plane crashes in Germany, a revolution takes place in Portugal (located about seven hours away by air), or when the king of Spain dies. On the other hand, we always know when an American president has a toothache, when a Hollywood star gets divorced for the third time, or when there is a rally for legalizing marijuana. This focus can be understood by the fact that the United States is a country at an intercontinental level, with several dozen states that function almost like European countries. Isn't it true that a middle-class American will spend his or her vacation in another American state? This virtual autism derives from another important factor within American daily life—the television. The American TV, a complex and overwhelming hydra, reports live on car accidents at the street corner, interviews the storekeeper on our block, or covers the "League of Friends" of something or another. The only international issues reported, in fact, are those directly related to the United States of America. Besides these, only natural disasters, revolutions, and air accidents are covered. The world is too far away: Europe is too distant, South America is not very close either, and only the immediate geographical space is subject to attention. TV imperialism and the enormous publicity machine suffer from umbilical narcissism, exploitable at any moment.

The American family is an enigmatic institution, both protective and uncaring. When I reflect on the concept of family, the transmission of values, and the conveying of parental authority, which is simultaneously rigid and relaxed, I feel that something is wrong; that is, there is something essentially different from these concepts in Europe. I admit my bias and some ethnocentrism, but I question the attitudes of American youth. For example, the obsession for alcoholic drinks when one reaches the authorized or legal age (which varies from state to state) appears to be in contradiction with family values conveyed to youngsters. I had many opportunities to observe young people, boys and girls, who used to get drunk, mixing various types of alcoholic drinks. When I asked several groups the reason for such mixtures, the answer was always the same: "We mix the drinks in order to get drunk as soon as possible." It is true that not all American youths proceed in this manner, but it is also true that the great ambition of a youngster eighteen years of age is to leave his or her parents' home. The wish for autonomy and freedom, and the obsessive thirst for alcoholic drinks, seem too radical and are a strange rupture within family tutorship. That is the reason I suggest that something is not going well in the family educational system in the United States. I hope to be forgiven by those who think I am generalizing too readily.

During my first visits to America, I thought there was a kind of empty space in relation to social control. I thought in these terms because I was a foreigner and apparently anonymous. In fact, in this respect American society is not so different from others. In large urban centers, naturally, interpersonal relations are marked by a great indifference, but that happens all around the world. By the same token, in American rural areas, as in rural areas worldwide, there are forms of social control, more or less visible, more or less subtle. What happens to the foreign visitor and observer is the initial blindness in the face of novelty and the unknown. Such blindness does not allow us to focus our dispersed attention on the analysis of social phenomena in their real proportions and profundity.

My son Carlos went to Los Angeles to spend a vacation. It was agreed that he would stay one and a half months in the house of our friends. Before his departure, I gave him some advice and information about the American way of life. During his stay he used to call me, but the tone of his voice did not sound very convincing when he informed me that he was truly enjoying his "American dream." After twenty-nine days, I received an unexpected phone call:

"Father, meet me at the airport, I'm coming back tomorrow!"

"But why so early?"

"I'll tell you later."

The next day, I went to the Lisbon airport. As soon as he saw me he gave me a hug and sighed,

"I wanted so much to return, but I already regret having come!"

That's exactly what America provokes in us: an ambivalent sentiment of love and rejection, in a type of overwhelming anguish that generates the ambition to go to America and the wish to come back quickly.

My son's thirty days in America were a unique experience that is a dream for many Portuguese and European youngsters of his age and that had also been the unreachable ambition of my own youth. Carlos wants to return to the States, and nowadays he is showing his intercontinental behavior with the consumption of many liters of Pepsi or Coca-Cola and enormous portions of ketchup, popcorn, and French-fried potatoes.

Meanwhile, I notice that he makes a show of using slang phrases that he has taken to his English classes. Naturally, this has not helped him earn good grades.

Since Carlos returned, he systematically uses coded expressions. He now says, "It's really good over there; there things are better; when I was there . . . ; there I could heat my orange juice in the microwave; there we can find everything." After some time, it was easy for me to conclude that for my son *there* means America.

A Portuguese of middle-class background can usually speak several languages. This situation is much appreciated by Americans, and we are normally well respected given our capacity to communicate in three or four languages: our mother tongue, English, French, and Spanish or German. For us, this was always a necessary or a natural thing: Besides our own language, it is not difficult for us to speak in Spanish; we have a long and great tradition connected with French culture and the French language; and in order to understand Americans, we need to speak English. Americans find themselves in an inferior position because neither history nor necessity has forced them to learn other languages. For some Americans, the ability to speak French is an indicator of incomparable prestige. I think that some Americans insist on enriching their vocabulary with French words and expressions, even if they cannot speak the language fluently. The Portuguese visitor wins some status and security given his or her role as a polyglot. However, in other situations, the Portuguese visitor gapes at the spectacular achievements (in terms of material culture and social pragmatism) of so-called American civilization.

We are amazed, for example, that the prestige of certain professions in America is not as low as is the case in Portugal. I think, in contrast, that Americans grant more dignity to the worker, regardless of the type of job performed. In the United States, a farmer, a taxi driver, or a traveling salesperson would not necessarily feel inferior; in Portugal, however, these are truly minor professions. In Portugal, too, an economist, an anthropologist, or a graduate in chemistry would almost never perform the aforementioned "lowly" jobs. "It does not become one" and "it looks bad" would be the first justifications.

In fact, this problem is linked either to the labor market or to the educational system, to access to the university, and to the total proportions of graduates, which are quite different both in quality and quantity in these countries.

The United States values community associations in a way we think exemplary. Cooperative projects, professional and sectorial associations, defense leagues, and friends groups proliferate in the heart of American society. In a land that has recently fomented excessive narcissism and individualism, it is interesting to note the conciliation of these two philosophies and postures.

Indeed, in the end, I know extremely little about the United States of America. Probably my American glasses have given me a blurred, out-of-focus image of reality.

The posture of a Portuguese can be ridiculous when in America. I remember that my son warmed his orange juice in the microwave to soothe his sore throat. Our difficulty in determining on which side a door opens is ridiculous. We Portuguese do not take showers after meals, we think it dangerous for our health to eat oranges at night, we make a lot of noise when we blow our noses, we rarely go to bed before midnight, and we spend enormous amounts of time at the table.

Any American, in turn, would grin at this strange behavior.

REFERENCES

Linton, Ralph. 1936. *The Study of Man.* Madison, WI: D. Appleton-Century.
———. 1937. One Hundred Percent American. *American Mercury* 40: 427–429.
Miner, Horace. 1956. Body Ritual among the Nacirema. *American Anthropologist* 58: 503–507.
Santos, José. 1989. *Entrevista a Octávio Paz.* Lisboa: Semanário (Setembro).

STUDY QUESTIONS

1. What evidence does Professor Ramos provide to display a rather impressive knowledge of America? How does that compare with your knowledge of his native Portugal? Or of any other European country for that matter?
2. What might be implied by the author's contention of American contradictions— that the "struggle is between the old Puritan morality and a new hedonism"?

3. How accurate is the author in his critique of the overuse and superficiality of the word *nice* by Americans?
4. What is implied by the author's comment that "TV imperialism and the enormous publicity machine suffer from umbilical narcissism"?
5. Is the author accurate in his generalities about the American family educational system? About the drinking patterns of American youths?
6. The author apologetically implies his own possible ethnocentrism in his views of American culture. Do you believe that Professor Ramos is ethnocentric? If so, in which of his assessments or opinions?

EIGHT

American Graffiti: Curious Derivatives of Individualism

JIN K. KIM
State University of New York, Plattsburgh

Professor Kim is visited by his closest high school friend, whom he has not seen for twenty years. During his visit, his friend, who hopes to immigrate to the United States, calls Kim an "American." In response and in order to aid his friend's transition to life in "this land of dreams," Kim writes him a letter. From a Korean cultural perspective, American issues of privacy, manners, sexual mores, individuality, interpersonal relations, and doublespeak are forthrightly and entertainingly addressed.

Jin K. Kim, *born and raised in South Korea, completed a B.A. degree in English at Sogang Jesuit University, Seoul, and came to the United States in 1972, where he pursued graduate study in communication at Syracuse University and the University of Iowa (Ph.D., 1978). Currently Kim is a professor in the Department of Communication, SUNY Plattsburgh. His teaching and scholarly interests include intercultural communication, communication theory, and mass communication law.*

*D*ear MK,
I sincerely hope the last leg of your trip home from the five-week fact-finding visit to the United States was pleasant and informative. Although I may not have expressed my sense of exhilaration about your visit through the meager lodging accommodations and "barbaric" foods we provided, it was sheer joy to spend four weeks with you and Kyung-Ok. (Please refrain from hitting the ceiling. My use of your charming wife's name, rather than the usual Korean expression, "your wife" or "your house person," is not an indication of my amorous intentions toward her as any red-blooded Korean man would suspect. Since you are planning to immigrate to this country soon, I thought you might as well begin to get used to the idea of your wife exerting her individuality. Better yet, I thought you should be warned that the moment the plane touches American soil, you will lose your status as the center of your familial universe.) At any rate, please be assured that during your stay here my heart was filled with memories of our three years together in high school when we were young in Pusan. It was indeed thirty years ago when we were as mischievous and curiosity-driven as any youngsters can be. Since then, your worst fear,

formed on the basis of my indefatigable appetite for books, has come true: "All you could achieve in your life is to become a stuffy scholar." In the meantime, riding smoothly on the rising tide of Korea as an economic power, you have amassed a small fortune, which you want to use as a down payment for an even bigger fortune in this land of dreams. Honestly, MK, an immigrant with a multimillion-dollar bank account is quite incongruent with the image of those millions who came to this country in response to the invitation: Send me your poor, your tired, your huddled masses yearning to be free." But then, the world has changed, especially in the past twenty years when we were separated from each other. If we could revive our friendship after all these years, if my twenty-year experience as an "alien" can contribute even one iota to making you less an "alien" in this country, and if your wealth can be justifiably used to the benefit of a new generation of the poor, tired and huddled masses of present economic hardships in my adopted fatherland, I will gladly sell my soul and volunteer to you every bit of my personal "wisdom" on what America is about. It is true that the peculiar pattern of life I have lived in the last two decades is likely to have tainted that "wisdom." But then, my old friend, do you know any wisdom that transcends its experiential boundaries?

During your visit, you called me, on several occasions, an American. What prompted you to invoke such a reference is beyond my comprehension. Was it my rusty Korean expressions? Was it my calculating mind? Was it my pitifully subservient (at least when viewed through your cultural lens) role that I was playing in the family life? Or was it my familiarity with some facets of the American cultural landscape? This may sound bewildering to you, but it is absolutely true that through all the years I have lived in this country, I never truly felt like an American. Sure, on the surface, our family followed closely many ritualistic routines of the American culture: shopping malls, vacations, dining out, holidays, weddings, funerals, summer camps, PTA volunteer works, community service, Little League baseball games, concerts, plays, movies, community youth orchestras, museums, art galleries, picnics, birthday parties, camping trips, Wrigley Field, state fairs, county fairs, jazz festivals, food carnivals, casinos, amusement parks, beaches, National Parks, fast-food chains, credit card shopping sprees, Nintendo games, board games, game shows, situation comedies, soap operas, hot dogs, apple pies (no Chevrolet yet), fundraising dinners, retirement parties, church potlucks, the health food craze, fitness programs, Tupperware parties, and, of course, Amway fantasies. I always considered my participation in these "rituals" as none other than the act of a half-hearted spectator who was being pushed by circumstances. My physical involvement in these activities was undeniable, but mentally I remained stubbornly in the periphery. Naturally, then, my subjective cultural attitudes stayed staunchly Korean. Never did the inner layers of my Korean psyche yield to the invading American cultural vagaries, I thought. Of course, I would not rule out the possibility of the outer layers being coated here and there with an American frame of reference. My subjective feeling about my cultural identity notwithstanding, when you labeled me an American for the first time, I felt a twinge of guilt.

Several years ago, an old Korean friend of mine, who settled in the United States about the same time I did, paid a visit to Korea for the first time in some fifteen years. When he went to see his best high school friend, who was now married and had two sons, his friend's wife made a bed for him and her husband in the master bedroom, declaring that she would spend the night with the children. It was not necessarily the sexual connotation of the episode that made my friend blush; he was greatly embarrassed by the circumstance in which he imposed himself to the extent that the couple's privacy had to be violated. For his high school friend and his wife, it was clearly their age-old friendship to which the couple's privacy had to yield. MK, you might empathize rather easily with this Korean couple's state of mind. But it would be a gross mistake even to imagine there may be occasions in your adopted culture when a gesture of friendship breaks the barrier of privacy. Zealously guarding their privacy above all, Americans are marvelously adept at drawing the line where friendship—that elusive "we" feeling—stops and privacy begins.

My first Greyhound bus trip in 1972 was a long one from Milwaukee, Wisconsin, to Syracuse, New York. During this twenty-four-hour trip, I met a divorced Catholic woman who confided in me the most intimate aspects of her private life, including her sexual hang-ups. By the time I got off the bus, she not only gave me her telephone number but also demanded I call her daughter, who was allegedly a student at Syracuse University. Two weeks after this incident, I rushed to Massachusetts to visit Michelle and Bob. You may remember these Americans whom I befriended at college in Korea; they had come to our university, in the midst of the Vietnam War, to do "peace" work instead of being involved in the acts of savagery in the Southeast Asian rice paddies. Our friendship, conceived and nurtured in the homespun Korean cultural climate, was indeed a special one. I ran, never without enthusiasm, the extra mile to make their life in a strange land comfortable and trouble free. They were equally intrigued with the intensely personal nature of the cross-cultural experiences I was providing for them. Our mutual respect and affection were such that Bob and I even showed unmanly tears at the airport when they returned to the States after three years. You can imagine, MK, how heartbroken I was when I arrived in that small New England city and was told they had been separated for several months. Their Korean-born son, Daniel, was on a biweekly parental-visit schedule. I had to ape Daniel's visiting schedule, seeing my old friends separately. On the second night I spent with Bob, he had a small dinner party for several of his friends, and I met an interesting woman with a radical political viewpoint. She was apparently a hard-core Maoist with a strong conviction that only a Mao-style revolution could solve America's mounting problems of the time. After dinner, she cordially invited me—me alone, that is—to her apartment, which was in the same building as Bob's. When I knocked on her door fifteen minutes later, I was greeted with a life-size poster of Chairman Mao hanging on the living room wall. (Remember, MK, this was in 1972 when I was in this country on a student visa. If the Korean CIA agents or their informants, who were known to be closely monitoring activities of Korean students in the United States, were tipped off about my "association" with a Maoist, I could easily have been blacklisted.) That gigantic red poster alone was sufficient to make my heart palpitate, but, my friend, it was nothing compared to what I was to discover next. On a more careful scrutiny of the woman with whom I found myself alone, I realized she was in a see-through evening dress with nothing under it! Admittedly, it was a hot summer evening, and even a most stoic Confucian disciple might have chosen relaxing attire. Even so, displaying the most private parts of her body to a virtual stranger completely threw me off. To be honest with you, I have no recollection of how coherent I was that night when I argued against the inhuman nature of Communist ideology, especially as it was practiced in the Chinese Communist Revolution, which claimed approximately eight million human lives.

These two encounters—that is, the one with the babbling woman on the Greyhound bus and the other with the naked Maoist revolutionary—led me to believe, however temporarily, that in America a voluntary abandonment of one's privacy precedes a long-lasting personal friendship. In Korea, as I remember, MK, it was always a lengthy friendship that was used as a pretext to forgo one's own privacy or violate that of another person.

Several days later, it was time to visit Michelle and her son. After spending a splendid New England summer afternoon on a beach where Michelle painfully explained how her separation from Bob came about, we headed home in her brand new Volvo. Out of curiosity and anxiety about my transportation problem in Syracuse, I asked Michelle, "How much did you pay for this car?"

"Michael, you do not ask a question like that in the States," said she, using my baptismal name.

"What do you mean?" I responded, perplexed.

"Because it is a matter of privacy. If you really need to know, 'Did you get a good deal for this car?' would be more appropriate," Michelle stated matter-of-factly.

As her voice or look did not indicate any sign that she was less than serious, I repressed my urge to protest against her apparent contradiction. What about our six-year friendship, I thought, and all the intimate facts of private life involving the imminent divorce, which she just had passed on to me at the beach? My perplexity and puzzlement were slow to diminish, since she never told me how much she paid for the car.

Indeed, one of the hardest tasks you will face as an "alien" is how to find that delicate balance between your individuality (for example, privacy) and your collective identity (for example, friendship or membership in social groups). Privacy is not the only issue that stems from this individuality-collectivity continuum. Honesty in interpersonal relationships is another point that may keep you puzzled. Americans are almost brutally honest and frank about issues that belong to public domains; they are not afraid of discussing an embarrassing topic in most graphic details as long as the topic is a matter of public concern. Equally frank and honest gestures are adopted when they discuss their own personal lives once the presumed benefits from such gestures are determined to outweigh the risks involved. Accordingly, it is not uncommon to encounter friends who volunteer personally embarrassing and even shameful information lest you find it out from other sources. Are Americans equally straightforward and forthcoming in laying out heartfelt personal criticisms directed at their friends? Not likely. Their otherwise acute sense of honesty becomes significantly muted when they face the unpleasant task of being negative toward their personal friends. The fear of an emotion-draining confrontation and the virtue of being polite force them to put on a façade or mask. The perfectly accepted social behavior of telling "white lies" is a good example. The social and personal virtues of accepting such lies are grounded in the belief that the potential damage that can be inflicted by directly telling a friend the hurtful truth far outweighs the potential benefit that the friend could gain from it. Instead of telling a hurtful truth directly, Americans use various indirect communication channels to which their friend is likely to be tuned. In other words, they publicize the information in the form of gossip or behind-the-back recriminations until it is transformed into a sort of collective criticism against the target individual. Thus objectified and collectivized, the "truth" ultimately reaches the target individual with a minimal cost of social discomfort on the part of the teller. There is nothing vile or insidious about this communication tactic, since it is deeply rooted in the concern for sustaining social pleasantry for both parties.

This innocuous practice, however, is bound to be perceived as an act of outrageous dishonesty by a person deeply immersed in the Korean culture. In the Korean cultural context, a trusted personal relationship precludes such publicizing prior to direct, "honest" criticism to the individual concerned, no matter what the cost in social and personal unpleasantry. Indeed, as you are well aware, MK, such direct reproach and even recrimination in Korea is in most cases appreciated as a sign of one's utmost love and concern for the target individual. Stressful and emotionally draining as it is, such a frank expression of criticism is done out of "we" feeling. Straight-talking friends did not want me to repeat undesirable acts in front of others, as it would either damage "our reputation" or go against the common interest of "our collective identity." In Korea, the focus is on the self-discipline that forms a basis for the integrity of "our group." In America, on the other hand, the focus is on the feelings of two individuals. From the potential teller's viewpoint, the primary concern is how to maintain social politeness, whereas from the target person's viewpoint, the primary concern is how to maintain self-esteem. Indeed, these two diametrically opposed frames of reference—self-discipline and self-esteem—make one culture collective and the other individualistic. It is rather amazing that for all the mistakes I must have made in the past twenty years, only one non-Korean American friend gave me such an "honest" criticism. In a sense, this concern for interpersonal politeness conceals their disapproval of my undesirable behavior for a time and ultimately delays the adjustment or realignment of my behavior, since it is likely to take quite a while for the collective judgment to reach me through the "publicized" channels of communication. So many Korean immigrants express their indignation about their American colleagues who smile at them but who criticize them behind their backs. If you ever become a victim of such a perception, MK, please take heart that you are not the only one who feels that pain.

At a societal level, too, the American tendency to close their eyes in an effort to avoid unpleasant realities surfaces in the form of a widespread use of euphemisms, especially in public life. Deaf people, for instance, become "hearing impaired." Proponents of abortion lace the dark reality of the actual acts with a glittering catch phrase, "pro-choice," while their antagonists, some of whom do not mind throwing bombs into abortion clinics, describe themselves as "pro-lifers." Americans take comfort at the rhetorical cosmetic surgery of calling housewives "domestic engineers." A simple tax raise transforms into "revenue enhancement," and American paratroopers invading another nation is called "a predawn vertical insertion." A hospital where an anesthetist kills a mother and her unborn child with an accidental overdose of nitrous oxide calls the deaths a "therapeutic misadventure." When potato chip delivery truck drivers are described in a "help wanted" ad as "executive snack route consultants," you realize how serious this epidemic is.

In a sense, Americans' reluctance and evasiveness in confronting unpleasant realities represent an inconsistent application of the meaning of individualism to a variety of human behaviors. The fundamental belief in the value and free will of individuals in pursuing the greatest good to the greatest number with minimal interference from state or societal constraints is vigorously advocated and even glorified when individual efforts bear fruit. Thus, when a rugged individual successfully overcomes adverse social and economic conditions, Americans elevate the man or woman to the status of hero for his or her spirit of independence. The individual is praised for fighting against the encroachment of collective forces. The individual is also likely to claim the well-deserved credit for achieving that status. However, when things go wrong, when those individuals fail to achieve what they set out to achieve, or when they become victims of circumstances, the same individualistic mentality takes a 180-degree turn; no individual accepts the responsibility or blame for the failure or admits the mishap was a reasonable consequence of risk taking in the normal course of life. Fearful of the immense cost of admitting one's failure, Americans too readily blame others for all sorts of things—from inadequate educational achievements (for example, "The school failed to teach me how to read" or "SAT questions are gender/race-biased") to murder (for example, "I plead not guilty by reason of insanity") to alcoholism (for example, "I inherited alcoholic genes"). The expression "I am sorry" comes out naturally from the mouths of Americans, as you will find out soon, MK. By no means do they use the expression indiscriminately, however. That apologetic statement is made mostly when the consequence of that gesture remains absolutely negligible. When matters of substance or legal responsibilities are involved, it would be virtually impossible to hear that statement. Admission of individual faults is such a precious commodity in the American cultural landscape! (As you will realize after your life as an immigrant progresses to an advanced stage, this reluctance in admitting fault also has to do with the prevalent role that litigation plays in American life.) More frequently than not, you are likely to wonder, "Where does the unwavering faith in individual spirit fade away to when problems arise?"

It was the summer of 1963 when you and I spent a month at a Buddhist temple preparing for the "Gate of Hell" (college entrance exam). Do you still remember our meeting with that Bee-goo-nee [unmarried female monk] who was "repenting" for her "sin"? Before she settled in the deadly silence of the Buddhist temple, she had passed a bar exam as the first female to do so in Korea and had become a trial judge. Her fate was such that she sentenced a murder suspect to death, but after the prisoner was executed, the real murderer was arrested. Tormented by the guilt and existential limitation of human reasoning, she, at the age of twenty-seven, changed her black judge's robe for a shabby gray monk's robe and cut off her connections to the secular world. At the time we faced her saddened eyes, she was approaching her sixties. "Thirty years of personal penitence for a collective error of the legal system? Was she insane?" I remember asking myself repeatedly.

Since then, however, MK, her eyes with those indelible marks of suffering have bothered me on innumerable occasions when I had to attribute my failure to external conditions. When my car was towed away from the no-parking stretch of that Montreal street near the Botanical Garden where you and I visited during your stay here, you personally witnessed my furious response. Unfortunately, I have no way of recollecting whether that was one of the times you called me an American.

MK—

The last facet of the individualism-collectivism continuum likely to cause a great amount of cognitive dissonance in the process of your assimilation to American life is the extent to which you have to assert your individuality to other people. You probably have no difficulty remembering our high school principal, K. W. Park, for whom we had a respect-contempt complex. He used to lecture, almost daily at morning assemblies, on the virtue of being modest. As he preached it, it was a form of the Confucian virtue of self-denial. Our existence or presence among other people, he told us, should not be overly felt through communicated messages (regardless of whether they are done with a tongue or pen). His most frequently quoted verse from Lao-tzu's *Tao Te Ching* was:

> *True words aren't eloquent;*
>   *eloquent words aren't true.*
> *Wise men don't need to prove their point;*
>   *men who need to prove their point aren't wise.*
>
> *The Master has no possessions.*
> *The more he does for others,*
>   *the happier he is.*
> *The more he gives to others,*
>   *the wealthier he is.*
>
> *The Tao nourishes by not forcing.*
>   *By not dominating, the Master leads.*

The Taoist principal, Park, was a fervent advocate of "conspicuous subtlety" in presenting oneself. He was not subtle at all about instilling in our budding minds his "messianic" message that self-advertisement was the worst form to let others know about "my existence." One's existence, we were told, should be noticed by others in the form of our acts and conduct. One is obligated to provide opportunities for others to experience one's existence through what he or she does. Self-initiated effort for public recognition or self-aggrandizement was the most shameful conduct for a person of virtue.

This idea is interesting and noble as a philosophical posture, but when it is practiced in America, it will not get you anywhere in most circumstances. The lack of self-assertion is translated directly into timidity and lack of self-confidence. This is a culture where you must exert your individuality to the extent that it would make our high school principal turn in his grave out of shame and disgust. Blame the size of the territory or the population of this country. You may even blame the fast-paced cadence of life or the social mobility that moves people around at a dizzying speed. Whatever the specific reason might be, Americans are not waiting to experience you or your behaviors as they exist. They want a "documented" version of you that is eloquently summarized, decorated, and certified. What they are looking for is not your raw, unprocessed being with rich texture; rather, it is a slickly processed self, neatly packaged and, most important, conveniently delivered to them. Self-advertising is encouraged almost to the point of pretentiousness. Years ago in Syracuse, I had an occasion to introduce a visiting Korean monk-scholar to a gathering of people who wanted to hear something about Oriental philosophies. After taking an elegantly practiced bow to the crowd, this humble monk declared, "My name is . . . Please teach me, as I do not know anything." It took quite a bit of probing and questioning for us to extract something to chew on from that monk with the mysterious smile. Contrast this with an American colleague of mine applying for a promotion several years ago, who literally hauled in two cabinets full of documented evidence of his scholarly achievements.

MK—

I am afraid this rambling letter really bored you with inconsequential topics, which might not have any bearing on your immigrant's life as a businessman. Seriously, however, if your business is such that you are dependent (both literally and figuratively) on Korean ethnic institutions in large cities such as Los Angeles, New York, or Chicago, none of these derivatives of the individualism-collectivism continuum may pose any threat or hindrance to your career. The "institutional completeness" of a contemporary immigrant society is so thorough that an immigrant who chooses to do so can lead a relatively undisturbed life thickly insulated from the mainstream. Because of a tremendous improvement in communication technologies and transportation, an immigrant living in a heavily ethnic environment—especially an immigrant from a country like Korea where the nation's communications infrastructure was developed in an American mold—maintains virtually the same information environment as the one in the original homeland. Daily satellite feeds of TV news programs, instant satellite transmission and subsequent reprinting of the newspapers from the homeland, videotapes of the popular TV dramas airlifted within one or two days after the original broadcasts, and the constant infusion of visitors from home all conjure to create a cultural climate radically different from the one that many earlier immigrants faced—a forced acculturation. It is becoming an increasing reality—a very tempting one indeed—to live in America without really leaving "home." Should such a home-away-from-home lifestyle become your choice, more than likely what I have scribbled here will not mean much for your immediate future as a businessman. But then, I may ask, what about your children when they start bringing home the debris of friction with the mainstream culture? The curious journey toward the American end of the individualism-collectivism continuum will be inevitable, I assure you. The real question is whether it will be in your generation, your children's, or their children's. Whenever it happens, it will be a bittersweet revenge for me, since only then will you realize how it feels to be called an American by your best high school chum.

SUGGESTED READINGS

Hyun, Peter. 1984. *Koreana.* Seoul, Korea: Korea Britannica Corporation.

Liu, Zongren. 1988. *Two Years in the Melting Pot.* San Francisco: China Books and Periodicals.

Lutz, William. 1989. *Double Speak.* New York: Harper & Row.

Mitchell, Stephen. 1988. *Tao Te Ching.* New York: Harper & Row.

Moore, Barrington, Jr. 1984. *Privacy: Studies in Social and Cultural History.* Armonk, NY: M. E. Sharpe.

Yoshikawa, Muneo Jay. 1988. Cross-Cultural Adaptation and Perceptual Development. In *Cross-Cultural Adaptation: Current Approaches.* Young Y. Kim and William B. Gudykunst, eds. Newbury Park, CA: Sage.

STUDY QUESTIONS

1. What are some differences between Korean and American customs relating to privacy?

2. Americans are ordinarily polite to friends, often reluctant to be critical. How does this differ from how Koreans would handle "honest" criticism? Which cultural practice appears to be most productive and truthful?

3. Can you think of public euphemisms other than those mentioned by Professor Kim? What are the societal functions of these euphemisms?

4. What was the poignant decision a female Korean judge made after she had made an error? How did she handle her fault? In contrast, how do Americans handle their faults?

5. How do the cultural principles of "asserting one's individualism" differ greatly between Americans and Koreans?

6. Can you understand why Professor Kim resented being called an American by his best childhood friend?

NINE

The Young, the Rich, and the Famous: Individualism as an American Cultural Value

PORANEE NATADECHA-SPONSEL
University of Hawai'i, Honolulu

From the point of view of a scholar raised in Thailand, Americans appear open and immediately friendly in their greetings. However, if one looks closely with a critical eye, these greetings are superficial and ritualized, and they tend to hide the more important aspects of American cultural values. The openness in greetings provides both contrast and contradiction to the closedness of social relations and family structures, especially when compared to traditional Thai cultural values. Further, the values of privacy and individualism and the attainment of wealth and fame are viewed as critical elements in relation to the nature of social relations and the kinship system.

Poranee Natadecha-Sponsel was born in the multiethnic region of Thais and Malays in the southern part of Thailand. She has lived in the United States since 1978. She received her B.A. with honors in English and Philosophy from Chulalongkorn University in Bangkok, Thailand (1969). She earned her M.A. (1973) in Philosophy at Ohio University, Athens, and her Ed.D. (1991) from the University of Hawai'i at Mānoa is in Educational Foundations with an interdisciplinary focus on Anthropology and Environmental Education. She currently teaches interdisciplinary courses in Religion, Environmental Philosophy and Ethics, Race and Ethnic Relations, and Gender Studies at Chaminade University of Honolulu where she is also an Academic Officer.

"**H**i, how are you?" "Fine, thank you, and you?" These are greetings that everybody in America hears and says every day—salutations that come readymade and packaged just like a hamburger and fries. There is no real expectation for any special information in response to these greetings. Do not, under any circumstances, take up anyone's time by responding in depth to the programmed query. What or how you may feel at the moment is of little, if any, importance. Thai people would immediately perceive that our concerned American friends are truly interested in our welfare, and this concern would require polite reciprocation by spelling out the details of our current condition. We become very disappointed when we have had enough experience in the United States to learn that we have bored, amused, or even frightened many of our American acquaintances by taking the greeting "How are you?" so literally. We were reacting like Thais, but in the American context where salutations have a different meaning, our detailed reactions were inappropriate. In Thai society, a greeting among acquaintances usually requests specific information about the other person's condition, such as "Where are you going?" or "Have you eaten?"

One of the American contexts in which this greeting is most confusing and ambiguous is at the hospital or clinic. In these sterile and ritualistic settings, I have always been uncertain exactly how to answer when the doctor or nurse asks "How are you?" If I deliver a packaged answer of "Fine," I wonder if I am telling a lie. After all, I am there in the first place precisely because I am not so fine. Finally, after debating for some time, I asked one nurse how she expected a patient to answer the query "How are you?" But after asking this question, I then wondered if it was rude to do so. However, she looked relieved after I explained to her that people from different cultures have different ways to greet other people and that for me to be asked how I am in the hospital results in awkwardness. Do I simply answer, "Fine, thank you," or do I reveal in accurate detail how I really feel at the moment? My suspicion was verified when the nurse declared that "How are you?" was really no more than a polite greeting and that she didn't expect any answer more elaborate than simply "Fine." However, she told me that some patients do answer her by describing every last ache and pain from which they are suffering.

A significant question that comes to mind is whether the verbal pattern of greetings reflects any social relationship in American culture. The apparently warm and sincere greeting may initially suggest interest in the person, yet the intention and expectations are, to me, quite superficial. For example, most often the person greets you quickly and then walks by to attend to other business without even waiting for your response! This type of greeting is just like a package of American fast food! The person eats the food quickly without enjoying the taste. The convenience is like many other American accoutrements of living such as cars, household appliances, efficient telephones, or simple, systematic, and predictable arrangements of groceries in the supermarket. However, usually when this greeting is delivered, it seems to lack a personal touch and genuine feeling. It is little more than ritualized behavior.

I have noticed that most Americans keep to themselves even at social gatherings. Conversation may revolve around many topics, but little, if anything, is revealed about oneself. Without talking much about oneself and not knowing much about others, social relations seem to remain at an abbreviated superficial level. How could one know a person without knowing something about him or her? How much does one need to know about a person to really know that person?

After living in this culture for more than a decade, I have learned that there are many topics that should not be mentioned in conversations with American acquaintances or even close friends. One's personal life and one's income are considered to be very private and even taboo topics. Unlike my Thai culture, Americans do not show interest or curiosity by asking such personal questions, especially when one just meets the individual for the first time. Many times I have been embarrassed by my Thai acquaintances who recently arrived at the University of Hawaii and the East-West Center. For instance, one day I was walking on campus with an American friend when we met another Thai woman to whom I had been introduced a few days earlier. The Thai woman came to write her doctoral dissertation at the East-West Center where the American woman worked, so I introduced them to each other. The American woman greeted my Thai companion in Thai language, which so impressed her that she felt immediately at ease. At once, she asked the American woman numerous personal questions such as, How long did you live in Thailand? Why were you there? How long were you married to the Thai man? Why did you divorce him? How long have you been divorced? Are you going to marry a Thai again or an American? How long have you been working here? How much do you earn? The American was stunned. However, she was very patient and more or less answered all those questions as succinctly as she could. I was so uncomfortable that I had to interrupt whenever I could to get her out of the awkward situation in which she had been forced into talking about things she considered personal. For people in Thai society, such questions would be appropriate and not considered too personal, let alone taboo.

The way Americans value their individual privacy continues to impress me. Americans seem to be open and yet there is a contradiction because they are also aloof and secretive. This is reflected in many of their behavior patterns. By Thai standards, the relationship between friends in American society seems to be somewhat superficial. Many Thai students, as well as other Asians, have felt that they could not find genuine friendship with Americans. For example, I met many American classmates who were very helpful and friendly while we were in the same class. We went out, exchanged phone calls, and did the same things as would good friends in Thailand. But those activities stopped suddenly when the semester ended.

Privacy as a component of the American cultural value of individualism is nurtured in the home as children grow up. From birth they are given their own individual, private space, a bedroom separate from that of their parents. American children are taught to become progressively independent, both emotionally and economically, from their family. They learn to help themselves at an early age. In comparison, in Thailand, when parents bring a new baby home from the hospital, it shares the parents' bedroom for two to three years and then shares another bedroom with older siblings of the same sex. Most Thai children do not have their own private room until they finish high school, and some do not have their own room until another sibling moves out, usually when the sibling gets married. In Thailand, there are strong bonds within the extended family. Older siblings regularly help their parents to care for younger ones. In this and other ways, the Thai family emphasizes the interdependence of its members.

I was accustomed to helping Thai babies who fell down to stand up again. Thus, in America when I saw babies fall, it was natural for me to try to help them back on their feet. Once at a summer camp for East-West Center participants, one of the supervisors brought his wife and their ten–month–old son with him. The baby was so cute that many students were playing with him. At one point he was trying to walk and fell, so all the Asian students, males and females, rushed to help him up. Although the father and mother were nearby, they paid no attention to their fallen and crying baby. However, as the students were trying to help and comfort him, the parents told them to leave him alone; he would be all right on his own. The baby did get up and stopped crying without any assistance. Independence is yet another component of the American value of individualism.

Individualism is even reflected in the way Americans prepare, serve, and consume food. In a typical American meal, each person has a separate plate and is not supposed to share or taste food from other people's plates. My Thai friends and I are used to eating Thai style, in which you share food from a big serving dish in the middle of the table. Each person dishes a small amount from the serving dish onto his or her plate and finishes this portion before going on with the next portion of the same or a different serving dish. With the Thai pattern of eating, you regularly reach out to the serving dishes throughout the meal. But this way of eating is not considered appropriate in comparison to the common American practice where each person eats separately from his or her individual plate.

One time my American host, a divorcée who lived alone, invited a Thai girlfriend and myself to an American dinner at her home. When we were reaching out and eating a small portion of one thing at a time in Thai style, we were told to dish everything we wanted onto our plates at one time and that it was not considered polite to reach across the table. The proper American way was to have each kind of food piled up on your plate at once. If we were to eat in the same manner in Thailand, eyebrows would have been raised at the way we piled up food on our plates, and we would have been considered to be eating like pigs, greedy and inconsiderate of others who shared the meal at the table.

Individualism as a pivotal value in American culture is reflected in many other ways. Material wealth is not only a prime status marker in American society but also a guarantee and celebration of individualism—wealth allows the freedom to do almost anything, although usually within the limits of law. The pursuit of material wealth through individual achievement is instilled in Americans from the youngest age. For example, I was surprised to see an affluent American couple, who own a large ranch house and two BMW cars, send their nine-year-old son to deliver newspapers. He has to get up very early each morning to deliver the papers, even on Sunday! During summer vacation, the boy earns additional money by helping in his parents' gift shop from 10 A.M. to 5 P.M. His thirteen-year-old sister often earns money by babysitting, even at night.

In Thailand, only children from poorer families work to earn money to help the household. Middle- and high-income parents do not encourage their children to work until after they have finished their education. They provide economic support in order to free their children to concentrate on and excel in their studies. Beyond the regular schooling, families who can afford it pay for special tutoring as well as training in music, dance, or sports. However, children in low- and middle-income families help their parents with household chores and the care of younger children.

Many American children have been encouraged to get paid for their help around the house. They rarely get any gifts free of obligations. They even have to be good to get Santa's gifts at Christmas! As they grow up, they are conditioned to earn things they want; they learn that "there is no such thing as a free lunch." From an early age, children are taught to become progressively independent economically from their parents. Also, most young people are encouraged to leave home at college age to be on their own. From my viewpoint as a Thai, it seems that American family ties and closeness are not as strong as in Asian families whose children depend on family financial support until joining the work force after college age. Thereafter, it is the children's turn to help support their parents financially.

Modern American society and economy emphasize individualism in other ways. The nuclear family is more common than the extended family, and newlyweds usually establish their own independent household rather than initially living with either the husband's or the wife's parents. Parents and children appear to be close only when the children are very young. Most American parents seem to "lose" their children by the teenage years. They don't seem to belong to each other as closely as do Thai families. Even though I have seen more explicit affectionate expression among American family members than among Asian ones, the close interpersonal spirit seems to be lacking. Grandparents have relatively little to do with the grandchildren on any regular basis, in contrast to the extended family, which is more common in Thailand. The family and society seem to be graded by age to the point that grandparents, parents, and children are separated by generational subcultures that are evidently alienated from one another. Each group "does its own thing." Help and support are usually limited to whatever does not interfere with one's own life. In America, the locus of responsibility is more on the individual than on the family.

In one case I know of, a financially affluent grandmother with Alzheimer's disease is taken care of twenty-four hours a day by hired help in her own home. Her daughter visits and relieves the helper occasionally. The mature granddaughter, who has her own family, rarely visits. Yet they all live in the same neighborhood. However, each lives in a different house, and each is very independent. Although the mother worries about the grandmother, she cannot do much. Her husband also needs her, and she divides her time between him, her daughters and their children, and the grandmother. When the mother needs to go on a trip with her husband, a second hired attendant is required to care for the grandmother temporarily. When I asked why the granddaughter doesn't temporarily care for the grandmother, the reply was that she has her own life, and it would not be fair for the granddaughter to take care of the grandmother, even for a short period of time. Yet I wonder if it is fair for the grandmother to be left out. It seems to me that the value of individualism and its associated independence account for these apparent gaps in family ties and support.

In contrast to American society, in Thailand older parents with a long-term illness are asked to move in with their children and grandchildren if they are not already living with them. The children and grandchildren take turns attending to the grandparent, sometimes with help from live-in maids. Living together in the same house reinforces moral support among the generations within an extended family. The older generation is respected because of the previous economic, social, and moral support for their children and grandchildren. Family relations provide one of the most important contexts for being a "morally good person," which is traditionally the principal concern in the Buddhist society of Thailand.

In America, being young, rich, and/or famous allows one greater freedom and independence and thus promotes the American value of individualism. This is reflected in the mass appeal of major annual television events like the Super Bowl and the Academy Awards. The goal of superachievement is also seen in more mundane ways. For example, many parents encourage their children to take special courses and to work hard to excel in sports as a shortcut to becoming rich and famous. I know one mother who has taken her two sons to tennis classes and tournaments since the boys were six years old, hoping that at least one of them will be a future tennis star like Ivan Lendl. Other parents focus their children on acting, dancing, or musical talent. The children have to devote much time and hard work as well as sacrifice the ordinary activities of youth in order to develop and perform their natural talents and skills in prestigious programs. But those who excel in the sports and entertainment industries can become rich and famous, even at an early age, as for example Madonna, Tom Cruise, and Michael Jackson. Television and other media publicize these celebrities and thereby reinforce the American value of individualism, including personal achievement and financial success.

Although the American cultural values of individualism and the aspiration to become rich and famous have had some influence in Thailand, there is also cultural and religious resistance to these values. Strong social bonds, particularly within the extended family, and the hierarchical structure of the kingdom run counter to individualism. Also, youth gain social recognition through their academic achievement. From the perspective of Theravada Buddhism, which strongly influences Thai culture, aspiring to be rich and famous would be an illustration of greed, and those who have achieved wealth and fame do not celebrate it publicly as much as in American society. Being a good, moral person is paramount, and ideally Buddhists emphasize restraint and moderation.

Beyond talent and skill in the sports and entertainment industries, there are many other ways that young Americans can pursue wealth. Investment is one route. One American friend who is only a sophomore in college has already invested heavily in the stock market to start accumulating wealth. She is just one example of the 1980s trend for youth to be more concerned with their individual finances than with social, political, and environmental issues. With less attention paid to public issues, the expression of individualism seems to be magnified through emphasis on lucrative careers, financial investment, and material consumption—the "Yuppie" phenomenon. This includes new trends in dress, eating, housing (condominiums), and cars (expensive European imports). Likewise, there appears to be less of a long-term commitment to marriage. More young couples are living together without either marriage or plans for future marriage. When such couples decide to get married, prenuptial agreements are made to protect their assets. Traditional values of marriage, family, and sharing appear to be on the decline.

Individualism as one of the dominant values in American culture is expressed in many ways. This value probably stems from the history of the society as a frontier colony of immigrants in search of a better life with independence, freedom, and the opportunity for advancement through personal achievement. However, in the beliefs and customs of any culture there are some disadvantages as well as advantages. Although Thais may admire the achievements and material wealth of American society, there are costs, especially in the value of individualism and associated social phenomena.

STUDY QUESTIONS

1. What are the social implications of the ways in which Americans greet each other? Is this a form of personal sincerity or is it, as the author suggests, to be viewed as similar to our fast food habits—simply convenient and lacking sincerity?
2. How do American greeting practices and Thai greeting practices differ?
3. What are some American subjects that would be taboo in a public meeting with friends?
4. How are eating habits different in Thailand?
5. If you grew up in Thailand, what class distinctions would dictate your expectations as to whether or not you would work to earn money as a youngster?

6. In relation to American individualism, how does the family financial expectations differ from those in Thailand?

7. What might the effects of "doing your own thing" in American culture have on the nature of American family structure? How does this reflect on differences between treatment of the elderly in both cultures?

8. What are the cultural constraints in Thailand that prohibit one from seeking to attain wealth and fame?

TEN

America and I

HERVÉ VARENNE
Teachers College, Columbia University

Having been a foreign graduate student at a prestigious American university, Professor Varenne reflects on differing interpretations of his own personal experiences. What others may have perceived as culture shock was anything but: There were more pressing issues, more important concerns. Now, after twenty years as a resident analyst of American culture, the professional outsider takes a penetrating look into the inside.

Hervé Varenne *was born and raised in France, where he completed his B.A. before earning his doctorate in Anthropology from the University of Chicago in 1972. He is the author of many books and articles on aspects of everyday life and education in the United States. His publications include* Americans Together *(Teachers College Press 1977),* American School Language *(Irvington 1983), and* Ambiguous Harmony *(Ablex, 1997). Professor Varenne is the editor and major contributor to* Symbolizing America *(University of Nebraska Press 1986). He is professor of Education at Teachers College, Columbia University.*

Many years after I finished graduate school at the University of Chicago, a friend who had started the same year I did, said something like, "Wow, you were in quite a state of culture shock that year!" My Michigan-born wife still tells me how poignant to her are the stories I tell of my eating my evening meals by myself, alone at a big table for eight at the International House, even when a group of my peers were loudly congregating in another part of the cafeteria. After all, I tell her, they had never specifically invited me, and anyway, I did not really feel comfortable in the midst of a group that seemed so assured of itself, noisily engaging in discussions in which I could not quite take part.

By the time people gave me these interpretations of my behavior, I had thoroughly learned what "culture shock" is meant to refer to in anthropological theory, and I was well versed in all the writings that highlight the difficulties "people from different cultures" have when they meet and have to do something together.

But that is now. Then, the time was September 1968; I was twenty years old. I had spent most of the preceding academic year in Chicago in the shadow of my parents.

We had made a comfortable nest that nicely filtered whatever was radically alien. We enjoyed ourselves. As for me, the heavy stakes were back in France where the important exams awaited me. I do not remember having sweated over my application to graduate school in anthropology. No one in my kin or acquaintance had ever applied to any American university. I did not understand the honor that had been given me when I was accepted, and I had no idea of the price I would have to pay.

By October 1968, everything was clearer. I was petrified with the fear that came with the recognition that I was among a very select few and that soon we would be much fewer. I was probably frozen in a quasi-catatonic silence. I now also suspect that it would be easy to analyze conversations with my fellow students and emphasize all the moments when I failed to recognize an invitation to join a group for dinner and all the moments when my requests for an invitation were ignored.

Yet I remember clearly that interactional mismatches were not my most pressing problems. My pressing problem was making sense of Talcott Parsons and of the ways in which my professor David Schneider agreed and disagreed with what he made us read. There I was, with several hundred pages to read a week—something I had never had to do in my college years in France—and three or four important papers to write within the next ten weeks. These assignments were important in all sorts of practical ways: My scholarship was on the line, as was the support my parents were giving me and my evolving recognition that cultural anthropology was something in which I was indeed passionately interested. I may not have fully understood what David Schneider had to say, but my cultural insensitivity to his ways of saying was the least of my concerns.

Eventually, my main concern was alleviated. The year finished and my scholarship was renewed. I was on my way, and I could go for a pure vacation in France as the children of the French petite bourgeoisie always do. The following year I wrote an M.A. thesis, my proposal was accepted, I received a grant, and after the ritual vacation, I "went into the field" in the bright yellow Pontiac convertible of my childhood dreams about America.

CULTURE SHOCK?

Can one be in "culture shock" and not know it? That depends, of course, on what one means by "culture shock" and thus, eventually, by "culture." Anthropologists generally define *culture shock* as a psychological syndrome, an actual state of a person when he or she is first confronted with the practical recognition that people do not all conduct their everyday life the way he or she has seen people conduct it until then. I still remember the way my heart clutched when I first got a glimpse of American suburbia from the Dan Ryan expressway in Chicago. It corresponded exactly to all the pictures I had seen of it in France, but now these little one-storied houses with their open front yards on tree-lined streets were all around me. They had moved from the world of my imagination to the world of my experience. They were now "here" and not "there."

And so my heart clutched. Often, I was unable and unwilling to perform acts that were routine to most people around me. Like many who first arrive in the United States, I had problems with forms of address. I gagged on calling my professors "Paul," "Cliff," "David," "Milton," and "Vic." My professors could only be "Friedrich" "Geertz," "Schneider," "Singer," and "Turner" in reference (as they still are to me when I talk or think about them) and "Professor . . ." in address (as I have stopped doing in deference to my understanding of American cultural proprieties). Fellow students could be addressed by their first names (but I often referred to them by their last). If I overheard them address professors by their first names, I inferred a familiarity that amounted to a professional anointment: I instinctively assumed that they could do so only because they had already been told that they had passed all the exams that would certify them as "the best." It took me several years to realize that professors could let students address them by their first name, still give them an extremely hard time, and eventually fail them.

These assumptions of mine, and the actual performances that accompanied them, could be interpreted as symptoms of something real that I could not name but that professionals might have helped me through. My friends had seen me, they had talked, and they had made a diagnosis: I was in "culture shock." Like depression or dyslexia, culture shock was an aspect of the world that human beings had failed to locate properly until science "discovered" the syndrome on its way to finding a cure for it.

There is also another possibility that an anthropologist must consider, and that is the possibility that culture shock is something that is "made in America" with miscellaneous pieces of human behavior that would be ignored anywhere else. Certainly I experienced something driving down Dan Ryan expressway that was not fully comfortable, and an empathetic therapist might have made me talk about it. Certainly, it appeared to my friends that I was puzzled, lost, silenced. America offers a pattern to bring all these things together, and they can be made into something that looks like culture shock. But this practical act of my friends when they used this pattern cannot be taken as evidence of a state of *my* mind. At most it is an indicator of what my friends could do—whether they were indeed aware of the logic of their act, whether they in fact believed in culture shocks. Other people in other parts of the world have institutionalized other ways of dealing with the odd behavior of the strangers they receive, and there is little evidence that the American organization of these manifestations more closely approximates "reality" than theirs do.

As far as I was concerned, I did not organize my various experiences in such a way as to recognize "culture shock" as something I was suffering from. I had other problems, and they centered on academic and economic issues. The more I sat in classes and the more I was certain I wanted to continue, the clearer it became that I indeed had a problem here. It was a familiar problem. I had sweated through five sets of major exams in France, and the part of my world in the United States that had to do with academic stuff was not so different. I recognized the fear, and I identified where it came from and what might resolve the problem: persistence. Four years later, I received a Ph.D., I was offered a position as an assistant professor at Teachers College, I married a woman who had been raised fifty miles from the town where I had conducted my fieldwork, and I moved to New York City. I was twenty-four years old then, something I sometimes have to downplay when people around me talk about the great advantage of taking breaks in one's education, experiencing the world, growing, and so on. I had graduated to a new set of problems as I worked toward tenure and at becoming an acceptable husband and father.

Would this four-year journey through the University of Chicago have been easier if I had been born in the middle-class areas of the United States whence came most of my friends? Many anthropologists would initially have to answer "yes" to this question. Individuals have cultures. They feel more comfortable in their own culture. They thrive best there, and they will experience great difficulty when they move to a "new" culture. Such statements have now become common sense, not simply among some anthropologists but also among the people of the United States at large. The anthropologist Michael Moffat once wrote that it may indeed be more enlightened to deal with foreigners through the constructs of culture difference ("After all, he has a different culture, so he can't understand what we are talking about") than through the constructs of intelligence ("He is really dumb").

Still, I believe I had a much easier time at the University of Chicago than many of my friends. Many of them now appear to me much more confused than I was about the fundamental condition of our life there. Then, of course, I thought they were the best and the brightest. After two or three years of studying America, I began to suspect that they could not see through the logic of liberal democracy, or perhaps that they could not organize their own behavior in terms of the vague understanding they must have had that things were not quite working the way they were dramatized to be. When our professors told us that they were treating us "like junior colleagues," they failed to specify that the basic condition of life for a junior assistant professor is (not) getting tenure. Democracy is about races on level fields and about fair competition among formal equals—it is not about universal success. Although every person may become president of the United States, most people will fail. For the vast majority of people in democracies, the fear of failure at the hands of personal interlocutors is the basic condition of everyday life. From the earliest, the persons that may be the closest and most familiar—parents, kindergarten teachers, Little League coaches, peers, and so on—are also the persons who can decide that we are not quite making it, that we need "help," "therapy," a "special" program, an environment "better suited to our needs." At school, on the job, and in most other endeavors, a middle-class person will continually be evaluated and, after a while, evaluating. Democracy is about the daily experience of inequality. In the long run, to mistake an attempt to make the competition fair (by evaluators making themselves "open," "friendly," "personable," and so on) for a sign that one has won is to leave oneself open to major difficulties when the race is actually run and announcements of the prizes are made.

THANKSGIVINGS

I am not so sure that I was in culture shock. From my point of view (and by comparison to my experiences in France), the faculty at Chicago were particularly nice in performing their appointed tasks, and I felt privileged when, in one instance, I could establish another kind of familiarity: the hierarchical familiarity of the adopted son who must continue to demonstrate the confidence his father has placed in him.

In any event, I had a few good friends. I could have extended conversations about structuralism, functionalism, models in the muddles, and other esoterica. I could ask what became and remains the fundamental question of my academic work: How can it make sense for someone to say, or do, this or that? What are the conditions that make this statement or sequence of behavior a reasonable response? What are the costs of other possible responses? How could someone perform something unexpected and not have it noticed as unexpected? In other words, how can one lie? How can one make something that had not been there before? How, perhaps, can one who is not American make it through the University of Chicago?

There happens to be another American myth about the fate of foreigners when they cross the boundaries of the United States. This is the myth of the immigrant who comes with nothing—not even the language—and "makes good" through hard work, self-reliance, and, perhaps, intelligence. This myth is now enshrined in the sacred space of Ellis Island. This is the myth now told about immigrants from the Far East or certain Caribbean islands. This is the myth that explains what is taken to be the success of Asian students in American universities, and it is tempting for me to couch my experience in these terms. I, too, did not speak English well when I came (through the corridors of Kennedy Airport rather than the halls of Ellis Island); I, too, worked hard. And I too made it into the upper ranks of my chosen profession. And so I could celebrate (as in fact I do) the institutions (enlightened admission procedures, generous scholarship funds, understanding professors, and so on) that made it possible for what I must be too modest to call my "talents" to flourish. For this and for many other gifts, I must give thanks every next to last Thursday of November.

There is enough verisimilitude in the Pilgrims' myth to couch my history in the United States in its terms. Still, like all myths, this particular origin myth tells us more about America and what it highlights and downplays than it tells about the experience of immigrants—except as the contents of this myth slowly become an aspect of their conditions that immigrants cannot ignore. For me, as perhaps for many immigrants, including the original Pilgrims, the United States started as the ideal of what France should be but, for whatever reason, could not achieve: a place where an intellectual interest in how human beings live could be comfortably served, with easily accessible libraries, concerned professors, financial help, and so on.

Only later did I understand that all this came at a price. The United States is not simply a more efficient version of France. It is a different place altogether, a different culture, and one cannot accept its gifts without also becoming a part of it. My first Thanksgivings were wonderful anthropological times when I was confronted with stylized, if not ritualized, dramatic performances that revealed America to me in its glory even when the actual details were altogether gross. There was the slightly ridiculous turkey, the continual tellings of overeating, the football games, the plateful of messy mush, and the interactional and physical struggles around the organization and realization of the event (at whose house? on what plane? with whose money?). Thanksgiving is not an easy time for most people in the United States, but it is also a moment of great social unison, a moment reimprovised in individual families, a ritual of beginnings and temporary endings, and a moment when the American spirit is celebrated and reconstituted, even as resources are redistributed.

Thanksgiving is a more encompassing product of America than the other sacred celebration of origins myth, the Fourth of July. I continue to delight in analyzing it, but I also know that it is now "my" myth too—that is, a myth that is being used all around me, for me, and possible against me. For my first two Thanksgivings at the University of Chicago, I was invited by a wonderful association with its headquarters in, of all places for a French man, Paris, Illinois, to come and spend the four days in a home there. Hundreds of certified "foreign students" in Chicago were picked up in buses and driven to various small towns of "downstate Illinois." The families, we were told, would "share their gifts" with us on Thanksgiving day. Only much later did I understand how this event itself recapitulated American culture in a manner that traditional social structural anthropologists would have loved. We stopped at all the sacred spots—including the "Second" Baptist Church, which happened to be our one contact with blacks in Paris. We attended a basketball game at the high school, we visited farms and a small factory, and we were formally asked where we wanted to go to church on Sunday and were taken there. Everything was perfect. There was an inside and there was an outside. My hosts and I safely constructed me as being "outside"—or so I thought.

I am not a certifiable foreigner anymore, and some look at me in a funny way when I tell them that I am not a citizen. After all, I have resided in the United States for more than 20 years; I married an American citizen and have three children who are all citizens; and I am a full professor at a major university. Even if I wished to place myself "out" when the time to give thanks for America comes, I would not get much cooperation. If I ever feel that I have "become" American, I will make the declaration of faith, the pledge of allegiance, the final statement of willingness to be born again civically in a process aptly named "naturalization."

There are many reasons why I will not take this step, why I cannot recite the immigrant myth any more than I can recite the "culture shock" myth. I cannot deny, however, the reality of the myth as something that concerns me. For a long time, I may have deceived myself into thinking that, because I was placed in the position of "foreigner to America," I was free of it. I know better now. From the day when I first entered an American consulate in Marseilles and began to respond to the practical requests of the culture, I have been "caught" in America. I yielded, and I continue to yield. I filled out the form and submitted to the medical exams. Later, I became fluent in English to the point that I cannot quite talk anthropology in French. Professionally, I have tried to be an "accessible" faculty member who addresses his students by their first names and lets them address him by his first name. I laugh understandingly when people talk about the state of culture shock I was in or about the way I still have a French accent, a French writing style, and a French way of arguing. I was never coerced. Indeed, I can say that I have chosen to remain caught by America. To tell the truth, when I was finally fully surrounded by America during my fieldwork in Appleton, I discovered that I fundamentally liked this culture and that I enjoyed the cultural manifestations that many of my student friends, at the end of the 1960s, were struggling so hard to escape.

AMERICA AS FACT

Enjoying America does not make an American. It does not make me one, and it does not make anyone else one either. This is the anthropologist, the professional outsider, speaking. Neither I nor anybody else in the United States can be explained by culture shock and its attendant psychointeractional traumas. I cannot be explained through the myth of the immigrant.

Still, both myths are real conditions of my life here. "American culture" is as present to me, and to everyone else in the United States, as the Atlantic Ocean, and I know by experience that landing at Kennedy Airport is not much different from plunging into water: Certain specific things had better be done fast if one does not want to drown (or be shipped back to the old country). It is not the case that

America is real because all of us in the United States "believe" it is real. America and its myths, rituals, customs, and institutions are real because people persist in placing us in conditions where we have to respond practically to the conditions according to their own logic.

Take a question like "Why are you not getting naturalized?" or a statement like "I guess you do not understand what we are trying to say because you are not from this country." The people who tell me such things are themselves caught in a cultural web that makes these statements commonsensical to the people who utter them. These questions and statements then become an aspect of the cultural web in which I now have to perform. I can make many different responses; I can even ignore the question. But other people will respond to me in the terms set by the question, and it will indeed make more sense to try and construct an answer—particularly if I expect to stay in the good graces of the people who asked the question. To the question about naturalization, I usually answer that I will not change citizenship because I believe that nationalism is one of the most dangerous ideas evolved by the human species (more dangerous than the atomic bomb). I believe that the process of changing citizenship puts a focus on nationalism and thus reinforces the institutions of nationalism that I wish to undermine. I cannot help being a French citizen because the current international order is based on every human being on the globe "having" a nationality. But I can choose not to carry an American passport.

This is a plausible answer even though many in the United States who have given a different answer, or who are the descendants of people who gave a different answer, do not like it. After all, the most powerful political statement of the 1960s was not "Make love, not war." It was "America, love it or leave it." Note, that to be meaningful, both statements depend on joining the concept of love with a proper social unit—couple, family, state, and country—for which one must eventually give thanks. This is the frame within which questions about one's relationship to America are placed, and to the extent that one cannot prevent the questions from being asked, this is the frame within which one's own answers, behaviors, and life history are placed; cross-referenced with other answers, behaviors, and life histories; and then evaluated.

I have been writing that I was "placed in the position of an outsider" rather than "I was an outsider," for precisely the reason that the framing of my actions, during my first years in the United States as well as now, has never been under my control. I was free not to apply for a visa to come to the country, but once I decided to apply, I placed myself within one of the categories defined by Congress and the State Department. So I got a "student visa," which gave me special rights, privileges, duties, and limitations. When I went to Paris, Illinois, on my Thanksgiving trips, the fact that I had such a category was used, by both myself and my hosts, as the essential aspect of my history that justified my trip. Once in Paris, the formal differences between my hosts and myself were further expanded: In their speech, their behavior, and their actions, they and I improvised a particular version of "the foreign student." That this was a special time tightly controlled by American patterns is perhaps best revealed by the experience of students from sub-Saharan Africa. In the practices of the town, they were, precisely, *not* black, and they were given access to parts of homes that other people of African descent never touched—except perhaps as domestics.

Later, when I finally received my doctorate, I could have left the United States. To stay, I had to redefine myself, administratively at first. And so I was a "resident alien." With this status, I was moved out of the position of outsider. My story was recast as it could now be said that I was "one of those foreign students who say they want to return home at the end of their studies but always find a way of staying here." There are flattering versions of this story and not so flattering ones. I never can quite control which version is going to be told when, and I may try desperately to argue—as I am doing here—that there is more to me than such stories. But I cannot prevent such stories from being told in the particular ways that make America unique and altogether beautiful.

FUTURES: PATHS NOT YET TAKEN

Cultural anthropology, uncomfortably, has a place within the behavioral *sciences.* What it writes about the fate of human beings when they get together is eventually judged by its power to enlighten us about the universal processes that are involved in the production of uniquely particular moments. What I write about America, to the extent that I consider myself a scientist of sorts, I could write about France. France, too, is a historically developed frame, a set of patterns used in France to handle the social world the French—and all others who cross the boundaries of the country—get to inhabit. The history of France has been different from the history of the United States, and the cultural worlds that have evolved in each geographical and institutional space are different. Not only are they different, but they are also at work maintaining a difference, since—as time has passed—each has become part of the historical reality of the other. America, for a long time, was a reproach to France ("Why can't we be like them?"). France, or at least the vague vision of Europe that may cross the Atlantic, can be, for America, either a cautionary tale about what people escaped, a reference point to measure "how far we have gone," or—more recently—an occasion to worry about competitors.

What one says, writes, and does is always framed by a cultural pattern that offers the phonology, vocabulary, syntax, rhetoric, style, and genre in which the statement could be expressed. As the Russian philosopher of language, Mikhail Bakhtin, wrote, we always speak in borrowed words on a marketplace crowded with others also struggling to make themselves heard over our own voices. I take this to be a major finding of scientific research in anthropology and sociology. No statement, however framed, is ever *determined* by its frame. Indeed, all statements are, wittingly or not, challenges to the frame, attempts to say more than is allowed by a stereotypical application of the pattern.

Certainly, here, I am writing in English, in the style of a quasi-scholarly paper, within the framework of anthropology, and so on. It would, however, be more accurate to my condition to say that I am struggling with all that has been given me to say something that will move us along. Whether it does is not really in my hands. As such a paper is read, it becomes a more or less temporary or powerful moment in the history of the reader. It may be disregarded or may cause one to stumble as one moves along one's path. It may also move someone to notice another path or to open another one. This response itself may then become a possibility for me. It may be ignored, or it may lead to a further reframing of my own life.

Nothing is standing still in human life. Neither America nor I, each as historical facts—albeit of an incommensurably different scale—can control each other or even our own future. We can answer questions about what was done, about the process through which things get done, but not about what is going to get done. There is no definite answer to that question except the one found in a famous phrase that summarizes best my first experiences of America, a phrase that nicely ties liberal democratic strivings with their biblical roots in their many manifestations: The answer is blowing in the wind.

STUDY QUESTIONS

1. How does Professor Varenne define "culture shock"? What were the initial aspects of the American university to which he had difficulty adjusting?
2. What do you suppose the author means by "Democracy is about the daily experience of inequality"?
3. How does the author envision myths in American culture? The Pilgrims? Thanksgiving? The Fourth of July?
4. Professor Varenne appears grateful for many things that he experienced as a graduate student. What do you think he implies when he remarks that "Only later did I understand that all this came at a price"?
5. After many years of living in the United States, the author has decided not to take the path to becoming a citizen. What reasons does he offer? What do you believe are his most profound reasons for not becoming naturalized?

ELEVEN

Encounters with
the Elderly in America

YOHKO TSUJI
Cornell University, Ithaca, New York

The surprises encountered in America by a Japanese graduate student are provided in a comparative framework. Wondering why the elderly appear invisible in American society, the author investigates our negative attitudes and reflects on the differences expressed toward the elderly in American and Japanese societies. Then she shares her fieldwork experiences at a senior center, further contrasting the attitudes and actions in the two cultures.

Yohko Tsuji *now teaches anthropology at Cornell University as Visiting Scholar. Raised in Japan, she came to the United States as a student in the mid-1970s. She received her Ph.D. from Cornell University in 1991, after doing fieldwork at the Lake District Senior Center in a small upstate New York city.*

INTRODUCTION

I was born and raised in Japan. I came to the United States in 1976 to attend college in San Diego. Before then, I had visited the country twice and also worked with Americans in Japan for six years. So my culture shock may not have been as severe as foreign students usually experience. Nevertheless, surprises and mysteries were abundant in my early days in San Diego.

I clearly remember my eye-opening realization of racial heterogeneity in the United States. A few days after my arrival, I was walking in a quiet residential neighborhood. I was taken aback by a Caucasian woman who came up to me and asked me directions. Didn't my Oriental face tell her that I was a foreigner? If a Caucasian walks in a Japanese city, no Japanese would regard such a foreigner as a local, much less ask him or her for directions.

My previous experiences did not prepare me for the casualness and lack of formality in my student life in California either. When I went to meet the dean, I put on a formal dress I had brought from Japan. Imagine my surprise when I learned that a man in blue jeans and cowboy boots, who had a huge mustache and was sitting on the secretary's desk, was the dean himself. I also assumed that there would be a formal entrance ceremony at the beginning of the academic year because the absence of such a ritual would be unthinkable in Japan. I was puzzled to see

"Admission Day" marked on the calendar a few weeks after classes were to begin. It turned out that there was no such a thing as an entrance ceremony. The "Admission Day" was to commemorate the state of California's admission into the Union, not freshmen's entry into college.

Surprises and mysteries diminished as I learned my way around. It did not take me long to start wearing T-shirts and jeans. During my first semester, I also obtained a driver's license. Driving was an absolute must to survive in Southern California, where, unlike Japan, public transportation was virtually nonexistent or incredibly inefficient. My initial inability to tell a brake from an accelerator surprised my driving teacher, but before long I found my old Buick indispensable.

One mystery remained, however. It was about older people. After a couple of months in San Diego, I noticed elderly people had disappeared from my life, though I could not imagine my life in Japan without them. Both the invisibility of the elderly and Americans' reactions to them puzzled me. When my American octogenarian friend visited me from Indiana, my roommates treated him nicely but shocked me by their comments after his departure: "I would rather die before I became like him"; "He has outlived his usefulness. He would be happier dead." Didn't they know some day they would also be old? What perplexed me most was that my roommates, who were kind and helpful to me, could say such cruel things about a sweet old man. Not surprisingly, my American friends had a pessimistic view of their own old age. One of them even said, "I will commit suicide before I become old, frail, and ugly." The incident made me realize that Americans had very different views of old age from the Japanese.

Knowing Americans' negative attitudes toward old age did not fully explain the disappearance of the elderly. It further mystified the issue because old people were kept hidden and I could not figure out why old age, a universal human experience, was viewed so differently in America. I was also curious how older Americans actually lived their lives.

Years later, in 1987 and 1988, these puzzlements and curiosities culminated in my eighteen-month-long dissertation research at the Lake District Senior Center in upstate New York. This essay illustrates what I discovered about older Americans as an outsider with anthropological training. To illuminate my comparative perspective, I will first describe my own experiences with the elderly in Japan.

THE ELDERLY IN MY JAPANESE LIFE

In the traditional Japanese family, three generations—grandparents, parents, and children—live together. It is called the "stem family" and is different from the "extended family" (found in China and India, for instance) in that each generation is represented by only one married couple. I grew up in one such family, which consisted of my widowed grandmother, parents, sister, and myself.

Old people occupied a significant part of my life in Japan. Because my mother was a full-time teacher, my grandmother took care of the children and household chores. Consequently, I shared more time and experiences with my grandmother than with my parents. My neighborhood had many old people, grandfathers and grandmothers of my playmates who also lived with their children's family. Though a few elderly men intimidated me by their authoritative manner, I regarded my elderly neighbors as people who would comfort me when I was crying or help me in my grandmother's absence. Japanese folk tales I repeatedly read reinforced this image of the elderly as good, nurturant people. Frequently, the heros and heroines in these stories were born magically, out of a bamboo or a peach, for instance, and raised by a tender elderly couple. The evil qualities of some of the elderly depicted in Western folk tales—for example, the witch in *Hansel and Gretel*—were foreign to me and made an enduring, frightening impression on me.

I was taught to be respectful and kind toward the elderly. Some of them, like my grandmother, were indispensable around the house, whereas others were too frail to do anything productive. However, I never developed a view of the latter as social parasites. I was told that their lifelong hard work consumed their bodies and they deserved special care in old age. I also learned that long life was something to cherish, not to dread. It is customary in Japan that special celebrations are held to honor the elderly on some of their birthdays, just like some wedding anniversaries—for example, the twenty-fifth and fiftieth—receive special commemorations in America. One's sixtieth birthday is called *kanreki* when two zodiac calendars, one with a cycle of ten years and the other with twelve years, meet again. Other rites of passage include the seventieth, seventy-seventh, and eighty-eighth birthdays, which are called *koki, kiju,* and *beiju,* respectively.

Until I moved to San Diego, old people had been an integral part of my life. I developed a generally positive image of old age through my frequent interactions with the elderly, Japanese folk tales, rituals to celebrate longevity, and absorbing what adults said about the elderly and did for them. It is with this cultural background that I plunged into my fieldwork at a senior center to explore old age in America.

MY PRE-FIELDWORK EXPERIENCES

My preparation for fieldwork intensified the negative image of old age in America. Hearing my research plan, one of my academic advisors exclaimed, "What a gloomy topic you have chosen!" Existing literature on old age abounds with the plight of elderly Americans. The stereotypical elderly person in America is described as "impoverished, socially isolated, and physically disabled" (Matthews 1979: 55). Also prevalent is the image of the elderly as someone who does nothing but wait to die. Most studies attribute old age problems to the wide gap existing between cultural ideals (the "ought," such as independence and productivity) and the realities of old age (the "is," such as infirmity, needing assistance, and being retired). Others regard the absence of cultural models for aging as problematic. In other words, studies show that American culture not only provides inadequate means for guiding the elderly, but also fails to provide any helpful models for the elderly to follow.

How can elderly Americans cope with this apparent cultural dilemma? Various strategies are suggested. One school of thought argues that staying active is the key to successful aging. However, because this model of aging is patterned after the lifestyle of American youth, it does not help the ailing, frail elderly. Some other studies assume that the gap between the "ought" and the "is" is unnegotiable and the best strategy, therefore, is to give up cultural ideals. They maintain that adaptation to old age is best made outside dominant American values through "disengagement" (withdrawing from social interactions), "deculturation" (*un*learning culture), or segregation of the aged (living in a community exclusively for the aged).

I was very skeptical of the validity of all these suggestions. Coming from another culture, I sensed in them an American bias of viewing the elderly as socially marginal. I wondered if these studies were colored by this preconception because most were done by American researchers. Common human psychology was another source of my skepticism. I had lived in several foreign countries—in China, Taiwan, and Thailand in addition to the United States—and encountered many cultural differences. At the same time, I also observed many basic similarities in human nature. Do older Americans lead as dismal a life as stereotypes depict? How could anyone live in such misery for a prolonged period of time and maintain sanity? I also suspected that, although old age might represent the antithesis of the ideals of a youth-oriented American culture, there must be ways to cope with this "cultural" problem. Otherwise, the country would be filled with helpless people.

My skepticism also derived from what I learned about culture through my anthropological training and my own experience of living in "other" cultures. Culture is indispensable for human survival. As we negotiate reality, we are guided and sometimes constrained by culture. Yet, no matter how significant culture may be, culture does not dictate to us, nor do we act as automatons. The interplay between culture and humans is complicated. At times, we may obediently follow cultural guidelines, but there are times when we interpret, manipulate, or even re-create cultural norms to suit our own situations. Also, culture and humans are mutually dependent. Just as we need culture for our survival, so culture needs human agencies for its continuation.

Culture is so deeply embedded in us that we normally take it for granted. However, my experience of living in other cultures not only made me aware of my own culture, but also showed me that I was a product of Japanese culture, not of any of the other cultures in which I had lived. As Professor Cerroni-Long mentions in this volume, "culture is not a sort of house we can enter and leave at will." Rather, "like a chronic disease, we always carry it with us" (p. 156). So, I carried Japanese culture when I lived in China, Taiwan, and Thailand and still do in the United States, no matter how comfortable I may have become with an American way of life. Understanding culture this way, I found it difficult to accept that putting oneself outside of culture was a viable solution to old age problems even if culture contributed to creating such problems.

My review of the relevant literature, though providing a lot of information, mystified old age in America even further. At the onset of my fieldwork, I felt like a detective attempting to solve a mystery or a homesteader challenging the unknown of the frontier. In fact, any organization exclusively for the elderly, including the senior center, was a totally unfamiliar social arena for me both in Japan and in the United States.

MY FIELDWORK AT LAKE DISTRICT SENIOR CENTER

Introduction

My "village" is located in a quiet, old, residential neighborhood near downtown in a small upstate New York city. The Center's two-story building is indistinguishable from other private homes in the area. Yet, once inside, visitors may feel they have crossed the threshold of a community that is very different from others. I vividly remember my initial shock, on first visiting in 1987, at finding such a concentration of the elderly in one place. The flood of short, curly, gray hair was in striking contrast to the brightly colored clothing they wore. This visual impression only served to accentuate my feeling of entering a different world, because I was used to Japanese grandmothers who habitually dressed in drab colors. In addition, many elderly at the Center were physically handicapped to some degree. Some used a cane to walk; others limped. Even those who showed no obvious signs of physical impairment moved slowly.

My "culture shock" did not last long, however. A cordial and pleasant atmosphere prevailed at the Center. Newcomers needing directions seldom were kept waiting for more than a brief period of time. They were greeted by wrinkled, smiling faces and encountered someone who volunteered help. The elderly at the Center extended to me the same friendliness and assistance. Once I started my fieldwork by attending a few classes (watercolor, clay work, and knitting), it did not take long for other groups and classes to invite me to join them. In this manner, the people at the Center adopted me into their community. I spent the next eighteen months at the Center conducting my research.

My Discoveries

Through my daily interactions with older Americans, I became friends with many of them and learned about their experiences. For the rest of this paper, I will discuss my findings regarding three of the questions I had before starting my research: (1) Do the prevailing stereotypes accurately portray the lives of older Americans? (2) Do older Americans need to "escape" their culture to deal with aging problems, as some previous studies suggest? (3) In what ways is old age in America different from old age as I had known it in Japan?

(1) *Stereotypes versus reality:* There were great discrepancies between the prevailing stereotypes and the old age I encountered at Lake District Senior Center. For example, I was initially surprised by the elderly's willingness to tell others their age. I never had to ask how old they were because most volunteered their age on telling me their names. It seems that the more advanced their age, the prouder they are. Obviously, being old has a positive connotation at the Center in contrast to the negative view held by society in general.[1]

This reverse attitude toward advanced age is evident in the way the Center people treat ninety-seven-year-old Mary, the oldest among them. Mary's appearance at the Center always commands the special attention of everybody present. People are happy to see her and greet her warmly. They also talk to each other about Mary's admirable qualities: maintaining independent life in a senior citizen's apartment, occasionally taking bus trips organized by the Center, making beautiful cards with pressed flowers she prepares herself, and so on. Remarkable as Mary may be, it is her age that makes her a "celebrity." The Center people treat her advanced age as an asset, not as a curse.

Likewise, the Center people's lives contradict the common assumption that the last stage of life is a quiet and static waiting period for death. I was amazed to find out how busy and active the Center people are. Though all of them are retired, it is rare to find them at home during the day. The coordinator of the local chapter of the Retired Senior Volunteer Program (RSVP) shared the same experience. She had not been prepared for the fact that 50 to 60 percent of the elderly registered in the program turned down volunteer opportunities. Their reasons for doing so also belied her expectations. Traveling and other volunteer work topped the list, not taking care of grandchildren, as she had assumed.

How busy they are is a frequent conversation topic at the Center, and people take pride in their busy lives. How do the elderly keep themselves busy? Basically, they adopt two strategies: filling time with activities and structuring time. For instance, Diane, age eighty-five, says, "On Mondays, I teach my class at the Center; on Tuesdays, I go to the nutrition class; on Wednesdays, I attend the Founders' group meeting; and on the third Thursday of each month, I am at the retired teachers' meeting."

Eighty-three-year-old Eleanor claims, "I am the happiest when I am busy." She has established a "second career" in her retirement. She has assumed some important leadership positions at the Center, including that of gift shop manager. She is also an avid bridge player. On Mondays, she is found at the bridge game at the Center and on Thursdays, at a local restaurant with another group of players. On Wednesdays, she is sitting at the Center's sewing machine as the central figure of the doll-making class. At home, she not only reads extensively, but also makes various kinds of stuffed animals and other handmade items to consign to the gift shop for sale. She also reserves a fair amount of time for her family: to get together with two daughters, grandchildren, and great-grandchildren living in the area and to keep in touch with family members living in other states. Surprisingly, Eleanor's "second career" includes another activity outside both the Center and the family circle. Every Saturday, she drives to the local hospital and works as a volunteer at the hospital's gift shop. With all these activities and responsibilities, Eleanor thinks she deserves a little time out. She says, "I [routinely] give myself Tuesdays off."[2]

It is not the Center people's active lifestyle alone that shows a striking contrast to the stereotypes. Their housing arrangements illustrate that "old people are in the course of a most dynamic changeable phase of life" (Hazan 1980: 37). Among eighty Center participants whose housing history I obtained, only twenty-eight stayed put after retirement. The majority, fifty-two, moved at least once. Among the latter, thirty-two moved locally, fourteen moved in from other parts of the country, and one moved to California. Some retirees moved more than once; ten, twice; and three, three times. In addition, a fair number of the elderly practice seasonal migration, spending winters in the south and summers in the north.

I had known of the mobile nature of American society. I had also learned that, unlike Japanese elderly, older Americans live apart from their children. Such knowledge, however, had not prepared me for this high rate of mobility among elderly Americans, because my own Japanese grandmother had continuously lived in our family home from her marriage until her death. Naturally, I wondered why elderly Americans change their residence.

My research indicates that the Center people moved after retirement for various reasons. Mary, a widowed octogenarian, moved three times, traversing the country twice just to live near her daughter. For others, however, having children nearby was not an important factor for their move. Some moved away from children to enjoy country living. Others changed their residence simply because they felt too "restless." Other reasons for retirees' moves included: to return home, to live in a community with better services and programs for the elderly, to lessen the burden of housekeeping, to cut expenses, and so on. The former president of Lake District Senior Center says, when it comes to the proper housing for the elderly, "No two situations are the same" (Morris 1987).

Nevertheless, one common factor underlies these variations: coping or anticipating coping with diminishing self-sufficiency. Hence, most changes of residence among the Center people involved a move to the kind of housing that requires less maintenance and/or provides easier access to assistance. Some, like Mary, moved closer to children in order to (among other things) secure emergency help. Housing for Judy, another resident, provides another example. Judy went through a sequence of moves following her husband's death: from her own house to a regular apartment and then to a senior citizen's apartment. Though she had no choice but to move to a nursing home when she became nonambulatory, her previous moves enabled her to maintain an independent life despite her declining health. Conversely, for some retirees, staying put is a way of dealing with shrinking financial resources. Emily, in her late seventies, maintains, "Living in my house is the cheapest for me because there is no mortgage."

In short, the elderly's choice of housing stems from their desire to maintain their autonomy in the face of declining resources. Their decision to move or not to move reflects their efforts to conform to a cultural ideal, being independent.

(2) *Conformity to cultural ideals:* When I came to know more about the actual lives of older Americans, what struck me most was their quest for independence. One inevitable aspect of growing old is declining health and shrinking resources. Simple tasks, such as eating, bathing, and cleaning, may become difficult and require assistance. Nonetheless, American culture emphasizes independence, creating a wide gap between the reality of old age and cultural ideals.

The Center people endeavor to negotiate this gap and conform to cultural ideals, thus nullifying some previous studies that propose putting oneself "outside" culture as a means of dealing with old age. How do the Center people remain autonomous in the face of diminishing self-sufficiency? The answer lies in helping each other. Let us examine a support relationship between Diane and Helen to illustrate (1) how crucial mutual dependency is for older Americans to maintain independence and (2) in what ways the elderly's desire to conform to cultural ideals shapes their behaviors.

Diane, age eighty-five, and Helen, a decade younger, both live by themselves in big houses on the same block. Members of the same church and of some of the same groups at the Center, they spend a lot of time together. They also share a ride, because Diane drives but Helen does not. In addition, they call every day at designated times to check on each other. Each has a key to the other's house. When Diane fell in the bathtub and was unable to move, Helen, alarmed when she received no response to her regular call, entered Diane's house and called for help. Because neither of them has been married nor has close relatives living nearby, this partnership is an essential source of support, security, and safety for them.

Forming support networks is an integral part of human life. Japanese society, for instance, is crisscrossed by many such networks. Yet, I discovered that support networks among the Center people operate quite differently from the similar system I was familiar with in Japan. For instance, in Japan, the network participation follows social conventions and is based on such factors as geographical proximity and membership in the communal or occupational organization. Hence, participation is often mandatory. Also, it is frequently the case that the group (that is, the family) rather than the individual is a unit of participation.

By contrast, among the elderly at Lake District Senior Center, forming or participating in support networks is always voluntary and based on individual choice. Consequently, there are many different ways or reasons to form support relationships. Some partners, like Diane and Helen, see each other almost every day, while others communicate primarily by telephone and seldom see each other. The criteria for choosing partners also vary: former colleagues, neighbors, shared interests or hobbies, shared experiences (for example, similar former occupations), and so on.

Despite these variations and the ad hoc nature of network formation, support networks among the Center people indicate some distinctive patterns. One such characteristic is their multiple participation in more than one network. For instance, although Diane and Helen have established a close, indispensable relationship, their involvement with each other is not exclusive. Diane claims that there are two other friends besides Helen she could not do without. One is Louise, with whom she spends holidays. Diane also exchanges books with her. The other is Marsha, an old family friend. She is one of the few people with whom Diane, the last survivor of her generation of relatives, can share memories of her family. Helen has friends of similar importance, such as those with whom she spends holidays and those with whom she exchanges hospitality. When Helen hosts a dinner party at home, Diane drives Helen to the grocery store. However, Diane is invited only on those occasions when she and the other guests belong to the same social circle.

If the Japanese were to have interactions of the extent and frequency of those between Diane and Helen, such social relationships would inevitably become total, exclusive, and enduring.[3] Therefore, I was puzzled at the beginning by the Americans' attempts to compartmentalize social ties among multiple friends. As I learned more about older Americans and their lives, I began to realize that what is behind this piecemeal participation in support networks is the elderly's quest for independence. By distributing their sources of support among different people, they avoid total dependency on any one individual. In addition, to minimize dependency, even the closest ties, like the one between Diane and Helen, do not involve economic commitment. They are limited to an exchange of favors and moral and emotional support.

The elderly's quest for independence is also manifested in their efforts to maintain an equal partnership in support networks. Growing old puts Americans in a double bind. They need to rely on others, but dependency is a cultural taboo. Egalitarian relationships with support partners enable them to circumvent this problem. The most common strategy is to complement each other's missing resources. Let us examine Diane and Helen's case again.

As noted earlier, Helen relies on Diane for a ride. In return, Helen serves as Diane's ears and legs because Diane is almost deaf and lame. While driving, Helen draws Diane's attention to the sound made by the turn signal, which did not stop automatically. When they go to an unfamiliar place, Helen navigates for Diane. Helen also walks for Diane by doing errands for her at banks and stores while Diane waits in the parked car.

The support relationship between Diane and Helen is mutually beneficial. Based on an equal partnership, their mutual dependency allows them to have a sense of independence. Though both find this partnership indispensable, they also try to minimize their reliance on each other. Diane occasionally walks to banks and stores on her own, using her cane and going slowly. Similarly, Helen sometimes walks to the Center. She also takes the bus. When Helen went to her hairdresser soon after recovering from a severe case of influenza, she accepted Diane's offer of a ride only after Diane's persistent attempts to persuade her.

In summary, Diane and Helen's case shows that forming support networks is essential for the very survival of older Americans. It also illustrates that three dominant values—independence, egalitarianism, and individual choice—guide the elderly's support relationships. In other words, the Center people deal with problems of old age *within* the realm of American culture, not *outside* it, as some previous studies suggest. Paradoxical as it may seem, culture creates problems for the elderly, but at the same time it offers resources for responding to them.

(3) *Old age in the United States and in Japan:* Old age in America is distinctively different from old age in Japan. Stereotypes of old age in these two societies are in complete opposition: strongly negative in the former and distinctly positive in the latter. Though my research at Lake District Senior Center has questioned the negative stereotypes of American old age, decisive differences still remain. Most important, cultural prescriptions of old age in the two countries show a striking contrast. For instance, American emphasis on independence demands intergenerational autonomy, and maintaining an independent lifestyle is viewed as an absolute must for successful aging. Hence, of all the Center people, only one widower lives in a two-generation family with his ninety-year-old father. Even in this case, all of the widower's seven children established their own separate households.

The typical Japanese reaction to such American attitudes was provided by a middle-aged Japanese housewife. When she learned that Dorothy, an eighty-four-year-old widow, lives alone in a senior citizens apartment even though she has several children, this visitor from Tokyo exclaimed, "If older people live alone in Japan, people blame their family for negligence." She deeply sympathized with the poor Dorothy.

As her remarks indicate, in Japan the dominant cultural value emphasizes mutual dependency, including that between parents and adult children, and creates the traditional view of old age as "a period of rightful dependency" (Fry et al. 1980: 127). Japanese tradition provides both structural and ideological support for taking care of the aged in the form of the three-generation stem family and the Confucian ethics of filial piety. As my late grandmother often said, a happy old age means a life surrounded by children and grandchildren. Needless to say, older Americans would detest such a life.

CONCLUSION

My research at Lake District Senior Center enabled me to observe and participate in the actual lives of older Americans and has clarified many unknowns about old age in America. The research was also personally rewarding. Though the way Center people behave and what they strive for are quite different from what I expect from Japanese elderly, talking to them and sharing their lifelong experiences gave me the same satisfaction and learning opportunities I had with old people in Japan. Looking behind physical decay and negative stereotypes, I discovered people with ingenuity, determination, and wisdom, who were able to make the best of their lives.

I also found out that the strong fear of old age, which my American roommates had demonstrated, was largely fear of the unknown. For many Americans, old age is a mystery due to the segregation of the elderly and lack of well-established cultural models of aging. Most American children, unlike their Japanese counterparts, grow up having little contact with their grandparents. The Center people shared with me some innocent but ignorant questions that young children had asked them: "Great-Grandma, are you dying?" "How come you can't run like me?" "Does your wrinkle hurt?" "How do you get old?" College students do not know much better. When I taught a course on aging, my students found Diane and Helen's support network almost as alien as, for example, an elaborate Moka feast practiced in New Guinea. Similarly, they had as little knowledge about change of residence among older Americans as about the mobile lifestyle of hunter-gatherers.

Old age in America is the "frontier." Growing old in America means exploring this frontier. Though my research indicates older Americans are guided by a cultural "map," the map does not provide a detailed description of this new territory. The Center people's courage and determination to challenge the little-known under these circumstances inspired me a great deal. I thought they were most suitably called "pioneers" and titled my dissertation "Elderly Pioneers."[4]

NOTES

1. According to Ward, in age-homogeneous communities, advanced age loses its saliency and thereby its negative connotation (1984: 228).
2. Why do older Americans keep busy? Why do they not sit back and relax now that they are retired? Most Center people find being inactive morally degrading and emotionally depressing. They honestly believe that keeping busy is the key to happy old age. Ekerdt explains their attitudes from another angle. He maintains that keeping busy provides the elderly with a sense of continuity in life. Just as the work ethic serves as "a weapon in the battle for status and self-respect" for the working person, the busy ethic, "an ethic that esteems leisure that is earnest, occupied, and filled with activity," honors the retiree's life (1986: 239).
3. This by no means indicates that the Japanese have only a small number of social networks. The fact is quite contrary. For the Japanese, the incorporation into social networks is not only essential both socially and psychologically, but virtually inescapable. However, patterns of social interactions in Japan and principles behind them are notably different from those in America. For instance, such factors as hierarchy, loyalty, and clear demarcation between those inside and outside play an important role in shaping Japanese social relationships.
4. Subtitled "A Cultural Study of Old Age in America."

REFERENCES

Cerroni-Long, E. L. 1998. Life and Cultures: The Test of Real Participant Observation. In *Distant Mirrors: America as a Foreign Culture* (3rd ed.). Philip R. DeVita and James D. Armstrong, Eds. Chapter 17. Belmont, CA: Wadsworth.

Ekerdt, David J. 1986. The Busy Ethic: Moral Continuity Between Work and Retirement. *The Gerontologist* 26(3): 239–244.

Fry, Christine L., et al. 1980. *Aging in Culture and Society: Comparative Viewpoints and Strategies.* South Hadley, MA: Bergin & Garvey.

Hazan, Haim. 1980. *The Limbo People: A Study of the Constitution of the Time Universe among the Aged.* London: Routledge & Kegan Paul.

Matthews, Sarah H. 1979. *The Social World of Old Women: Management of Self-Identity.* Thousand Oaks, CA: Sage.

Morris, Fred B. 1987. Pick Your Retirement Home Ahead of Time. *The Ithaca Journal,* 14 October, p. 12A.

Ward, Russell A. 1984. The Marginality and Salience of Being Old: When Is Age Relevant? *The Gerontologist* 24(3): 227–232.

STUDY QUESTIONS

1. Contrast both the status of the elderly and the traditional family structure in the United States and Japan.
2. How are the ways Americans and Japanese treat the elderly different?
3. What were the significant discoveries that Professor Tsuji made during her eighteen months of research in a center for the elderly?

TWELVE

Neighborly Strangers

HONGGANG YANG
Southeastern Nova University

Dr. Yang spent two years doing fieldwork in a private cluster homes neighbor-hood in Florida. In this essay he focuses on how American homeowners both resist and come to terms with the ownership of common property by contrast-ing his experience in Florida to his experience in urban China. He clearly articulates the barriers that American individualism creates for the develop-ment of community among his neighbors in "Pondtrees."

Honggang Yang *currently teaches in the Department of Dispute Resolution at Nova Southeastern University. He worked as a research associate in Conflict Resolution Programs at the Carter Center of Emory University and taught at Antioch College. He did medical training in undergraduate education and studied social psychology in graduate school in China. Before coming to the United States in 1986, Honggang Yang was a faculty member in the Depart-ment of Sociology at Nankai University. He earned his Ph.D. in Applied Anthropology at the University of South Florida in 1991. Dr. Yang's research interests are in the fields of legal anthropology, community organizations, and management of common property resources.*

I spent almost two years doing fieldwork in an American neighborhood with a homeowners association. My ethnographic curiosity is about how American homeowners in a private cluster homes development share and manage common property resources, such as neighborhood fences, swimming pools, tennis courts, picnic sites, parking lots, entrance areas, playgrounds, and clubhouses. Like many anthropologists engaged in fieldwork overseas, I was often puzzled by the foreign patterns of social relations in this modern residential corporation in the United States, since I had grown up in China where communal life was quite different. At the beginning of my field endeavor, I could not see the "problems" in what were considered problems by my informants, and I could not understand why what I per-ceived as problems were not regarded as "problems" by the residents.

In my writings, I call my field site "Pondtrees"—a fictitious name. Pondtrees is located in a suburb of the Tampa Bay area. The development was started in the mid-1970s and completed in the early 1980s. There are now about five hundred homes in Pondtrees. As the place name indicates, there are several ponds and lakes and plenty of trees. The development has two kinds of homes: the single-family house or detached building and the townhome or contiguous unit. The larger lake in the area serves as a marker: All of the single-family homes are on the west side of the lake, whereas most of the townhomes are on the east shore. However, homeowners of both groups are mandatory members of the association. There are also a considerable number of absentee homeowners and renters in Pondtrees.

When I started fieldwork, I was first struck by the legalistic and commercial multiplicity of the residential organization. In Pondtrees, homeowners are obligated to pay dues to the association for maintaining the common facilities and common areas. Owners of townhomes pay more because they receive more services, such as pest control, mowing, roofing, siding, and repairing exterior parts of their property. The board of directors, consisting of five volunteers elected from among the homeowners, contracts a property manager to do the jobs. A set of documents are the legal basis for the operation and governance of the association. The highly specialized rules and regulations for Pondtrees are contained in documents entitled "Restated Articles of Incorporation; Bylaws; Restated Declaration of Easements, Covenants, Conditions, and Restrictions; Master Declarations; and Townhome Declarations." I was astonished by the complexity as well as the quantity of the collection. There are a multitude of signatures and stamps on the documents, imprints of approval and witness. In one of the documents, the Restated Declaration, there are at least twenty-three signatures and seven stamps.

Pondtrees is quiet. Residents are seldom well acquainted with one another, in sharp contrast to my residence in China where every neighbor knows each other. In the Chinese urban neighborhood where my parents still reside, the residential setting and communal atmosphere appear characteristic of *Gemeinschaft* (traditional community). Residents in such a community are often employed in the same work unit. There exists ongoing mutual aid among neighbors, which includes watching the stove, buying vegetables, helping move furniture, and taking care of children for each other. As a child, I customarily addressed my neighbors in senior generations by the kinship terms *uncle* or *aunt*.

Different from the American counterpart, urban houses in China are usually not privately owned but are provided by the government through work units. Migration into cities is restricted, unless one is recruited by the government. Urban residents are all legally required to register to gain jobs, housing, food, health care, school, and the like. The neighborhood is geographically bounded, consisting of several adjacent blocks with from one hundred to a few hundred households. There is a resident committee in each neighborhood, which is a semiautonomous multifunctional organization. I call it "semi" because of its political affiliation with the party and state and its folk ties with local residents. It is organizationally different from the board of directors of American homeowners associations in many ways. In China, the committee members are chosen or elected from among volunteers, most of whom are retired elders and housewives with charismatic authority carrying social respect, credit, and trust. They assist the local government in conducting household registration, inspecting block sanitation, supervising individual immunizations, family planning, handling minor criminal cases, mediating civil and domestic disputes, coordinating a neighborhood watch, and holding some social activities.

While my family and I were in Pondtrees, my wife often expressed to me her personal reactions to the neighborhood. She sometimes complained that our immediate neighbors never invited her over to chat, visit, or have supper together. I remember that last year when we were moving from one house to another within Pondtrees, my wife intended to look for help from the neighbors and wished that someone had given us a hand.

Undoubtedly, the prevalence of high residential mobility in U.S. society is a factor contributing to the existing lack of communal sentiment. Around my house in the townhome section, there are several adjacent buildings with four units each. My neighbors change almost constantly, moving in and out. There are quite a few vacant units, and on several are signs of "For Sale" or "Assumable Owner." I found that residents rarely get to know each other. One of my informants in the single-family section told me that his next-door neighbors have changed three times in the past two years. But my fieldwork experience also taught me that most of the residents do not have intentions or expectations to know each other beyond saying hello in the street. Some of them believe that Pondtrees is simply a place to live; others consider it an investment; still, a few of them refer to it as a "community." Despite the cognitive differences, they always seem ready to move.

I describe the residents in Pondtrees as "neighborly strangers." "Neighborly" used here has two meanings, one referring to the physical vicinity or the spatial contiguity of their residence and another connoting a routine presentation of self as "nice." A good neighbor in this context is expected to be "friendly" with others, rather than a friend. "Strangers" implies the remote interpersonal distances among the neighbors, as distinct from my neighbors in China, who not only know each other's ages, occupations, ranks, economic conditions, family histories, relatives, and personal hobbies but also often offer help. My neighbors in Pondtrees, on the other hand, seldom have that kind of knowledge and trust, since such knowledge may entail a sort of invasion of privacy. Their shelters are too close to allow them to be friends in such a living domain, perhaps due to what I term "privacy considerations." My wife once commented that maintaining surface interaction without a greater sense of community was almost meaningless, and it would lead to feelings of uncertainty and indifference among neighbors. Not having neighbors as friends doesn't mean that the residents have no friends but that they make friends somewhere else. When I approached the residents, asking questions about neighborhood concerns, they often responded very briefly with common expressions of "You know what I mean" or "You know what I am saying." They seemed reluctant to talk more and were politely on guard. There seems to exist an invisible interpersonal boundary that is almost impossible for "nonfriends" to penetrate.

The mobile and anonymous conditions of life in Pondtrees significantly affect the harmony of communal life. The neighborhood atmosphere is sometimes marred by the prevalent apathetic attitudes and frequent complaints about the commons shared and managed by residents themselves. One informant, who had been vice president of the board, told me his experience: "No matter what you do, everybody hates you." While I was in the field, I attended every monthly board meeting, and there were only about one dozen participants. I was surprised at the beginning because I expected more residents to be active in their neighborhood. One of my informants told me that low attendance is a good sign that means fewer complaints and less trouble. Later, I found that my informant was right about those who came to the meetings. Most of the participants usually have ideas, concerns, confusions, problems, or issues on the maintenance and services. For example, some of the common complaints were about the inconsistent decorative colors of homes, curtains, windows, and fences, which in my eyes could have been ignored. Typically, there are more complaints than constructive suggestions about the commons in the neighborhood, and there are fewer residents willing to volunteer for the board or committees than critics. For several consecutive years, the annual meeting, the most important activity of the association (election, budgets, and finance), could not reach a quorum and had to hold a second meeting with a lower quorum.

In Pondtrees, I presented myself as a resident as well as a student, and I volunteered in quite a few ways to get more involved. For example, I served as a clubhouse coordinator. One day when I was on duty at the clubhouse, I found an interesting newspaper clipping titled "Motto":

> Stay away from meetings. If you come, find fault and never offer an alternative. Decline office or appointment to a committee. Get sore if you aren't nominated.

> After you are nominated, don't attend board or committee meetings. If you get to one, despite your better judgment, clam up until you get outside, then sound off on how things should have been done.

> Don't work if you can avoid it. When the old reliables pitch in, accuse them of being a clique.

> Oppose all banquets, parties, seminars, conferences, and trade missions as being a waste of the attendees' money. If everything is strictly business, then complain that the meetings are dull and officers belong to the old guard.

> Never accept a place at the head table. If you aren't asked to sit there, threaten to resign because you aren't appreciated.

> Don't rush to pay your dues; let the directors sweat—after all, they wrote the budget. Read the mail from the association only now and then; never reply if you can help it, and then ask why you were not informed.

This "motto" is an exaggerated depiction of some common dilemmas involving sharing in such an environment. It reflects, in a dramatic way, an embedded contradiction between the individual and the commons. The essence of the commons is to provide resources that are needed but are difficult or impossible to provide individually. I asked some of my informants for their comments on the "motto." They told me that it was true but varied per particular individual, for a particular period of time, on a particular issue, and in a particular context. The cynical attitudes in the "motto" expressed implicit tension and disharmony, and these attitudes were, in fact, not less influential in neighborhood life than apathy. Neither the cynicism nor the apathy, in my opinion, are constructive or healthy.

There were also occasional legal battles that reflected another aspect of the neighborhood—communal politics and interpersonal tension in Pondtrees. About two years ago, a number of the homeowners found that a board member was delinquent in his monthly dues but was somehow permitted to take part in the association election at the annual meeting. This incident happened at the time when a controversial, extraordinary assessment was proposed by the board. The dissatisfied homeowners decided to hire an attorney to sue the board of directors for permitting the board member to vote. According to the bylaws, homeowners failing to pay assessments prior to the meeting are not entitled to enjoy the benefit of association membership, including electing and getting elected. But the tricky part of the dispute centered around the fact that the delinquent board member submitted a check for payment just before the meeting and then requested that the check be returned to him the following day because he was not financially able to meet his obligation. To defend the stand taken, the board also sought legal counsel from the association attorney. The association attorney held that the board's permission was legally legitimate and did not influence the voting.

Facing such legal threats and possible court action, the board of directors decided to indemnify its members, which meant spending additional money on buying insurance—a guarantee against personal liability in conjunction with board service in the nonprofit corporation. This episode illustrates a painful and complex aspect of the usually quiet situation in Pondtrees. It reveals that going to court more or less becomes one of the standard facts of communal life in a neighborhood like Pondtrees. This whole issue perplexed me. I thought that life in an American suburban common property development would be peaceful and economical. To achieve harmony, however, the residents need to work to solve their problems while maintaining communal unity.

In China, neighborhood mediation is one of the distinctive functions of the resident committee, and it is characterized by an informal, decentralized, self-governing approach on a face-to-face basis at the grassroots level. Under the state ownership of housing and with the dominance of the cultural value of kinship, not many residents concern themselves with the maintenance of the common resources they share or other nonkinship, public matters. These are the recurrent problems and issues in such scenes. The inside of individual homes may be tidy and in good order, but the shared areas like corridors and entrances are sometimes messy and vandalized. In such cases, the committee members will approach the responsible residents directly, explain the problem, and persuade them to correct it. Conflict resolution within the neighborhood remains relatively undifferentiated between communal matters and family affairs. For example, if a couple has a big quarrel and one of them seeks a divorce, the neighbors who hear it may tell the committee members and then the committee members may mediate between the two sides, reminding them of the happiness of their marriage and helping them understand each other in that emotional situation. This pattern of neighborhood dispute resolution correlates with the emphasis on "harmony of life" in Chinese culture as well as with the socioeconomic context where urban mobility is low.

Even in Pondtrees, against the background of apathy and cynicism, there has been a successful community organization operating without interruption—the garden club. It came into being on the partial completion of the development and is still running. It demonstrates the convergence of individual interests and communal benefits. Every home has a courtyard, and greenery is found throughout Pondtrees. Either the individual or the association must take care of the gardens, yards, and common areas one way or another. Also, the increasing environmental awareness in society reinforces the positive perceptions of the role of this organization.

Basically, the garden club is autonomously organized for the informal exchange of ideas, information, and help in the maintenance and beautification of the surroundings within individual courtyards or in front of homes. Starting with some individual horticultural hobbies, the club extended its activities to natural preservation and neighborhood landscaping in Pondtrees. It was loosely organized, so there was little pressure. It served as a popular arena for residents' interests and provided some enjoyable labor for members in their leisure time. The club activists responded to my curiosity about its success with "We just love doing it." The club introduced plants and shrubbery suitable for the soil and seasons and managed to get a good deal for the plants. They also offered their expertise and made recommendations to the association and individual residents for the selection of plants both in the common areas and in individual backyards. The club also invited local speakers for water, land, and other natural conservation campaigns and helped distribute the information.

Although there is a separate committee in charge of landscaping in Pondtrees, the tasks are sometimes closely combined with those of the club. In the last two years, the garden club has selected four "Yard-of-the-Month" designations. The award is based on overall attractiveness and improvement and is intended to recognize and honor those promoting natural beautification on their property and in Pondtrees. The selection goes on smoothly except that two of the honorary signs were once stolen. These special efforts improve the communal atmosphere while contributing to community formation, and some of the residents even purchase plants for the common areas. Quite a few of the club members volunteered for other neighborhood committees and later got elected to the board of directors. To my surprise the other day, I saw one of my neighbors (renting in the building next to mine) taking care of the plants in the common area the day before he moved out of Pondtrees.

The homeowners association in Pondtrees is a fascinating sociocultural and economic construct. I find that the management of common property by the residents themselves shows a convergence of individualism and volunteerism, although there exist ambiguities concerning the commons, leading to a variety of disharmonies and conflicts. Individualism is a way that people look at and are adapted to their world. An individualistic worldview considers the individual as the elementary unit of primary order, whereas society is viewed as a secondary or artificial construct.

Like any other cultural value, individualism is effective only in some contexts. In some ways it is liable to produce alienation. I see individualism as a reaction to the constraints of society and nature that tries to solve the contradictions between self and the outside world by assigning primary importance to the individual. Residing in a neighborhood with a homeowners association entails cooperating and sharing, which is sometimes incongruent with American ideals of individuality and independence. American individualism is quite like a two-edged sword: on the one edge, trying to gain something always pursued, such as individual freedom and happiness; on the other, taking a risk of losing something still needed, such as a trusting human community and togetherness.

Compared with the community life in my Chinese neighborhood, interpersonal relations among neighbors in Pondtrees were aloof, cold, and lacking of an expectation for future interaction. However, human problems and issues are ubiquitous and embedded in sociocultural institutions. Furthermore, communal life indeed varies in different societal structures. Both Chinese and American cultures have their weaknesses and shortcomings as well as their strengths and advantages. The headaches suffered by my Chinese neighbors were different from the complaints expressed by my American neighbors in Pondtrees. I believe that the neighborly strangers in my neighborhood could benefit by becoming more aware of their common ground and communal needs, while the quality of life in my Chinese community could be enhanced by overcoming institutionalized political and economic barriers and sociocultural weak points. After all, we are transients, as Chinese-American anthropologist F. L. K. Hsu points out, and what we need is a pleasant journey through this world. We should try our best to gain benefits from cross-cultural knowledge and to be free from those physical and psychological sufferings existent in both of our cultures.

ACKNOWLEDGMENTS

I am grateful to Professors A. W. Wolfe, M. V. Angrosino, S. D. Greenbaum, J. E. Jreisat, and E. G. Nesman for their direction and comments during my studying and writing at the University of South Florida. I am also thankful to Ron Habin for his editorial assistance.

STUDY QUESTIONS

1. What are some of the residential differences between rural lifestyles in China and Dr. Yang's Florida research site?
2. What is intended in the description "neighborly strangers"?
3. What are the social and personal reasons for the residents of Pondtrees being "strangers" to each other?
4. Contrast communal conflict resolution practices between Pondtrees and China.
5. In which way is the American value of individualism incongruent with the neighborhood requirements of Pondtrees?

THIRTEEN

País de mis Sueños: *Reflections on Ethnic Labels, Dichotomies, and Ritual Interactions*

GISELA ERNST
Washington State University, Pullman

Ethnic categorization and labeling are questioned as abstractions of either reality or accurate features of the persons or groups to which these labels are attached. The author explores the polarizing and negative applications of English language qualifiers relating to "race" and ethnicity, viewing them as system-maintaining devices in service to the hierarchical structure of American society. The essay concludes with some of Ernst's impressions of American friendliness viewed as ritual.

Gisela Ernst grew up in Lima, Peru, coming to the United States in the 1980s to study sociolinguistics and anthropology at the University of Florida. She is an associate professor in the College of Education, Department of Teaching and Learning at Washington State University.

Some of the most interesting questions are raised by the study of words whose job it is to make things fuzzier or less fuzzy. (Lakoff 1972: 195)

Like Saint Paul, I have seen the light. It happened while I was finishing my master's degree, when I was introduced to sociolinguistics; what I learned about language, language use, and culture literally changed the direction of my career. I had found an area of study that allowed me to grapple with the interplay of linguistic, social, and cultural factors in human communication. During my doctoral program at the University of Florida, I had the opportunity to think more deeply about why people use language the way they use it and why language can be clear and precise. At the same time, language often can be characterized by vagueness, ambiguity, and imprecision.

Perhaps nowhere is the interplay of language and culture more "fuzzy" (to use Lakoff's term) than in the labels we use to define ourselves and others. In this chapter I will share some of my experiences, and my subsequent reflections upon those experiences, with the use of labels and terms used to refer to a person's ethnic, cultural, and racial background. Within this context I will share my feelings about, and explore the connotations of, the made-in-the-U.S.A. label "Hispanic." Then I will explore the use of dichotomies and negative constructions in English. These structures will be better understood by contrasting them to Spanish. This comparison will illustrate that the existence in English of extreme dichotomies can often influence how native English speakers voice and manage their relations with others. Finally, I would like to illustrate how some of us "foreigners" can often be taken in by the friendliness of people in the United States.

ETHNIC LABELS: "I CAME AS A PERUVIAN AND IMMEDIATELY BECAME A HISPANIC"

I was a fortunate child who grew up in Lima, Peru. I was brought up in an upper-middle-class environment, attended private schools, lived in a handsome neighborhood, and was surrounded by a protected haven of mostly well-educated friends and acquaintances. Like many others in Peru, I was a *mestiza,* the daughter of an Austrian father and a Peruvian mother, the product of an encounter of two continents, of two races. Like many others, I had European names and Peruvian looks, spoke more than one language, and was proud to be a Peruvian who also had knowledge about and appreciation for her father's homeland.

In spite of my good fortune, I also encountered my share of problems, sorrow, and broken dreams. This is why, like many others who leave their familiar lands in search of better lives, I too left mine in search of *el país de mis sueños* (the land of my dreams). I had little money but lots of hope, confidence, and a clear sense of national identity as a Peruvian woman. Therefore I set off happily, in June of 1985, unaware of the need for "clear" labels to identify my ethnicity, race, and culture. Soon after my arrival in Florida, I did what many other foreign students have to do if they want to get into graduate school in the United States: fill out multiple forms. Throughout this process I discovered two things: first, the momentousness of the written word in this society, and second, the importance of race and ethnicity as forms of social classification in the United States. It quickly dawned on me that my avowed national identity was of little relevance to the society at large. I realized that I was seldom considered a Peruvian but was most often either "Hispanic," "legal alien," "Latino," "Spanish-speaking," "South American," "Spanish," or, what is worse, "Other"! Within the context of official forms, institutionalized inquiries, and government requirements, I was faced with having to find the appropriate label to describe my nationality, culture, and background. The following question about ethnic origin will help illustrate my feeling of dubiousness, doubtfulness, and diffidence as I attempted to answer what, for some, might be just another question on a form.

Ethnic Origin (mark one)

__ White (not Hispanic origin)

__ Asian or Pacific Islanders

__ Black (not Hispanic origin)

__ American Indian or Alaskan Native

__ Hispanic

__ Other

Not only did I find the emphasis on racial categorizations in the United States perplexing, but I felt that the selection offered was limited and problematic. I felt that I had to summarize my nationality, ethnicity, upbringing, language, culture—in sum, my whole existence—in one fixed and unappealing label. I was not only appalled but also confused. For example, given the categories mentioned above, I could have marked the first option since I appeared "white" in both of my passports (Peruvian and Austrian). Yet, at the same time, that option would be incorrect since I am also what could be called "Hispanic."

I thought about marking "American Indian" or "Alaskan Native" since, in fact, I was born in (South) America and there is some Indian blood in my mother's ancestry (even though she might not want to admit to it). But these labels did not reflect all my other influences: my mother's descent from Spain, my father's Austrian and German blood, and the fact that I do not speak the languages nor share the cultures of Peruvian Indians. Because I had to use my European passport, on which I appeared as "white" (it included my visa and my "alien" number), I felt that no available categories encompassed my national and cultural identity.

My confusion grew as the smorgasbord of categories changed—from form to form and from institution to institution, and I often found myself spending considerable time trying to select the most appropriate label. After several months and many more forms, I opted to leave the question unmarked (when possible) or to mark "Other" (if there was such an option). On some occasions, depending on my mood, when the question asked for "race," I would write "Cocker Spaniel," "German Shepherd," or "unknown" on the blank line next to "Other." Because there often was an indication that this information was optional, I did not feel any remorse for perhaps skewing some demographic data. On the contrary, this simple act provided me with an opportunity to show my dissent toward questions that limited my individuality to a generic label.

Do the classifications recognized by the U.S. Census Bureau offer us a useful way of understanding our national and cultural experiences? Do terms such as *black*, *Asian American*, and *Hispanic* have any real substance to them, or are they the creation of media czars and political impresarios? Let's examine the official definition of Hispanic (according to the 1990 U.S. census):

> A person is of Spanish/Hispanic origin if the person's origin (ancestry) is Mexican, Mexican-American, Chicano, Puerto Rican, Dominican, Ecuadorian, Guatemalan, Honduran, Nicaraguan, Peruvian, Salvadoran; from other Spanish-speaking countries of the Caribbean or Central or South America; or from Spain.

The ethnic label "Hispanic" began to be used heavily by state agencies in the early 1970s to refer to all people in this country whose ancestry is predominantly from one or more Spanish-speaking countries. As a result, millions of people of a variety of national and cultural backgrounds are put into a single arbitrary category.[1] No allowances are made for our varied racial, linguistic, and national experiences, nor for whether we are recent immigrants, long-time residents, or belong to an associated territory. Furthermore, using "Hispanic" to refer to those who are of Spanish-speaking origin can be problematic in that it excludes a considerable sector of the population in Latin America for whom Spanish is not a first language. Many "Hispanic" immigrants come from regions that are not necessarily predominantly Spanish. This is the case of those who speak Nahuatl and Tiwa in Indian villages in Mexico; Kanjobal and Jacaltec in the southern part of Guatemala; Quechua and Aymara in the highlands of Peru and Bolivia; Guarani, Chulupi, and Mascoi in the

Chaco region of Paraguay; Tukano and Tuyukaf in the swamps of Venezuela and Colombia; and others from predominantly non-Spanish-speaking regions. Thus, given that their native language may not be Spanish, it is inaccurate to call these people of "Spanish-speaking origin."

Furthermore, as Berkeley social scientist Carlos Muñoz writes, the term *Hispanic* is derived from *Hispania,* which was the name the Romans gave to the Iberian peninsula, most of which became Spain, and "implicitly emphasizes the white European culture of Spain at the expense of the nonwhite cultures that have profoundly shaped the experience of all Latin Americans" through its refusal to acknowledge "the nonwhite indigenous cultures of the Americas, Africa, and Asia, which historically have produced multicultural and multiracial peoples in Latin America and the United States" (1989: 11). It is a term that ignores the complexities within and throughout these various groups.

DICHOTOMIES AND NEGATIVE CONSTRUCTIONS: "I DIDN'T REALIZE I WAS A MINORITY UNTIL I CAME TO THE UNITED STATES"

As mentioned earlier, I always felt special and different among my fellow Peruvians. However, it was only when I came to this country that a label for being different was assigned to me: I became a minority! I must say that being labeled as such has not always been that bad; on occasion I have received some special treatment just because I fit the category of minority. However, the term *minority* has heavy connotations, especially when we realize that it signifies differences from those who make up the majority in this county. In other words, my status was assigned to me because I am not part of the majority, so therefore I should be part of the minority. The term *minority,* like other terms used to identify people's racial, ethnic, and cultural backgrounds, is defined in opposition to another term.

The same can be said about the term *Hispanic.* In contemporary discourse the term *Hispanic* has come to be used as a nonwhite racial designation. It is not unusual to read or hear people use the terms *whites, blacks,* and *Hispanics* as if they were mutually exclusive when, in fact, the 1990 census states that 52 percent of Hispanics identify themselves as white, 3 percent as black, and 43 percent as "other race."

The English language is constructed as a system of differences organized as extreme dichotomies—white/black, majority/minority, good/bad, dark/fair, and so on. The existence of this polarization influences how English speakers manage their relations with others. Consider the case of qualifiers or adjectives. The heavy emphasis on opposites often compels speakers of English to use one of two opposite adjectives when formulating questions. As a result, people in the United States commonly use evaluative terms in questions and descriptions, and find it easier to be critical rather than positive or neutral. For example, let's compare pairs of adjectives in English and in Spanish:

English		*Spanish*	
old	young	viejo	joven
long	short	largo	corto
far	near	cerca	lejos

At first, it may seem as if both the English and Spanish pairs contain words that are opposite in meaning but equal in their power to describe a point on a continuum. However, this is not the case. Consider how the English adjectives are used in asking questions: "How old is he?" "How long is that ruler?" and "How far do we have to go?" Questions are not phrased using the secondary term, as in "How young is he?" (unless in reference to a baby or small child), "How short is that ruler?" and "How near do we have to go?" In all of these questions one of the terms is designated as the defining term—for age, *old;* for size, *long;* and for distance, *far.*

To the Spanish speaker, these same dichotomies do not have the same dependent hierarchy; rather, these pairs enjoy symmetry. This weaker polarization of Spanish pairs is evident in the way questions are phrased. In Spanish, "How old is he?" becomes *"¿Qué edad tiene él?"* which can be literally translated as "What is his age?" The question "How long is that ruler?" becomes *"¿Cuánto mide esa regla?"*—that is, "What's the measurement of that ruler?"—and so on. In Spanish, the emphasis is placed on the middle ground of the continuum rather than on one of its ends.

Thus, one important aspect of opposing adjectives in English is that the primary term appears as the defining term or the norm of cultural meaning, while the secondary term is much more specific or derives its meaning from its relation to the first one. Examples of the "good-bad" dichotomy help to illustrate this point. If you ask a friend to help you with a new software program, you will probably say, "How good are you with MacMisha 5.1?" rather than "How bad are you with MacMisha 5.1?" That is, the use of the term *good* reflects a more general qualifier, while the use of the term *bad* already suggests that something is not good; thus this latter term is more specific (in a negative sense).

This same polarity can be applied to some of the qualifiers used in discussing issues of race and ethnicity. For example, in the case of pairs of labels, as in white/black, majority/minority, resident/nonresident, white/colored, and American/other, the defining term of the norm is given by the primary term; the secondary term represents what is different, alien, or abnormal.

The negative precision of English qualifiers yields a linguistic base for qualifying as negative whatever appears to be different. Thus, the labels and distinctions made among different ethnic and racial groups perpetuate a hierarchical system where some groups are the norm while the others, by default, do not fit the norm.

RITUAL INTERACTIONS:
"PEOPLE ARE INCREDIBLY FRIENDLY!"

My brother, who recently visited me from Peru, shared with me his thoughts about American friendliness after spending two days wandering around a large northwestern city. He was taken aback by the Pacific Northwest because he found people to be "incredibly friendly." He went on to say that during his three-week stay in this part of the country, a number of people on the street, on the road, and in the parks had smiled or said "hello" to him. He found it "kind of strange because you just don't see that in Lima, New York, Vienna, or Paris." I was a bit taken aback myself when I heard the story, thinking to myself, "Is the difference tangible?" After pondering a moment, I answered my own questions, "Absolutely!" There's a unique, friendly spirit you find throughout the Pacific Northwest. I think we sometimes lose sight of that fact. When you live something every day, there's a chance you'll start taking it for granted. My brother's comments were somewhat of a wake-up call for me and reminded me of my first months in the United States.

Although at that time I was in northern Florida, I can recall having similar feelings about this unusual kind of friendliness. I clearly remember feeling incredibly special when someone would welcome me to the town, ask me how I was feeling, and wish me a pleasant day. Furthermore, I still remember how shocked I was when an auto mechanic spent almost two hours trying to install a tiny plastic hook in the door of my 1966 VW bug and charged me only $1.50 for the part. And, in perhaps the most startling demonstration of American "friendliness," I vividly recall how, just two months after my arrival in this country, a smiling police officer said, "Welcome to America" after she gave me two (undeserved, I must add) traffic tickets.

Instances like these remind me of an incident recounted by British-born journalist Henry Fairlie in an article entitled "Why I Love America":

> One spring day, shortly after my arrival, I was walking down the long, broad street of a suburb, with its sweeping front lawns (all that space), its tall trees (all that sky), and its clumps of azaleas (all that color). The only other person on the street was a small boy on a tricycle. As I passed him, he said "Hi"—just like that. No four-year-old boy had ever addressed me without an introduction before. Yet here was this one, with his cheerful "Hi!" Recovering from the culture shock, I tried to look down stonily at his flaxen head, but instead, involuntarily, I found myself saying in return: "Well—hi!" He pedaled off, apparently satisfied. He had begun my Americanization. (1983: 12)

For Fairlie the word "Hi!" had an important meaning:

> (I come from a country where one can tell someone's class by how they say "Hallo!" or "Hello!" or "Hullo," or whether they say it at all.) But [in America] anyone can say "Hi!" Anyone does.

Like my brother and Henry Fairlie, I was also very impressed with the friendliness of people in this part of the globe, in particular the friendliness and concern of store clerks and waiters, who would often introduce themselves by their first names and treat me in a casual, friendly manner, even asking how I was feeling today. I was really taken by this caring manner. I remember thinking, How can you not feel special in this great nation if everyone is always trying to see if you are okay? In Lima, where everyone is in a hurry (and sometimes trying to take advantage of others), store clerks and waiters barely say "thank you," if they speak to you at all. And of course, as a customer, you would not spend time chatting or exchanging greetings with those who are in such unsuccessful positions.

One day, however, I was struck by a somewhat sad discovery: What I thought was true concern and friendliness was just a ritual interaction. On that day, I had just learned that Max, my roommate's Golden Retriever, was at a veterinary hospital; he had been run over by a car. On my way home, I stopped by the grocery store to get some milk. As on other days, a friendly clerk checked my groceries, and when she asked me, "How are you?" I responded, "A bit sad." To my surprise, the friendly clerk said, "Great! Have a nice day." After a few seconds of puzzlement, I grabbed my paper sack and left the store. Later, my roommate, a native Floridian, explained that this type of greeting was routine and that stores often require their employees to display "extreme friendliness" with customers. It was only after this explanation that I realized that the caring tone used by clerks and others working with the public was routine chat, part of a ritual exchange.

Ritual exchanges such as "How are you?" "I'm fine, thank you," "Nice meeting you," "Hope you have a nice day," and other similar phrases are, like any ritual exchange, more about form than substance. In other words, questions and answers are (or should be) the same, regardless of the participants in the interactions and their feelings. In the above incident, even though I responded candidly with an unscripted answer to the customary "How are you" questions, I got a conventional short and scripted answer.

The brevity and formulaic aspects of these ritual exchanges, I believe, have little to do with whether people are friendly or not. Rather, this behavior might be related to an informal, egalitarian approach to others characteristic of American culture. It might also have to do with the brevity, informality, and practicality that characterizes the American style of communication (which, by the way, reminds me of the typical monosyllabic answers that I receive from my students when I ask even complex questions: "Sure," "OK," or "Nope").

Ritual interactions, like many other aspects of language and communication, vary from culture to culture and from country to country. This becomes evident when contrasting the little and often impersonal ritual exchanges of Americans with the long and personal ritual interactions of Peruvians. In Peru, ritual exchanges like those mentioned above are not as common as in the United States. When they do occur, however, one generally asks about family members' health. On these occasions, one needs to be accurate in one's questioning and attentive in one's listening, not only in terms of asking about the appropriate family members (for instance, not asking a widow about her husband's health), but also in relation to the substance of the answer (for example, showing some empathy when someone mentions an illness in the family).

SOME FINAL THOUGHTS

The study of communication and miscommunication across cultures is a relatively new area of research and one that holds much promise in terms of what it can teach us about language and intercultural communication. In this piece I have shared my experiences and reflections about the powerful role played by some terms and ethnic labels in the construction of people's social identity. In addition, I have also discussed some aspects of face-to-face interaction that vary from culture to culture and, as in the case of ritual interactions, provide fertile ground for miscommunication. My intent has been not only to illustrate how individual misunderstandings emerge but also to signal how these interactional processes reproduce and reinforce larger patterns within a society.

All in all, my years in the United States have for the most part unfolded like a dream. Sure, I encountered some problems, misunderstandings, and barriers, and often I had to adjust my expectations and appeal to my flexibility in order to keep going. But then, that is life. I am still learning about how to survive in this, my new home, and in the process I am trying to figure out why we use language the way we use it and why language can make things fuzzier and or less fuzzy.

ACKNOWLEDGMENTS

I am grateful to Professors Cynthia Wallat at Florida State and Ginger Weade and Allan Burns at the University of Florida, who introduced me to the study of sociolinguistics. Appreciation is also due to Kerri Richard, David Slavit, and Elsa Statzner for feedback on drafts of this essay.

NOTE

1. Ethnic labels, like all names, are constructs, abstractions of a reality. In this respect, social scientist Suzanne Oboler (1995) argues that perhaps the inevitable use of ethnic labels includes singling out particular socially constructed attributes, whether related to race, gender, class, or language. The attributes are assigned to be common to the group's members and used to homogenize the group—regardless of whether this designation corresponds to the reality of the group to whom the label is attached.

REFERENCES

Fairlie, H. 1983. Why I Love America. *The New Republic,* July 4, 1983, p. 12.
Lakoff, G. 1972. Hedges: A Study in Meaning Criteria and the Logic of Fuzzy Concepts. In *Chicago Linguistic Society Papers.* Chicago: Chicago Linguistic Society.
Muñoz, C. 1989. *Youth, Identity, Power.* London: Verso.
Oboler, S. 1995. *Ethnic Labels, Latino Lives: Identity and the Politics of (Re)presentation in the United States.* Minneapolis: University of Minnesota Press.

STUDY QUESTIONS

1. Why are there problems with the designation "Hispanic"?
2. What is the original derivation of the word *Hispanic,* and why is the contemporary use of the word incorrect?
3. How do the English and Spanish languages differ in relation to the primacy of defining terms? Which language is more culturally accurate, positive in content, or sensitive?
4. What did Professor Ernst eventually learn about the true cultural meaning of "extreme friendliness" in America?

FOURTEEN

Giving, Withholding, and Meeting Midway: A Poet's Ethnography

SALEEM PEERADINA
Sienna Heights College, Adrian, Michigan

A Westernized Indian, stubbornly resistant American, poet, teacher, and participant observer compares the customs of his native Bombay with those he experiences while coming to terms with American life. Values associated with hospitality, social reciprocity, the concept of neighborhood, and higher education are critically and lyrically evaluated.

Saleem Peeradina is a poet who grew up in Bombay, India. He came to the United States as a student in the 1970s, living for three years in the South. He returned again in the 1980s to teach writing at Sienna Heights College.

*B*efore I lead the reader into my chosen landscape, let me offer a wide-angle view of the terrain so that my antecedents become clear and my intent and direction are laid bare.

What will become immediately apparent is that I speak out of a double consciousness: a Westernized Indian, a stubbornly resistant American, a poet-teacher, a migrant-expatriate looking over his shoulder, a participant-observer. Even bureaucratese offers a gem: resident alien! My thesis is that this is the contemporary condition, even without the fact of migration; that the clash of multiple choices complicates but also enriches our life. And what we work toward is a balance, a synthesis.

I hope the reader will bear with me if the opening section of this essay feels like a bumpy ride in a crammed vehicle. I can assure you the voyage will be smooth once we settle down.

Moving in 1988 from Bombay's congested, noisy, vibrant metropolis of ten million (the 1995 figure is fifteen million) to a small midwestern town of twenty-two thousand people can set the stage for multiple layers of dislocation. Subjectively speaking, the levels of contrast fall into the following categories: the massive scale, fast tempo, stimulus and stress of big city life versus the diminished size, peacefulness, and dull pace of small town living; the year-round heat and humidity of Bombay versus the temperate and freezing temperatures of the lake region; the hard, daily struggle for survival under deteriorating sociopolitical conditions in modern India versus the comfort and ease of a stable, new professional and domestic environment;

the exchanging of family ties, connectedness with the community, and abiding friendships in the homeland for the alienation and isolation of the adopted country; the escape from oppressive cultural dictates of a tradition-bound society to a more liberating social framework. And so forth.

The pluses and minuses fall on both sides, even vary with the passage of time, changing circumstances, past histories, and modulations of desire. In the case of my family, individual responses and equations running the gamut of gender and generational differences were balanced by a collective wish for a "new" life.

In my own particular instance, a previous stay of three years in the American South, as a student in the early 1970s, propelled by a lifelong aspiration to cross the bright waters, made my earlier quest (as it does my present one) an adventure. Through this mind-set, what could be potential "dislocations" were really altered states of being in different geographical and cultural locales. I was ready to encounter and eager to participate in the new ethos.

I offer this as a preamble to establish the backdrop against which I will make my pitch. As a poet and social commentator I am always in the field. The gestures, products, and the systems of culture are my raw material, the vital signs of life. Cultural jousting is work, play, and a fine art. Every setting presents itself as a watering hole, an arena; every encounter becomes an enactment in which articulate informants vocalize, whether they realize it or not, a script. I am simultaneously witness, participant, and scribe. I am never off duty.

The mix and rush of metaphor in the foregoing paragraph is intentional. It attests to the dramatic possibilities residing in cultural scenarios.

From the global to the local everything flows into my funnel. (As an Easterner, my metaphors are still pretechnological; an American poet would say, "Everything beams into my screen!") My sources include international politics, big business and service industries, the consumer marketplace; television, movies, advertising, and other media; literary, artistic, and intellectual endeavors; and, finally, street-level activity, neighborhood existence, and the realm of the domestic and personal. Because it is the last I observe most closely on a daily basis, and whose immediacy forces radical adjustments of lenses in my own cultural biases, I will develop some themes that grow out of this. Besides, I am a hands-on kind of writer, preferring the concrete and particular to toying with abstractions. I work from the ground up, allowing the experiential to lead to the conceptual. So I will peer into the pond and hope to find in the teeming life there the distant sky intertwined in it.

Although all this may approach the methodology practiced by anthropologists— and I am aware the field is rife with contending ideologies—I must disclaim any intent of making my viewpoint carry the weight of researched and scholarly accounts. Still, while operating firsthand, I have constantly applied checks and references from a wider set of testimonies not necessarily limited to the experiences of other foreign culturalists. My jottings find analogues and parallels and therefore the backing of numerous and diverse "authorities."

To put it another way, the poet's speculations, arrived at from a different angle of perception, complement the "scientific" and other angles. In the poet's way of seeing, there occur certain revelations and disclosures from the world that, in their particularity, offer themselves as epiphanies. Perhaps it would be more correct to say that although the poet revels in the unique, the idiosyncratic, the strikingly new or the strangely different, his poetic creed nudges him toward a double consciousness of the universal-in-the-local. Often there is no overt or visible separation between the center and the margin: It is one encompassing moment, one encapsulated value striving for poetic validity.

One final disclaimer: From the very nature of the historical "position" and the local "presence" that informs my ethnography, what results is an inevitable comparative approach between the subject (that is, myself) and two cultures (that is, American and Indian). This can be perceived as circumscribing locational boundaries, or simply as defining those boundaries: a point of origin and subsequent shifts. I see it as relational rather than binary, a connection that catalyzes the interplay of two mirrors. The use of contrast between cultural forms and practices, between disparate geographies and belief systems, allows both writer and reader to construct several additional layers of significances beyond the ones unfolded.

This stance, however, is not as clear-cut as it appears. In India, the place of origin, my view of the home culture is far less partisan, much more critical, influenced by the ideologies of the West. Once that self is replanted in the West, the cultural winds and temperature strike at an angle more oblique than the one imagined, inviting a more critical stance. Simultaneously the place of origin and the past does not remain static. It turns fluid, then reassembles to other shapes and colors. Another paradox emerges: Subject and place share an extra physical and extra temporal space. The culture is out there and embedded in me; I carry its imprint wherever I go. It fades, flames, or erupts like a chronic skin condition. In the face of local imperatives, it subsides, like water seeking its level.

The whole point of laying open my antecedents, the unmasking of my proclivities and vulnerabilities, is to let the reader in, to reveal the persona, to clear roadblocks, and leave a trail. The reader can then see not only the conclusions, but also how they were arrived at.

If the general tone of this article tends to be critical of American culture, it is a result of the choice of themes. It does not define or exhaust my view or appreciation of the culture's many attractive features—features that continue to draw a cast of thousands to the ongoing show.

After one has flown in and found a spot to set up camp, the sizing up begins almost immediately. So, this is America. Or is it? The distant rumblings of America speak in the superlative accents of history, myth, and media images: unrestricted freedom, unlimited opportunity, constant mobility and rush, crime figures, fast food, casual sex, and AIDS. A 360-degree tour of the local habitat reveals a small, quiet campus, friendly people, and a somewhat run-down town that boasts of a symphony orchestra but no bus station.

The rumblings soon fade as more pressing daily concerns surface: how to make oneself at home, how to belong to the campus community, how to get to like the food, how to find one's bearings in the supermarket, how to conduct oneself with students, colleagues, friends. The small but friendly and supportive Indian community eases the transition in many ways, providing kitchen stuff, transportation, and welcoming us into their homes.

In one year we make three changes of location and four changes of residence (contributing our share to raising the national average), creating corresponding degrees of instability for the children and the household economy. It is easier for me since the job is the driving impulse, while the family has to cope with its dislocating rhythms.

Settling down, acquiring the accoutrements of American living—a used car, television, microwave, yard sale odds and ends—prepares us for the real business of living: understanding American ways, finding acceptance for Indian ways, investing in friendships, giving meaning to our lives, figuring out the stacked aisles in the supermarket!

No matter what the material gains manifested or how the external changes shaped our lives, the satisfactions or the lack thereof, the heartaches and the spiritual disquiet always centered on the following clusters: notions of generosity and reciprocity; interpretations of what constitutes hospitable gesture, selfless action, helping behavior, and "the deal"; issues of independence and interdependence; intolerance of ambiguity and mistrust of those attributes of personality that tend toward the indeterminate or the inscrutable; surrender of the subtle and the complex in the public sphere to the onslaught of the crass, the simplistic, and reductionist.

Let me jot down a set of "quick and dirty" impressions harvested from a site that might be considered a natural starting point for my inquiry: the home.

To an Indian, Asian, or Easterner (henceforth, each term will be used inclusively), home is a shelter with open doors, privileged space for communal use. Hospitality not assumed or turned down by the visitor is cause for offense. The guest is an honored figure, be it a relation, friend, or stranger.

For most white, middle-class Americans (and those who have been assimilated into that group's value system), home, as the prime embodiment of private property, is a protected area, an armor against intrusion into personal space. The business of hospitality is often deflected into public places—in restaurants and at park picnics. Stayovers are to be accepted only when offered and are time-bound. Even then, Americans grumble incessantly about putting up with family relations visiting during the traditional holidays.

Within the Indian house, all spaces are accessible. In our small apartment in Bombay, we often sat company on the bed; our small living room was too small for furniture. Even when the conveniences are limited, the best is placed at the guest's disposal. If company stays over, the hosts will sleep on the floor, insisting that visiting guests take the bed. Even a poor family will share its food and order or make special items that are normally beyond its means to buy or consume. Sharing is a given. Two of my colleagues and several students who have visited poor communities in Mexico and Central America attest to identical notions of hospitality among the people there. For instance, guests had first dibs on scarce resources like bathwater.

In the American home, the bedroom is always off-limits; even within the family, territorial markings are explicit though not rigid. No great fuss is made over food; self-help is encouraged. Visiting relations are clearly directed to neighborhood motels.

According to Indian protocol, invitation to a home is the first of a series of renewable gestures toward establishing ties of friendship and better mutual understanding. It is also a statement of acceptance and dependability. Walking in and out of each other's home ground is the outward sign of easy exchange of confidences and support in times of need.

An early, now almost archetypal portrayal of this relationship occurs in E. M. Forster's *A Passage to India*. For Aziz, to open his heart to Fielding comes naturally after he has befriended him; it proves somewhat of an embarrassment to the Englishman to be the recipient of such confidences. On his own part, Fielding finds it difficult to return the familiarity that Aziz assumes will flow as a logical outcome of the equation of hospitality he has established with the guest. Among other things, the novel is a classic statement of cultural misunderstandings and the cross-purposes under which individual and political relationships labor.

In the American view, the home visit is a single event entailing no obligation to reciprocity. Our American friends are often flattered, touched, and sometimes leery of undeserved (in their eyes) invitations to our house. We do this routinely, but our expectations are often frustrated because we see ourselves trying too hard to extend warmth and receiving no such gesture in return. Evidently, we are being unreasonable given that we are not singing out of the same hymn book.

Under Indian auspices, the gifts that friends bring are usually for the host family's use, not for serving up to company. Similarly, the spread that the host provides is ample, thoughtful, and an expression of genuine sharing to delight the guest.

Americans usually carry gifts (other than flowers) of which they will be co-consumers. Not only that, they will take back what is left! The menu is most often spare and functional unless it is that glorious American invention, the potluck, or the annual Thanksgiving meal. Oftentimes, items like steak will be counted one to a person—no seconds available. At first we were outraged at what appeared to us to be small-heartedness; now we laugh it off.

In India, dropping in is celebrated, taken for granted, existing as it does in a culture that thrives on contact, that generously devotes its time to serving the needs of others. Besides, the absence of telephones in most middle-class homes in India rules out calling ahead: You assume the party at your destination will greet you with smiles when you show up at the door. Because you have trudged halfway across town to accomplish this, the host is in fact delighted. Improvisation is the rule, for the welcome you are given. I can vouch for the wide application and validity of this practice.

In America, dropping in is taboo, violating codes of etiquette connected with privacy, personal time, and planning; thus, springing of social surprises is not welcome, not even at short notice.

For years, we lived without a telephone in the distant suburbs of Bombay. We woke up on Sundays playing the guessing game of anticipating visitors during the day: It could be parents, cousins, brothers, sisters, or friends. On days when no one appeared at our door, we went to bed feeling let down.

It is not as if the codes for privacy or personal space are not recognized or not valued by Asians; they are simply set aside voluntarily to honor more sacred obligations. From the domestic sphere to the larger social framework, what makes for the greater interdependence between individuals and the group is a higher degree of tolerance, accommodation, and sacrifice, which balances out individual claims against community goals.

In the American family and social network, support is limited to whatever does not interfere with individual space, time, and freedom of choice. When these lines are overstepped, the vote cast is always on the side of individual rights, the pursuit of personal fulfillment and profit, defined from a peculiarly self-driven standpoint.

So lost are some self-evident truths that researchers actually have to conduct studies to demonstrate that service toward others, devoting oneself to another's well-being, can be good for one's own psychic welfare! So unfashionable is conventional wisdom that the bringing together of the elderly and very young children in a supervised setting is seen to be a revolutionary idea. So misplaced are family memories that stories of sons and daughters taking in sick or disabled parents actually make news! Americans *en masse* tend to abdicate common sense and intuition in their reliance on "scientific data" and "experts" to help them monitor their personal lives. The diet industry's periodic "findings" (usually backed by drug-industry-funded "research" and bandwagoned by other ancillary enterprises) is another example of this mindless conformity. For a culture that prides itself on individuality, this conformity is shockingly routine in many areas of life.

Language is the first casualty in this broadside of jargon and rhetoric, the leveling of conceptual thought. For a country with a flair for developing the most colorful Americanisms out of the English language, there is the flip side in which language is constantly under assault and subject to trivialization. Words like *stress, disorder,* and *abuse,* for instance, are currently the most abused words in the language. They are applied loosely and across the board, and they infect and distort discussion leading to abbreviated thinking. Everywhere, labeling is handy, a quick way of slotting opponents, polarizing issues, and preempting any complex examination of gray areas. Look at the battle lines drawn between pro-lifers and pro-choicers.

In schools, the condition of "disorder" runs rampant, an assumption that underlies the representation of students' abilities and deficiencies, their diagnoses and prescriptions for cure.

Often I enjoy the use of sports terminology in the forecasts on the Weather Channel. The use of athletic metaphors, which is pervasive in all walks of American life, from boardrooms to bars, became quite offensive and dehumanizing when applied thoughtlessly—"kicking butt"—to the "enemy" in the Gulf War.

Reliance on learning tools such as the calculator and spell checking function on computers has virtually dried up mental arithmetic and versatility with language. I have seen friends incapacitated without a tape measure when rough-and-ready estimates of size and fit are called for. The indiscriminate use of words like *pretty* and the generic verb *bug,* for example, grates monotonously on my sense of proper usage as it strikes me as a teacher and writer. Definitely not "cool" in my book.

But I am not yet done with the domestic. Having children sleep over, which they do all the time in the homes of classmates, is a good way of infiltrating into the domestic stronghold. The vantage point that invisible informants have is priceless. The same applies to our children's friends who sleep over at our house—we have the benefit of examining ourselves from their insider viewpoints. Some revelations: As parents we rated easygoing, liberal, unfussy. So there is some truth to the suspicion that this is a conservative town! The other possibility is that this particular set of families makes up rules that are stricter than ours.

I must confess that my score as a husband fell a lot lower than the American standard set by my wife's peers and coworkers in relation to decision-making and independence in financial matters enjoyed by them. *Mea culpa.* On the other hand, my wife's friends inquire if she will rent me out for my domestic reputation as a cook and baby-sitter. They are also somewhat astonished that we give each other permission to go out for dinner/movies with friends of the opposite sex. We also did this in Bombay, totally horrifying our respective parents.

Food cropped up again on the children's list of noticeable differences—specifically, a reluctance to share. The father of one of my daughter's friends will say within my daughter's hearing when she comes over unannounced to do homework: "What is she going to eat? We didn't make enough." The two parents work five jobs between them, carry their badges of affluence, and, reports my daughter, their kitchen shelves and freezer are stacked with food.

When my daughters' friends drop in unannounced after school and there isn't enough food or nothing to their taste, we generally concoct something without any fuss. In our house, our children's friends enjoy the same status as other guests with the attendant services due to them. Most of them, to our delight, have become connoisseurs of curry and Indian *chai* (a strong concoction brewed with tea leaves, to which is added sugar and milk).

Reluctance to share food: two more images vie for attention. People solemnly munch brown bag lunches in company without the least bit of self-consciousness. Same scenario among Indians—an impromptu and jovial division of the spoils from bags and tiffin boxes to everyone present is undertaken, especially for those who haven't brought their own.

There is the example of a good friend of ours for whom our doors have always been open and a meal guaranteed, and who has regularly partaken of our hospitality. Once, when my wife dropped in on her at noon, she was lunching on fast food but showed not the least bit of courtesy by sharing even a french fry. I am not offended, simply amused to see such narcissism with respect to food. Of course, our friend, in her own way, has been generous to us on plenty of occasions. The modes have varied; the terms have differed.

Before moving from the present locale to the classroom, let me, by way of transition, make a quick stop in the neighborhood.

Having spent between two months to four years in five different residential areas, having seen a pattern replicated in the lives of friends across the country, my impression about small town, suburban living is one of overwhelming desolation. While appreciating the logic behind the rapid growth of suburban living as a retreat from the busier, centralized, and faster-paced pattern of urban planning; while enjoying the benefits of space, quiet vistas, clean air, safety, and other perks that I would never give up; while empathizing with the American desire to shut in the self and shut out the world, I am still left with missing pieces.

To start with, the suburban neighborhood hardly qualifies as "user-friendly," to borrow another one of those cryptic American terms. "Neighborliness" as a concept has all but been erased from what used to be understood as community life. There is only mild concern or interest in who lives next door; there is hardly any at all in who lives down the block. Greetings in passing and a quick wave of the hand are the standard modes of communication; carpools are the common mode of interaction. The appearance of utility vans in the driveway or the arrival of ambulances is the only spark generating curiosity. In warm weather, more faces and bodies become visible, but exchanges remain superficial or ritualized over the drone of the mower. Many properties have no fences—an attractive feature, despite Robert Frost's ambivalence in "Mending Wall": "Good fences make good neighbors." But appearance belies the reality: The walls between neighbors are impenetrable, unscalable.

Sometimes, I think Americans have succeeded only too well in realizing their dream of living in private paradises that resemble solitary confinement cells.

It is true that ties with the broader community, not the immediate one, continue to be maintained. But it is often from a consumer orientation that these exercises are conducted: out of the security of home and into the comfort of the car to make a trip to the store, the mall, the sports stadium, the aerobics class, the vacation, the fast-food stop, and back to the nest. To be fair, the real moments of America at leisure not dictated by everyday exigencies or the enticements of the leisure industry take place in restaurants, bars, bookstores, theaters, music and movie halls, parks, pools, beaches, nature trails, and above all, in front of the television set. Americans love "the good life" and work hard at having fun.

It might also be a truism that the whole point of domestic striving is to shut in and to keep out. I enjoy my share of it, and indeed, it is a change from the traditionally intrusive mode of neighborhood living in Indian cities and suburbs. Apartment and condo building in big cities has somewhat discouraged the old-style, open, in-your-face living arrangements, sometimes with traumatic consequences for tenants used to more informal and cluttered lifestyles. A recent study undertaken in Calcutta describes the depression experienced by women living in skyscrapers whose contact with ground-level existence and joint family dynamics is cut off for prolonged periods because of the husband's upward mobility, and migration into a nuclear family setup.

It is this deep conditioning that, in time, makes the Asian-American long for the vitality of a neighborhood alive with children, vendors, cyclists, shops, surprise, drama. Some of this is on vivid display in ethnic enclaves in New York, San Francisco, and other big cities—Dearborn, near Detroit, and Devon Street in Chicago are sights familiar to me. Not so long ago in American memory, Jane Jacobs in *The Death and Life of Great American Cities* described the texture and tone of sidewalk contacts as the "small change" out of which grew the community's wealth of public life. The props and paraphernalia of city property are designed to stimulate this growth. When this high-pitched vitality degenerates into an environment of noise, dirt, congestion, and crime, suburbia offers a welcome alternative.

But suburban subdivisions and layouts are designed as closed, static systems. With all of their attractions, conveniences, and gratifications, they seal the American soul in an ingrown, selfishly guarded, deadbolted cell, insulated and detached from the principle of a shared community life. Where this principle comes into effect, it is through the structured network of church, club, bingo group, or work-related interests, with established and limited goals.

In good weather, when children spill out on the lawn, an exchange of sorts takes place. In one of our former settings, where two houses in the same yard were rented out to two families, stay-at-home mothers and children provided the glue for interfamily contact, exchange of recipes and food items. The relationship between these families continues—now that one family has moved to the Upper Peninsula—through mail and telephone, gift exchanges, and summer visits. In our present neighborhood, however, our friendly overtures have worked with only two out of twenty households. Superficiality reigns; anonymity is the norm.

Let me see if the shift to the third locale will help me round out and culminate the themes I have unfolded.

Having begun by identifying the context from which I speak, I went on to examine the notion of hospitality, reciprocity and related behaviors, and the withholding of these gestures. I tried to link these with wider historical and cultural patterns. From there I looked at the idea of "neighborhood" to find out if there was a cause-effect relation between designs and systems of living and social interaction. Now I intend to focus on how some of these manifestations affect the educational system and the lives of students, and what lessons we may learn from a renegotiation of current realities.

For me, the impulse to write comes out of the same source as the desire to teach—giving voice to a shaping spirit. In one, the speaking self constructs a text and in the other, the self lends its voice to give life to other texts. Both are inner-driven and outer-directed: They presume an attentive consciousness, a longing, and an active intent at both ends of the process.

I picture the classroom as a crossroads, the place where worlds collide; where, along with the dismantling and rupture of theories and practices, a fusion is also taking place in a series of continuous, dynamic moments in the act of reading, writing, and conversation. The ruling principle here is *connectedness*—a network of links between teacher, learner, materials; worlds occupied, abandoned, yet to be born; ideas, stories, dreams.

Here, again, I find myself in a place of dissonance. Although theoretically as well as in practice, American higher education functions in a more stimulating, liberal atmosphere than comparable systems elsewhere, its pedagogical bent militates against any deep-rooted, sustained *engagement* between teacher and learner. Textual learning is elevated above everything else, performance and scoring are the highest rated values, development of "skills" the ultimate goal. Individual success, which is evidenced through completed assignments and secured grades, is emphasized more than the quest for meaning. The idea of personal growth is touted loudly and ritually, but often revolves around the notion of self-acceptance and "feeling good"—almost totally denuded of the refining edge of critical self-scrutiny.

Although the educational system is differentiated enough in terms of programs, value orientation, and choice of schools to allow for a more humane scale of interaction (a focus on intellectual and humanitarian pursuits), the attempt is effectively undermined by the habits and structures of American mass culture. The grain of American life, its temper and tempo, its headlong rush into short-term, goal-centered styles of living, the dependence on products of technology and the agendas set by it, the media's subversion of sacred and rational discourse, and any number of related phenomena ensure that intellectual and humane concerns always get the short end in a culture driven by innovation, consumption, profit, and self-serving motives.

In this climate, to define one's calling as a teacher as that of a friend, guide, and philosopher raises eyebrows, arouses suspicion, and generates disbelief. Coming from an ancient "guru" culture, I am branded by that tradition that still thrives in the spheres of music, theater, dance, and religious training. Admittedly, even in India, higher education has become mechanized to the point where any possibility of negotiated relationships between student and teacher has been virtually eliminated.

Over here, although my commitment as a teacher and the energy I invest in the life of students is appreciated, my attempt to invite partnerships, to offer apprenticeships, appears like a sad and touching anachronism. There are few takers. Any arrangement showing any sign of mutual dependence produces distinct discomfort in the American ego. On the part of the younger generation, this fear is often based on a general distrust of teachers and of the adult population. Because I am forced to deal with this every day, I have struggled with trying to come to terms with this resistance.

Some observations: Helping behavior, especially of the unsolicited voluntary kind, is regarded as presumptuous, almost a judgment of another's ability; in the eyes of some, it amounts to an insult. Since independence is such a prized virtue, looking out for oneself is the prime value.

Because, in the American rule book, selfless behavior is suspect, actions are viewed as always having a motive. Similarly, if help is acknowledged or accepted, the recipient assumes that an unspoken obligation or demand may ensue. Because this will impinge on the freedom to make up his or her own mind, the helpful action is declined. When a "favor" is accepted, it is sought to be quickly squared off through payment. Nothing is as easy and businesslike in personal dealings between Americans—even in marital and intimate family transactions—as settlements worked out in dollar amounts for specific help or gain. Money is the great leveler.

Nothing is as touchy to Asian-Americans as the equating of acts of friendship and gestures of goodwill with monetary value. An act of generosity is meant to be accepted as a gift, a token of affection and esteem for the one on whom it is conferred. The receiver waits for the right occasion to show appreciation in return. When the smell of money intrudes, the deed is paid for, bought, and concluded. The future of giving is nipped.

For Americans, the most universally understood metaphor for transactional behavior is "the deal." Although this originates in the dominant, male, competitive culture, women get drawn into it easily. You get fair exchange, or you get the better of the other. In competitive relationships, you work toward gaining an advantage. In unsavory situations, you screw someone; in outright exploitative ones, you do worse. No wonder my wish to function outside these tried and tested parameters invites suspicion and mistrust.

Students, as well as colleagues, prefer an up-front accounting, a visible contractual relationship rather than one with latitude that may have a hidden agenda. I suspect issues of autonomy, control, trust, and vulnerability have a lot to do with this holding back. In today's climate, the legality of roles and functions and the status of what is "appropriate"—another one of those words running loose—also probably inhibit the following of one's own drumbeat.

If giving, generosity, bestowing on others the gifts that arise out of doing one's duty or out of one's temperament is frowned upon, what is propelling the spreading cult of "random acts of kindness"? Why is there such a yearning for groupism? Wherever you turn, whatever you tune into, the language is saturated with "support," "caring," "self-worth," "growing." But this is a halfhearted yearning, an artificially contrived cure played out in the atmosphere of a hothouse. It evades the bedrock ideology of American individualism: An assumption, though vaguely questioned from time to time, has not quite become problematic enough for a radical reappraisal. Indeed, support groups subvert their own logic by offering a ritualized, rehashed kind of community (shades of the encounter group from an earlier era?) that makes no onerous demands but panders to individual-focused agendas that suit perfectly the self-centered habits and aims of its followers. As such, these genuine but misplaced attempts are doomed to failure—the residue of another lost art.

The need for periodic reviews of values, attitudes, and behaviors seems to be ongoing—clearly, a sign of health—in the life of the culture. But it invariably takes place through the agency of a passing fashion or fad, only to be replaced by the next one.

Limitations of space have constrained me from a fuller examination of the excursions I've made. My hope is that readers will be motivated to look more deeply into the psychological and cultural ground on which these sightings have been made. In wrapping up this narrative, I'd like to linger awhile in the inviting space between giving and withholding.

The solid core of American values—the good old standbys of self-reliance, industry, profit and pleasure, good humor, an incurable optimism, and the need to move on—remains unshaken.

Despite the frictions and misunderstandings—it is unrealistic after all, to expect complete harmony or thorough understanding among diverse groups, classes, genders, and national cultures—there is a drive and a level of coherence that makes this society run.

Signals and prophecies of doom are announced at regular intervals. But if history is any comfort, this tendency is a well-established cultural trait. Except that at this historic moment, the culture will have to invent a more active ingredient than the stale formula of "tolerance" in order to accommodate current and developing realities. Tolerance is easy when it issues from a privileged source. Tolerance distances and separates because it is patronizing and benevolent; it is the gruel dished out to those who have sought asylum. Tolerance ultimately retreats to its high ground. The active ingredient now needed to shake the tolerant out of their torpor is an invitation to embrace, to meet midway, to take by the hand, to sit face to face.

The exponents of American culture who make brave attempts to understand "the other" in their midst succeed to a degree through the simple, ubiquitous device of "acceptance"—that all-American gesture and nod to the stranger arriving on their shores. They welcome, make room, and delight in the strangeness of the creature they have adopted. It is evidence of the dash of pragmatism in the American recipe for survival. But deeper understanding eludes these exponents, particularly as the stranger resists easy labeling and categorization, defies familiar models of behavior and norms of conduct.

The Asian and other foreign representative will always remain elusive to some degree; his or her heart and soul will always seem inscrutable. In day-to-day dealings, this mystery will often pose barriers, give rise to minor annoyances and misinterpretations. Such simple issues as permissible eye contact, physical proximity, and touching can raise unanswerable questions. Inevitably, these are tied up with differences in professed values and styles of communication.

The Easterner lives comfortably with ambiguity of personality as well as language, without hankering after absolutist or categorical statements of position at all times. He is at home with contradictions, even unresolvable ones, since they are part of life's unsolvable problems back home or part of the larger mysteries of the universe. The indeterminate is a very real, fascinating, even venerated category of experience. This other world sits on a stalk and sways between the *yes, no,* and the *maybe;* it is poised between the *this* and the *not this.* The language of paradox is that native's natural medium. The state of uncertainty is not threatening; it is fertile, a state that entertains possibility.

This is clearly misunderstood, dismissed, and proves to be a source of provocation to a culture that insists on clear-cut definitions, scientific accuracy, statistical data, and the belief that inquiry must yield firm results, evidence must lead to truth. It is not so much the methodology that is inadequate but the underlying dogmas that make the process flawed.

Surely the challenge and exhilaration lies in the coming together of complementary viewpoints of the familiar and the strange, the mysterious and the intimately known, the distant and the close-at-hand. The question we must ask ourselves is: Can we hear the hum of the universal in the heartbeat of the particular? Despite the burning focus on undeniable particularities of difference—histories, heritages, communities, voices—we need to salvage the possibility of universal connection. This is our stage, our arena, our field of vitality. This is where we must meet to recover our faith, to find ourselves renewed.

Given the conditions of displacement, expatriation, and exile (in more than the geographical sense), what speaks to me is a statement by Novalis that I have rephrased: Poetry, travel, anthropology, is for me an endless homesickness; it is the urge to be at home everywhere.

STUDY QUESTIONS

1. What are the basic differences between American and Indian concepts of hospitality?
2. Compare Indian and American codes of privacy and personal space.
3. How does Professor Peeradina describe the concepts of the suburban American neighborhood?
4. What are the author's main criticisms about teacher-student relationships in higher education? What does he find to be the basic problem with the value system indicated by students' attitudes?
5. Do Americans have, as the author has suggested, an "urge to be at home everywhere"? Why or why not?

FIFTEEN

A Russian Teacher in America

ANDREI TOOM

This article contrasts Russian and American systems of higher education, focusing on the teaching of mathematics and the attitudes of students. Toom reveals for us some unsettling aspects of American culture, such as our excessive concern with credentials but seeming lack of concern with competence. Competition and the grading system are taken to task, as is our market orientation in learning—trying to get the highest grade for the least investment.

Andrei Toom *grew up in Russia (then the Soviet Union). He taught mathematics and did research for nearly twenty years at Moscow University. He came to the United States in 1989 and taught mathematics at Rutgers University and at Incarnate Word College.*

I am a Russian mathematician and teacher. For nearly 20 years I did research and taught students at Moscow University. Now I have moved to the United States, as have many other Russians. This article is about some of my experiences of teaching both in Russia and America.

Americans' ideas about Russia are as contradictory as Russia itself. For many years Soviet Russia was perceived as "The Evil Empire." On the other hand, there was a *Sputnik* movement in America, which claimed that the Russian educational system was much better than the American one. Obviously, these images did not fit together. A lot of effort is needed to give the real picture. I am just going to make a few comments to explain my background.

Communist rule in Russia emerged from the collapse of the obsolete Tzarist autocracy, under which most people were deprived of education. Early Communists enthusiastically sang the *"Internationale,"* which claimed: "Who was nothing will become everything." Nobody ever knew what it meant exactly, but many were excited. Many Russian revolutionaries sincerely believed that it was their mission to redress all the social injustices immediately, but ignorance crippled all their efforts. A telling example is described in the novel *Chapayev* by the Russian writer Furmanov.

This article was originally published in the *Journal of Mathematical Behavior* and is reproduced here with permission.

The hero Chapayev, a Red Army commander, insists on giving an official certificate of competence in medicine to a poorly educated man, naively thinking that having such a certificate really makes one a doctor.

Communists made promises that looked very democratic, particularly that children of "proletarians" would be given unlimited educational opportunities. Children of manual workers and poor peasants really were given privileges to enter all kinds of schools, and professors who gave them bad grades might be accused of antirevolutionary activity. Only a generation later, Russia had thousands of hastily coached engineers and scientists of proletarian descent. One of these "proletarian scientists," an academician named Lysenko, gave fantastic agricultural promises that he never kept. However, Lysenko impressed Soviet rulers from Stalin to Khrushchev because they also were pseudoeducated. A major branch of biology, namely genetics, was declared a "bourgeois pseudoscience" because Lysenko was against it.

The ambitions of pseudoeducated "proletarian scientists," their haughtiness toward bourgeois science, their pretensions of superiority because of having had poor parents and being led by "the world's truest teaching" (that is, Marxism) caused a lot of industrial and ecological disasters. However, Communists never admitted the true causes of these disasters; all of them were attributed to some "enemies'" sabotage. A number of alleged "enemies" were arrested and reportedly confessed. Masses of people, although declared "educated" by that time, believed these reports. But disasters continued, and to explain them away the authorities needed more and more "enemies." Meanwhile, Russia became the world leader in wasted resources and polluted environment: *Chernobyl* is just one (but not unique) example.

I was 11 when Stalin died. For many years all Soviet people, especially youngsters, had been indoctrinated that they should never doubt the Communist tenets. All media had been filled with verbose praises to Stalin, who was called "the greatest genius of all times and all peoples."

However, much of Russian and foreign literature was available, including American authors. Foreign authors were published under the pretext that they "criticized bourgeois society." Mark Twain, Jack London, Ernest Seton, O. Henry, Edgar Allan Poe, Paul de Kruif, Ernest Hemingway, and Ray Bradbury were among my favorite authors.

I vividly remember reading a book about a scientist who proved that insects have no reason; they only have instinct. What he actually proved was that the behavior of insects was effective only in situations usual for them. When the experimenter artificially arranged unusual situations, the insects did the same standard movements although they evidently could not be of any use in that new situation, because it was different from those to which the insects had become accommodated through evolution. I was impressed: I understood that propaganda tried to turn us into some kind of insects. I thought then and think now that it is a most important duty of a teacher of humans to teach them to be humans; that is, to behave reasonably in unusual situations. When I taught in Russia, I was thanked most explicitly for this. But I met a lot of resistance from some of my American undergraduate students especially when I tried to give them something unexpected. On tests, they wanted to do practically the same as what they had done before—only with different numerical data. This is why I decided to write this article.

I always believed that really good education is the most valuable contribution that intellectuals of a country can make toward its democratization. Remember that the great French Revolution was prepared by the Age of Enlightenment. It was evident that the worst features of Soviet rule were connected with the power of the pseudoeducated who got their certificates for being "proletarians," but cared only for their careers. Understandably, Soviet authorities always were suspicious about independent thought and real intellectuals.

In return, good teaching, intended to develop real competence of students, always had a flavor of resistance to Soviet authorities, as it involved realism, open-mindedness, and critical thinking. When a good mathematics teacher tried to move his students to think independently, he was aware that his real influence went far beyond mathematics: He tried and succeeded to keep alive the critical spirit. Learning recipes without thinking was associated with the Communist tyranny; learning to solve nontrivial problems was associated with independence and criticism. For this reason, for example, George Pólya's writings on teaching were perceived in Russia as books on openmindedness and critical thinking rather than just on the teaching of mathematics. We knew that Pólya was not alone: He referred to other scientists, for example to Max Wertheimer's notion of "productive thinking."

In the years of Khrushchev's liberalism, some new foreign books also became available in Russia. Russian thinkers read very attentively all the foreign authors they could find. Many valuable ideas came from Americans: authoritarian personality (Theodor Adorno); group pressure (Solomon Asch); obedience to authority (Stanley Milgram). Eric Berne's *Games People Play* moved us to see which dirty games our rulers played with us. Thomas Kuhn's book about scientific revolutions was about ideological revolutions for us. Milton Rokeach's idea of open and closed minds opened our minds. John Holt's criticism of American schools made us understand that our schools deserved much harsher criticism.

My parents belonged to artistic circles, and pressure of censure [censorship] was a constant theme of conversations. If trimming a tree went too far, they would say with regret: "Look, how we have edited this tree!" Exact sciences provided the greatest available degree of independence from authorities, and my parents spoke with envy about mathematicians who could afford to say the exact truth and even be paid for it rather than punished. They could not guide my study of sciences, but they expected intellectual efforts of me, and it was important.

Later, my school teacher of mathematics, Alexander Shershevsky, helped me a lot. He strived to become a mathematician, but could not obtain a research position because in his student years he had gotten into some political trouble. (The trouble must have been minor; otherwise we would never have seen him again.) I was especially impressed by his responsible attitude to his mission. He urged me to attend informal classes in mathematics at Moscow University. The main business of these classes was solving nonstandard problems. Students were free to drop in and out; using this, I changed several groups until I found a teacher, Alexander Olevsky, whom I liked most. Every year students at Moscow University arranged a competition for high school students in solving problems. Every problem was new and unlike others and demanded a nontrivial idea and a rigorous proof to solve. There were five problems and five hours to solve them. Typically, everyone who solved at least one problem was rewarded. In this way I got several prizes. This convinced me that I could succeed as a mathematician. When I moved from high school to the mathematics department of Moscow University, solving problems naturally led me to research.

From my first year in the university I took it for granted that a competent mathematician should participate in the teaching of mathematics because I had excellent examples to follow. The famous Kolmogorov organized a mathematical college affiliated with Moscow University, and I taught there. Academician Gelfand organized a School by Correspondence, and I instructed its teachers. In the computer club I headed the teaching program.[1] Aleksandrov, Arnold, Boltyansky, Dobrushin, Dynkin, Efimov, Kirillov, Postnikov, Sinai, Tzetlin, Uspensky, the Yaglom brothers, and other first-class mathematicians were willing to lecture and to communicate with students. A lot of new and original problems from all branches of mathematics and at various levels of difficulty were invented for all kinds of students from young children to graduate students and young professionals. Now, I was among those who invented problems. When I advised Ph.D. and other students, I gave them problems that interested me, and we solved them together.

The main pressure that students put upon teachers was to tell them something new. A vivid example was Leonid Vaserstein (then a student), who would declare in the middle of a talk: "All this is trivial." Taken out of situational context this may seem impolite, but actually this was quite *productive*. He pressed lecturers for more competence. Soon he had to emigrate. (Now he is a professor at Penn State University.) His fate is typical: Top officials of Moscow University, very poor scientists but bombastic Communists, used all pretexts (notably anti-Semitism) to get rid of competent young scientists to ensure their own positions. Now, they do the same without Communist paraphernalia; they recently elected a notorious hardliner, Sadovnichy, president of Moscow University.

Whenever the purpose of learning was real competence, it had nothing to do with good standing with the authorities, who were feared and despised by intellectuals. Grades were just a nuisance, like any extraneous control. For example, when I taught in the college organized by Kolmogorov, I simply gave an A to every student because all of them deserved A according to average Russian standards, and I wanted to save them the trouble of dealing with the authorities. But they knew perfectly well that we expected much more of them than of the average student, and they worked very hard.

Every advanced school, where independent and creative thought was cultivated, became a breeding ground for political dissent. The mathematics department of Moscow University was no exception. From time to time there were political clashes, and I took part in them. This caused me problems with the Soviet authorities and eventually led to my emigration.

Most of my sixty publications are in mathematics; the others pertain to education and humanities. Not one article of the latter part was published as I wanted it, because of censure [censorship] restrictions. Most of them would never have been published without the willingness of a particular editor to take a certain, well-calculated risk. Whenever I brought an article to the newspaper *Izvestia,* my cautiously courageous editor, Irina Ovchinnikova, exclaimed: "Oh, Andrei, do you really think that this is publishable?" And she had to cross out the most critical statements to save the others.

My research in mathematics could not improve my position in the university because Communist bureaucrats always (and correctly) understood that I would never *solidarize* with them. The adviser of my Ph.D., Ilya Piatetski-Shapiro, emigrated to Israel and thereby became *persona non grata* for the Soviet establishment:

Even referring to his papers was not easy. My papers were known abroad, but were not recognized as anything valuable by my supervisor, because I gave him too few chances to appropriate my work. I received several invitations from foreign universities, but the authorities never allowed me to go abroad. Only by chance, I got to Italy in 1989 and decided to accept all the invitations I had, without going back and subjecting myself to the same arbitrariness. From Rome I went to Rutgers University, then to other American universities.

It is a common opinion that the United States of America supports democracy. Democracy always was connected in my mind with good education for all people, and I knew that American thinkers also believed in this connection. Thus, when I came to this country, I expected to have rich opportunities to teach students to think critically, independently, and creatively and to solve nonstandard problems without hindrance from authorities.

My first experience in teaching in this country did not contradict this expectation. It was proposed that I give a course called "Analysis of Algorithms" to graduate students of the computer science department of Boston University (BU). The textbook *Introduction to Algorithms* by Cormen, Leiserson, and Rivest was excellent. The department applied to me a wise rule—to give full freedom to the lecturer— and I used it to the benefit of my students as I understood it. In one semester I covered most of that rich book. I believe that the mathematical introduction was especially useful: I filled many gaps in my students' former education. My nineteen students came from all over the globe, and most of them collaborated with each other in an excellent way. After every lecture they came to one room, discussed the problems that I gave them, and solved them together. Some problems I gave them were from the book; some were invented by me. I tried to miss no opportunity to make my students think, and they accepted it. Also there was no problem with grades. The department gave me *carte blanche,* and I used it benevolently: Almost all of my students learned a great deal, and I rewarded them with good grades.

But in the next year, when I came to a huge state university and started to teach the so-called business calculus[2] to undergraduates, I got into an absolutely new situation. All my ideas about teaching students to think became completely out of place. Never before had I seen so many young people in one place who were so reluctant to meet challenges and to solve original problems. All they wanted were high grades, and they wanted to get them with a conveyor belt regularity. Suppose that a worker at a conveyor belt gets inspired by some interesting idea and tries to implement it into his work. You can guess that he will get into trouble. This is what happened to me when I started to teach American undergraduates.

In my student years, I hated teachers who simply repeated textbooks: It seemed to me that they wasted my time. Naturally, as a teacher, I avoided that practice. This worked well until the last year, when I started to teach business calculus. Then I found quite a different attitude among my students: Many of them would be most satisfied if the teacher simply repeated and explained what was written in the textbook. It seems that some of them have problems in reading by themselves what is written there, although most textbooks are quite elementary (but verbose). At first I failed to understand this, and one student wrote about me: "He should teach from the text and give exams based on the text or similar problems."

The voluminous book I had to use in teaching the business calculus course may impress nonprofessionals, for example, parents of students. Its chapters are named after really important mathematical theories. But everything nontrivial is carefully eliminated. In fact, every chapter contains a recipe, as in a cookbook, and problems do not go beyond straightforward applications of the recipe. The book carefully avoids connecting the material of different chapters, presenting the subject from different sides, giving problems in which a student should choose which method to apply. And this book was chosen among others, some of which were quite usable. Why? I see one explanation: Because this book perfectly fits the *max-min* principle of the market: maximal pretensions with minimal content. All the other textbooks are not so perfect in this respect.

I was astonished by the fact that I could find absolutely no nonstandard problems in the textbook. But I said to myself: This is a good case for me to show what I can do! I *can* invent nonstandard problems! And so I *did!* And my first test was a total failure. It turned out to be so difficult for the students that most of them got very low grades. I had to learn that every technical calculation, which I was used to ignoring, was a considerable obstacle for my students. It took a considerable amount of time for me to understand how poor they were in basic algebraic calculations. Every time I prepared another test, I tried to make it as easy as possible, and still several times I failed: The tests turned out to be too difficult. As time went on, I came to the following rule: As long as a problem was interesting for me, it was too difficult for the students; only when a problem became trivial, might it be given in the test.

It was good luck for me that one of the students auditing my precalculus course, Robert Tufts, was a retired engineer who had lived much in Europe and Japan and had an extensive experience of learning and teaching. For him my style of teaching was not unusual; in fact, he liked it and told other students about it. Thus, they chose the label, "European teacher," for me, and this softened their shock. Still, another student wrote:

> Please inform Mr. Toom about the grading system and instruction methods of THIS country. Mr. Toom assumes that his students were taught as he was. I earned a grade of A in my college algebra and trigonometry courses so it makes no sense for me to be doing so poorly in this course. Please straighten this man out.

In the next semester I straightened myself out: At every lecture I took the textbook into my hand and explained some examples from it. And nobody complained.

As I had often done before, I gave out to students lists of additional problems arranged by me, and as before, these problems were useful as they moved many students to think. But I had not got used to caring about grades, and this time grades—not math problems—were the center of attention. My carelessness created a lot of trouble for myself and for the department. Those students who solved my problems wanted extra credit, while those who did not solve them wanted full credit also. Several times I was called to the official in charge to clarify my grading system. In the next semester I decided not to give any extra-credit problems, and no trouble arose. The less I teach, the less trouble I have. In Russia we used to joke: No initiative will remain unpunished. Now I saw this rule working in American education.

I had to learn by trial and error how much of elementary mathematics was taboo in the business calculus course. It took a while before I realized that I was lecturing about exponential functions to students who were not required to know about geometrical progressions. Also I confused my business calculus students by trying to explain errors in the textbook. Many of them would prefer to accept every word of it without criticism.

Another mistake made by me was to include a trigonometrical function in a test problem. I could not imagine that students who take "calculus" were not supposed to know trigonometry, but it was the case. Of course, I was called to the official in charge and rebuked. Thus, I could discuss the equation $y'' - y = 0$, but not $y'' + y = 0$. In addition, I received a telephone call from someone who had graduated from the school of law; referring to a decision made by the authorities, he accused me of wasting taxpayers' money by teaching students what they did not need to know (trigonometry). After several lapses of this sort, the department decided not to invite me for the next year, although they knew that I was a competent scholar, that I was interested in teaching, and that I needed a position. All they wanted was not to have problems with the students.

I noticed that research mathematicians treat the business calculus courses like Russians treated Communist meetings: Nobody dares to criticize openly, but everybody tries to sneak away. That is why foreign lecturers such as myself are needed to do this dirty job. But foreigners adjust to the system pretty soon, so that American students have almost no chances of becoming aware of their ignorance. For me, a few months were sufficient: The pressure from those students who wanted good grades with minimal learning, which was supported by university officials, made me care more about my safety from complaints and less about the real competence of my students.

One foreigner, experienced in teaching Americans, advised me in a friendly manner "Listen, don't ask for trouble. Education in this country is not our concern. Nobody will care if you fall short of the syllabus, but never go beyond."[3] And he went home with dollars earned honestly; that is, by doing to Americans just what they—both students and officials—wanted him to do. Of course, he teaches in a much more productive way in his own country.

Suppose you fly in a plane. What is more important for you: the pilot's real competence or his papers that certify he is competent? Or suppose you get sick and need medical treatment. What is more important for you: your doctor's real competence or his diploma? Of course, in every case the real competence is more important. But last year I met a large group of people whose priorities were exactly the opposite: my students. Not all, but many. Their first priority was to get papers that certify that they are competent rather than to develop real competence. As soon as I started to explain to them something that was a little bit beyond the standard courses, they asked suspiciously: "Will this be on the test?" If I said, "no," they did not listen anymore and showed clearly that I was doing something inappropriate.

I had to learn also that American students want to be told exactly from the very beginning of the course what percentages of the total score comes from homework, from tests, and from quizzes. First I thought that it was some nonsense, as if I were requested to predict how many commas and colons I would use in a paper I was going to write. But later I understood that these percentages make sense for those students who do not care about the subject and take a course just to get a grade with minimal learning.

Of course, students are different. Many really want to learn, because curiosity is inherent in human nature. But selfless curiosity is illegal (at least in the business calculus course) in the sense that it is neither expected nor supported officially. On the contrary, officials cater to those who want to learn as little as possible, and percentages are a telling example of this.

It seems that some parents urge their offspring to get high grades by any means, but fail to add that they care about actual competence, too. I understand that some students are the first in their families to get a higher education. Their parents did monotonous work all their lives, tried to make more money for less work and were right, of course. Now, their offspring do monotonous exercises at universities, try to make more grades for less work, and nobody in the family sees anything wrong with it. Indeed, parents may perceive this as a great achievement when their offspring graduates, and they may think that they now have an "intellectual" in the family, while this is simply someone who bought a discounted degree at a university sale! Discounted not in the sense of money, but in the sense of intellectual effort and development.

The grade looks like the ultimate value, and neither students, nor parents, nor university officials see anything wrong with this. In fact, all officials completely support the top priority of official records. It seems to be generally taken for granted that students normally learn as little as possible for a certain grade. Only by a misunderstanding may they learn more, and when this happens due to an undetailed syllabus, they blame the teacher like people who blame an official whose neglect caused them a loss.

It is the basic principle of the market that everybody tries to get as much as possible and to pay as little as possible. There is nothing wrong with this: When I buy something, I try to save money, and everybody does the same. What is wrong is that some students apply the same rule to learning: They seem to think that they *buy* grades and *pay* for them by learning. And they try *to pay* as little as possible! In other words, some students seem to think that it is a loss whenever they learn something. This looks crazy when put in such straightforward terms, but there are students who behave as if they think this way. (I do not know what they really think.) And there are officials who take this behavior as normal and arrange the learning environment according to it.

The attitude "learn as little as possible" is not totally wrong, however, because a good deal of the stuff students are taught indeed deserves minimization (business calculus, for example). A good deal, but not all—there are excellent books and teachers—but many students are not sophisticated enough to discriminate.

After every test, I explained correct solutions. Many a student said: "Now I understand." I was glad: The purpose of my teaching was achieved. But some said it with regret, which meant: "This understanding is useless because it came too late to provide me a good grade." To me, tests were just a means to promote understanding; to them understanding was just a means to get a good grade. To some students it made no sense to understand anything after the test.

Some students are so busy and anxious counting points on tests and predicting grades that they have no "mental room" left to think about mathematics. It seems even irrelevant both for them and for the university whether they have learned anything at all: What matters for both sides is that the students overcame another barrier on their obstacle race toward graduation (and wasted some more months of their young and productive years).

At one lecture I wrote a theorem on the blackboard and said to the students: "Look what a beautiful theorem it is!" Some laughed. I asked what was the matter. Then one explained: "Professor, it is nonsense, a theorem cannot be beautiful!" And I understood that these poor devils, who had always learned under the lash of grades, never from natural curiosity, really could not imagine that an abstraction might be beautiful.

Any creative activity (including learning) needs at least tempory independence from external rewards and pressures. Peaks of creativity (which are essential in learning and solving nontrivial problems) need so much concentration on the subject that any sticks and carrots can only disturb them. Only when the intimate work of creative faculties is over and has produced a finished result, may one think how to sell this result most profitably. Pushkin, a Russian poet, said: "Inspiration is not for sale, but a manuscript may be sold." The same applies to learning: Those who lack intrinsic motivation and are guided only by external rewards, learn poorly. They are never carried away by the subject's charm for its own sake, as they believe that they must be "practical"; that is, never forget their points and grades. As a result they never use the powerful potential of creativity given to them by nature. Everybody's natural abilities are rich, but their use depends on individual priorities.

It seems that some students just cannot imagine that learning might be of intrinsic value, besides official graduation. And they might go through many years of schooling, communicate with teachers and officials, graduate from an elementary school, middle school, high school, and a university, and never have a chance to question this! Unless they meet some irritating foreigner!

Foreigners, however, soon understand that to survive in this country they have to adjust to the system rather than to criticize it. At various levels and in various ways, newcomers are shown clearly that this country wants intellectuals, but not those who are too independent. This may be one reason why so many immigrants who were excellent mathematics teachers in Russia have done much less than their best to reform American education.

In my case, pretty soon the pressure from students made me deviate from my principle to do my best: I was forced to care about my safety from students' complaints at the expense of their own best interests. Although my personal experience is limited, I think that this situation is typical. In another state, students complained about their mathematics teacher, another newcomer from Russia: "We pay as much as others, but have to know more than they for the same grade." Still in another state, another newcomer from Russia found an effective way to calm his students; when they asked how he would give them grades, he answered that he would do it "on the curve." I asked him what he meant, and he answered that he did not know: What mattered for him was that the students got relaxed and became willing to listen to lectures and solve problems.

Well, I can imagine a situation in which learning for a grade makes sense. If students are ultimately disappointed with the teacher, if they have given up any hope of learning anything valuable from him, if they not only disrespect, but actually despise him—then, and only then, it makes sense to learn for a grade—to get at least this if there is nothing better to get. In the final analysis, learning for a grade is the deepest offense to the teacher, because it implies the thought: "I know in advance that nothing valuable will come from real contact with the teacher; so let me at least get a grade." But, according to my experience, students who learn for grades do it in all courses. They seem not to be aware that they offend teachers; they simply take this mode of behavior for granted. (And most American teachers and officials also take it for granted.)

At one of my lectures on business calculus, when asked why I gave problems unlike those in the book, I answered: "Because I want you to know elementary mathematics." I expected to convince students by this answer. In Moscow, a university student who was told that he or she did not know elementary mathematics, got confused and checked into the matter immediately. Elementary mathematics was normally taught to children who looked like children. Now imagine my astonishment when right after my answer, an imposing train of well-grown adults stood up and tramped out. They decided (correctly) that they could graduate from the university without knowing elementary mathematics. And they knew that they would easily find a lecturer who would teach them from the text.

And the one who had to change was me. In the next semester, I never scared students away by checking into basics. I understood perfectly that teaching an advanced subject like calculus without filling gaps in basics was like building on sand. But I could not afford to care about my students because I had to care about my safety from their complaints.

I have examined the American Constitution and found no statement that guarantees the right of ignorance for students. Nevertheless, some students behave as if such a statement existed. And some officials behave as if they had no other choice than to comply with them. Why? One official explained to me that some students had sued universities for better grades and won. (I have never heard of a student who sued a university for better or more knowledge.) Now the main concern of officials is not to have this trouble again. One evident result of this is that bright students lose a lot of opportunities to learn more, but they never complain (regretfully), and officials do not need to care about them.

I do not propose to put all the blame on students. In fact, their priorities reflect the cynicism of educators who design courses not for the sake of students' best interests, but for other aims: for example, to put another artificial obstacle in their way, to keep teachers busy, etc. The business calculus course seems to be deliberately designed just as an obstacle for those who want to graduate in the business school.

I understand that I have very little experience with the bulk of the Russian population. Most of my students in Moscow were children of intellectuals, because in Russia (as in most countries) a much smaller percentage of youngsters than in the United States go into higher education. In fact, what is going on in America is an experiment: to give higher education to those strata of society which remain deprived of it in most other countries. My concern is that this should be really an education, not an imitation.

I was astonished to find that many of my American colleagues, although very competent as scientists and quite decent as persons, had absolutely different ideas about education and teaching than I had. When I spoke to them about education, they answered something like: "This is not my concern. There are special people to care about all that," as if I spoke about some important but remote activity. According to my experience, the prevailing attitude among American mathematicians is to avoid teaching. When these American mathematicians say that they have a "good position," this typically means that *they do not have to teach*. And if a mathematician with (substantiated or not) research ambitions has to teach, he often tries to do it as mechanically as possible. And students take this for granted, and they try to learn as mechanically as possible. The result is a tit-for-tat between teachers and students, which may reduce mathematical education to wasteful bureaucratic mirages. And the system (as any system) is robust: If a recent immigrant, inexperienced in American ways, happens to be different (for example, to love teaching), he or she does not fit into the system and only causes troubles.[4]

The attitudes of some mathematicians toward teaching form a perfect counterpart to the attitudes of some students toward learning. Some, but not all. It certainly is not exciting to teach those who invest more efforts into pushing for grades than for understanding. But, on the other hand, students as a whole are not nearly as hopeless as some smug teachers pretend.[5] It is true that there are a few nasty students who can put anybody off teaching, and it is true that some indifferent bureaucrats prefer to yield to their pressures (at the expense of those who want to learn). But in every course there are students who are really interested, and I think that these students are the most valuable. In every one of my courses there were students who were excited by those very nontrivial problems that moved others to complain. My former students came to my office to thank me. They said that after my course the next courses were easy for them. Some asked if I was expected to teach something in the next year and advised me to publish the problems I had invented. But bright students never complain (regretfully), and officials do not care about them. More than once I had to say to one student or another: "You did very well in my course, and I gave you an A. But this does not mean much, because what I teach you is not really mathematics."

Some people excuse bad teaching by saying: Since students buy it, it is OK to sell it. But pushers of drugs say the same. It is the responsibility of specialists to do the right things even if laymen cannot discriminate between right and wrong. It is the responsibility of teachers to teach in a way that really develops students' intellect. Imagine that a noneducated person is sick. Is it fair to prescribe him a fake medicine just because he cannot tell it from a good one? Of course not: This is not only inhuman, but also dangerous for the reputation of the medical profession. The same about teaching: Fake teaching is unfair and breeds anti-intellectualism. The moral status of those who designed the business calculus course is like that of colonial-time hucksters who sold cheap beads, mirrors, and "firewater" to ignorants, whose role is now played by students. (I do not blame rank-and-file teachers, because many have no choice.)

For many years, the Soviet authorities tried in vain to reduce scientists' concerns to their job and were irritated when someone interfered with public affairs. Sakharov is the most well-known example of a Russian scientist directly involved with politics, but I am sure that educational efforts of many others were equally important. In this respect, the free American job market seems to intimidate dissenters more effectively than Soviet despots ever could: Most American mathematicians try to deal with education as little as possible, because of the existing system of rewards.

Most students are young people. They are not yet quite mature, and their priorities are in the process of formation. Every school not only teaches particular subjects, but also suggests certain ideas of what learning and mental activity should be.

In the present situation, the idea most often promoted by authorities is that official records are the most important results of learning. Many students are not independent enough to defend themselves against this bad influence and get phony education at the expense of real time and money. Their motivation shrinks to external sticks and carrots, and they fail to develop independence from external rewards of the social system.

I love to start my courses at the precalculus level by asking students to vote on the following question:

> Take the infinite decimal fraction 0.999. . . . [T]hat is zero, then decimal point, then an infinite row of nines. Is this fraction less than or equal to one?

Often the majority votes that the fraction is less than one. Then I ask, how much less, and students give different answers according to which calculators they use. This starts a useful discussion in which all the students participate because they feel that this really pertains to them. Every student tries to prove that his answer is correct, which allows me to convince them that all are wrong: This fraction equals one.

You may ask me: Why do I start my courses by provoking students into making a wrong decision in such a dramatic form? Because it is absolutely necessary for a teacher to keep his or her students alert and critical of themselves. If I simply informed my students that this fraction equals one, they would easily agree, but forget it by the next lecture. This is just one example. In fact, when I teach as I want, I try systematically to show that something that seems evident may be wrong. Experience of this sort, I believe, is essential as a psychological prerequisite for studying rigorous mathematics. In Russia, students were delighted whenever I succeeded to bamboozle them. Even children understood that it was a pedagogical device to make their knowledge and thinking more robust. My graduate students at BU also were excited when I proved that no algorithm can solve the sorting problem in linear time and right after that presented an algorithm that seemed to do this.

This is understandable: Wise nature has made people, especially young people, in such a way that they love challenges. That is why people (especially children) enjoy performances of magicians whose job is to cheat. Many love mysteries and detective stories whose authors intentionally mislead the reader. Why shouldn't the teacher use the same device? Creative students are happy to meet something puzzling or misleading, because it gives them a chance to become tougher as thinkers.

But many undergraduate students are oversensitive to everything that they perceive as a failure, even a small one. Whenever intonations of my voice led them in a wrong direction, students took it as a violation of some gentlemen's rules. It looks like some American students cannot afford the natural human love for intellectual challenges because of the pressures of grades and formal records. If the teacher's recommendations do not lead them straight to the right answer, they perceive it as the teacher's fault, not as a pedagogical device. But with this attitude one cannot develop intellectual independence.

Some seem to think that they should be perfect from the very beginning, and if they are not, this is a fatal failure—like an incurable disease. They seem to feel obliged to give the right answer as quickly as cowboys shoot in Westerns, and if they miss, they just feel themselves to be losers and have no ways to deliberately and systematically develop themselves.

Officially, certain prerequisites are requested for every course. I wanted to check students' actual prerequisites and found that many of them could not solve simple, almost arithmetical, problems.

I included in my courses a problem that I had solved in middle school:

Tom and Dick can do a job in two hours. Tom and Harry can do the same job in three hours. Dick and Harry can do the same job in four hours. How long will it take for all three of them to do this job?

This problem can be solved by elementary algebra and a few arithmetical calculations. Most of my students could not solve it. One of them wrote the following system of equations:

$$T + D = 2, T + H = 3, D + H = 4$$

The student got a bad grade and asked me why. I asked in return, which parameters she meant by T, D, and H—time or something else. She said that she meant no parameters, just Tom, Dick, and Harry. I replied: "This is illiterate." A Russian student would grasp the chance to learn something new, but the American took this as a fatal failure, left the room with tears in her eyes, and dropped from my course. I regret this even now, but what else could I say?

This case is typical in the sense that many students avoid discussing their mistakes; it looks like a useless pain for them. If you learn for competence, which is valuable for you as such, you can benefit from your mistakes. But if you learn for grades and your self-esteem completely depends on external evaluations, it is plain masochism to keep in mind lost opportunities.

At the last lecture of my business calculus course, I gave a problem:

When 1,000 pounds of cucumbers were brought to the shop, they contained 99 percent water. But while they were kept unsold, some water evaporated, and the percentage of water dropped to 98 percent. How many pounds do they weigh now?

The students grabbed their calculators, but seemed not to know what to calculate. After a while, one produced a complicated and wrong answer. And it was pretended that these students had learned to solve differential equations! Of course, they had not! All they had learned was to follow a few recipes without thinking—a bright start for their careers!

Well, let us admit that most people can manage without being able to solve differential equations. But why did the students waste their time? The syllabus, the textbook, all the course design aped those for future professionals, but with one *small* change: applying recipes instead of solving problems. But this change annihilated the whole enterprise.

Thus, students lost several months, but had not learned to solve any problems at all, because to solve problems means to think productively, that is, to produce ideas that are not given in advance. And this is what they were completely deprived of.

The problems given above should be solved in high school or even middle school. Solving problems like these and writing down the solutions are a valuable experience of productive formal thinking that is hardly avoidable for every man or woman in modern civilization. All normal teenagers have brains mature enough to solve such problems, and those who solve them at 14 really can learn calculus at 18.

But most of my students seemed to have no such experience. What had they done throughout their many years of schooling?

It seems that to a great extent they had filled in boxes, that is to say, chosen the right answer among several ready-made ones. Multiple-choice tests are convenient because their results are easy to process. This seems to be the main reason why such tests are so often used. Perhaps such tests give valuable information to educators, but they grossly limit students' initiative, fragment their activity, and deprive them of self-organizational experience.

Suppose that you are an average student. If you write solutions, even wrong ones, you can analyze them and learn something from your mistakes. But if you just put tallies into boxes, you don't remember why you made the choice; so you cannot analyze your mistakes and cannot benefit from them. All you hope is that your conditional reflexes will gradually improve, but you cannot control this process, like an animal in a problem box.

Well, better late than never, that is why I gave the problems mentioned above to my students. But I could not give more than just a few problems of this sort, because I had to follow the syllabus.

Nowadays, throughout the world, every youngster is assigned to learn some mathematics, but most of those who are in charge of this huge enterprise cannot explain in reasonable terms what all this is for and what is meant by "mathematics" in this context. What is the purpose of mathematical education for those many who will not become professional mathematicians? This is an enormously important question, but too comprehensive to discuss here in detail. Let us at least understand that it has no straightforward utilitarian answer. Very little of mathematics is used by most people in their work or other activities. Managers and lawyers, social workers and police officers, drivers and farmers, politicians and officials, doctors and nurses, cooks and barbers, writers and artists, sportspeople, businesspeople, salespeople and showpeople do not solve quadratic equations, do not use set theory, the theory of numbers, functions or algorithms, analytical or projective geometry, and do not differentiate or integrate.

Please, do not think that I am *against* teaching mathematics. I am *for* it. What I want to emphasize is that a teacher should never expect that students will have a chance to apply recipes literally. If you teach nothing but recipes, you teach nothing. This is especially true when teaching such an abstract subject as mathematics: It makes sense only when it is teaching one to think, to learn, and to solve problems. When this takes place, teaching mathematics may be enormously useful for everybody.[6] Here (as elsewhere in this paper) I do not pretend that my opinions are original. A lot has been said in the same vein, for example: "In mathematics 'know-how' is the ability to solve problems, and it is much more important than mere possession of information."[7]

But thinking and solving nontrivial problems are conspicuous by their absence in many developmental courses. (Nobody knows what these courses actually develop.) Many courses of mathematics in liberal arts settings are made up by the following simple rule: Take the professional course, keep the shell, and eliminate the kernel. That is, keep the pretensions, terms, even some formulations, but eliminate everything that needs thinking. At first sight, it may seem easy to avoid this, because there are lots of problems in various textbooks; solving these problems would certainly benefit students much more than business calculus, which is neither business nor calculus. But this won't do because of the market pressures. Suppose that some author writes a textbook with problems that need thinking for their solution, and some college gives a course using this book. Instead of learning recipes with bombastic labels, students who take this course will have to adopt the modesty that is required for concentrating on the real difficulties of a subject. The college will have to admit that its students simply learn to solve some mathematical problems and thereby just become more intelligent. Which parents will send their offspring to it? Which firm will hire the students? What will they boast of?

To survive against competition, every university and every college has to pretend that it gives something modern, advanced, and immediately marketable. But is it possible to give advanced courses to students who are ignorant in elementary mathematics? Of course not. What to do? Very simple! Emasculate the course by excluding everything nontrivial, reduce the students' task to applying ready-made recipes without understanding—and you will survive and succeed. Your pretensions that you teach something advanced will allow the students to pretend that they are educated, and this will allow the firms and departments that hire them to pretend that they hired educated people. But at some point, this chain of pretensions will have to break.

The American ability to get things done has become proverbial. The question is what should be done. I have no panacea, but I invite Americans to at least see the problem. Many seem not to see any problem at all. I tried to figure out what political leaders of this country think about the quality of education and concluded that they think nothing about it. They speak of giving everyone an opportunity to obtain an education, but they say nothing about the quality of that education.

Now many Americans say: "We have won the Cold War." This is wrong. The Soviet rulers certainly lost the Cold War, but this does not yet mean that Americans won. The Soviet bureaucrats lost because they lived in the lunatic world of "advantages of the Soviet system," "Soviet type of democracy," "building of Communism," "enthusiasm of the Soviet people," and other slogans of their own propaganda. Lack of realism, fear of any independent opinion, enormous discrepancy between reality and official versions undermined the Soviet rule. Much can and will be said about the collapse of the Soviet Union, but I am sure that the dominance of bureaucratic fictions at the expense of reality certainly played a major role.

Regretfully, all the same can be said about some part of American education. There are people among students, their parents, teachers, and officials who do not understand what education is about. They anchor their aspirations and priorities to the bureaucratic form rather than to the substance of culture. Let me repeat that there is nothing special about Americans in this respect. There are lots of countries where the average education is worse than in America (in Russia, for example).

There is rule *by* the people in America, but not always *for* the people. People command to the intellectuals, in a sovereign way, something like the following: "Give certificates of competence to our offspring without any delay! And don't waste taxpayers' money by teaching students too much! And don't you dare to discriminate against ignorant ones." Intellectuals obey implicitly and give out bombastic graduation papers with an open hand. Everybody is glad: Scientists return to their research having paid as little effort and attention to teaching as possible. Bunches of youngsters get impressive certificates that are the most marketable results of their studies. Parents have realized their dream to "educate" their children. Some of the richest and smartest parents are also glad: They find special ways for their children to get *real* education, so their future is ensured. But what about the future of others? Is it ensured as well?

Those who learn for grades expect to succeed in their business. *Today* they are right insofar as almost every American who has a degree, however ignorant, can live better than even competent people in much poorer countries around the world. A person with a diploma should not fail to find a job in his or her field of competence: This is a common belief in this country. But this cannot last long in the situation when "competence" and a diploma tautologically mean each other. The advantages enjoyed by Americans are the results of real competence and real efforts of previous generations, whose heritage is now getting devaluated as a result of the bureaucratic character of the educational system. And someday, ignorant people with degrees and diplomas may want power according to their papers rather than their real competence. We Russians have some experience of this sort, and it is not unique. In all countries (including America) activists of ignorance try to dictate their will to universities, and sometimes they succeed—at the expense of those who really want to learn.

How much of American education really develops students' competence and how much—like business calculus—comes to pretentious trivialities? I don't yet know. And I don't know who knows. I am learning about it by experience, and it will take a long time to learn. But it is clear to me right now that the winners in the modern world will be those countries that will really teach their students to think and to solve problems. I sincerely wish America to be among these.

NOTES

1. Many thinkers were read with interest in our club. Reading Seymour Papert's *Mindstorms,* we thought: "If small children are taught to think with such care in America, they must develop into tremendously competent university students."
2. Full title: *Calculus II for Business and Economics.*
3. Remember that throughout my business calculus course, I never went beyond into something more advanced; I simply tried to cover up gaps in my students' basic knowledge. And exactly this caused all the trouble.
4. Most advertisements about positions request what they call "commitment to excellence in teaching," especially teaching undergraduates. But what does it mean: commitment to teach thinking or commitment to waste one's time for pseudoteaching? And according to my experience, if an applicant claims that he or she loves teaching, he or she only moves others to think that he or she is failing in his or her efforts to do research.
5. A typical game (in Berne's sense): "It is profanity to make such a genius as I am, waste my precious time on teaching."
6. One small example of a successful solution of a practical problem: Once my daughter (who was 12) needed a dictionary, and we went to a bookstore. She chose one but could not find any printed indication of the number of words it contained. Then she chose a page that looked typical, counted the number of words in it, looked at the number of the last page, rounded both numbers to the first digit and mentally multiplied them. Thus in a few seconds, she obtained an adequate estimate of what she needed. I was delighted. This may be called "mathematical common sense." What a contrast with most of my business calculus students who were

helpless without their calculators and without a detailed instruction of what to do and in which order!

7. George Pólya, *In the Curriculum for Prospective High School Teachers.*

STUDY QUESTIONS

1. What were some critical problems in postrevolutionary Russia once education was opened to the children of "proletarians"?

2. What does Professor Toom believe the first duty of a teacher to be? Why did he find resistance to this in Russia?

3. What had incompetent Russian scientists traditionally done to rid themselves of competent young scholars?

4. What are the basic faults that Professor Toom finds with the attitudes and expectations of American university students?

5. What happened to this "European teacher" when he attempted to teach his students to think?

6. What distinctions does the author make between competence and the American value of high grades at minimal effort? What are the dynamic consequences of such values in learning?

7. What are Professor Toom's sincerest wishes for the focus of American education?

SIXTEEN

First Impressions: Diary Of a French Anthropologist in New York City

FRANÇOISE DUSSART
University of Connecticut

Moving from the solitude of the Australian outback, where she had been studying Australian aboriginal culture, a French anthropologist finds herself living in New York City in a multiethnic neighborhood characterized by poverty, homelessness, and drug dealing. From reflections of seven months, excerpted from her diary, she not only describes the neighborhood, the apartment complex, and some of its residents but also comments on some aspects of the culture of the neighboring, wealthier residents of "The City."

Françoise Dussart *was raised in France, Africa, England, and the United States. She received her B.A. and Masters in Anthropology from the Sorbonne University in Paris (1980, 1982) and her Ph.D. in Anthropology from the Australian National University at Canberra (1989). Professor Dussart is an associate professor of Anthropology at the University of Connecticut at Storrs.*

*A*nthropologists are, by nature, note-takers. What follows are slightly neatened excerpts from the diary I kept when l first reached New York City in the fall of 1988.

ARRIVAL

The plane will be touching down soon. After five years of working in an Australian aboriginal community, I suspect I am prepared to handle the "exoticism" of New York. How much stranger can the ceremonies of Manhattanites be than those of the Warlpiri Aborigines? Certainly the system of kinship will be a lot easier to handle. Here you do not have to marry your mother's mother's brother's daughter's daughter. I will try to suspend judgment. But is that possible?

The plane banks over New York. I have to stop thinking of the city's geography in terms of aboriginal culture. I look out the plane's oval window and, seeing the sparkling skyline, recall the fires burning in the central Australian desert. This kind of obsessive comparison-making is the observer's kiss of death. Still, the temptation is always there.

On landing, I am confronted by more differences. Stopped by an immigration official, I am asked to prove that I have adequate funds for my stay in the United States, and then I am questioned about my profession. I respond in the most general terms that "anthropology is the study of people, their history, their habits, and their rituals." The official seems satisfied with my answers. I have money and a profession, the twinned necessities of American acceptance. (I guess that's why they call the man at the airport a customs official!) Back in Yuendumu, the settlement at which I conducted my fieldwork, those questions would have had little meaning. Arrival would have been marked by a long and involved interrogation about my family genealogy.

The ride into Manhattan is marked by general discussion of "The City," as if there were no other city in the world. In this regard, residents of Manhattan seem particularly geocentric. (I am taught over time the specialized lexicon of the region. Brooklyn, the Bronx, and other boroughs are part of New York City but are never referred to as "The City," a term restricted to the borough of Manhattan.)

I am told what I should do ("The museums are nice, and the art galleries are fantastic") and what I should not do (a much longer list that includes not going to Harlem alone, avoiding confrontation, and carrying enough money to satisfy muggers, robbers, and other petty criminals).

Two words linger in my head as we snake through the traffic into New York: danger and inequity. The danger arises from all the talk of robbery, burglary, and rape. I am told to fear the city before I've even had a chance to explore it. The inequity arises from the scenes outside the window: the shelterless populations next to neatly kept homes. These two words figure into the storytelling tradition of the city's residents. Real estate and crime are the subject of many conversations. Perhaps this is the modern-day legacy of the fireside storytellers of central Europe.

FIRST DAY

I will be staying in the very part of town I was told to avoid: the southern tip of Harlem. As I walk around the neighborhood (the environs of West 107th Street), I am confronted by the speed with which the affluence of neighborhoods changes. From one block to the next, you can switch from doorman apartments to tenements populated by people of predominantly Central American origin. My accommodations are found in the second form of habitation.

The rectilinearity of Manhattan is an impressive quality of this city. All the streets are on a grid that denies natural geography. Local residents do not understand notions of uphill and downhill. Their awareness of which way is north or south is based on the numbering of the streets, not on any geographical sense of the terrain. This is so unlike aboriginal culture, where location is defined by terrain. (The urge to compare, I guess, is inevitable.) "Go to the water hole and walk east until the mulga trees area" is replaced by the simplicities of consecutive numbering (though I am told that lower Manhattan rejects the grid completely).

Even before I arrive, I am told of the drug addicts and mentally disabled homeless who walk the streets. In my new neighborhood, I discover that the homeless situation is quite depressing. Unwed mothers with children also make up a part of this migrant army of despair. The scenes remind me of the "Courtyard of Miracles" in the French novel *Notre Dame de Paris,* but we are not in the sixteenth century. How can it be that such a rich city has so many beggars? Perhaps that is why it is so rich.

I have already started to notice that different ethnic groups dominate different street activities. It is obvious that the Koreans run the fruit stores on Broadway. There are also other groups overseeing specialized markets. A small group of South American Indians sells flowers out of shopping carts they roll around the West Side of Manhattan. One Peruvian woman sells native sweaters and dolls from the inside of a heated car. Dozens of impoverished black men sell castaway clothing, books, shoes, lamps, and junk salvaged from the garbage of wealthier locals. Even in junk selling there are differences to be observed. The better-off vendor uses a table and has prices marked with little stickers, whereas the more desperate street people line up their wares on the cement and take pretty much what is offered. The homeless tend to avoid corners because corners are too windy, and their clothing is ragged at best. The slightly more upscale salesperson, on the other hand, will gladly set up a stand on a corner.

I observe more links between ethnicity and occupation. Most of the taxi drivers in New York seem to be Haitian. A driver named Jean Jean from Port au Prince describes the difference between being a cabbie in Haiti and being a cabbie in New York. "The passengers are much more trusting in Haiti," he tells me in French. He says that New York passengers, fearful of being overcharged, almost always provide detailed instructions of exactly what route they wish to take. I let him choose the path he wishes, all the time trying to test myself on the orientation of east, west, north, and south.

FIRST WEEK

I have settled in the top-floor apartment of a five-story walk-up on the Upper West Side of Manhattan, just south of Columbia University. The university's presence is not felt. This is a Spanish-speaking world. Most of the residents come from Central and South America. The food, the smells, the language, and the way in which life is played out on the streets are all wholly Latino.

The rent in the apartment where I am staying is low, and this fact dominates much of the conversation I have with native New Yorkers. Sometimes I feel that real estate and safety are the only two topics of conversation. Safety is discussed because a number of nonminority acquaintances are made nervous by the "unsafe" nature of my new neighborhood. When I ask what constitutes "unsafe," they seem to associate predominantly white neighborhoods with protective environments, even though they admit to having been confronted in those areas as well.

Back at my apartment building, I ask a Puerto Rican neighbor (as best as I can without speaking Spanish) where he feels safe. He points to our building. Safety, clearly, is relative. In this "dangerous" neighborhood, he can buy food, pitch pennies, and go to church. He says he would never go to Brooklyn.

I could picture a map of New York City with "safe" areas shaded in by different ethnic groups. I suspect that the whole of the city would be covered. Likewise, "unsafe" shading would produce similar results.

SECOND WEEK

I have been spending my time trying to map out the cultural geography of my neighborhood. Never have economic discrepancies been so dramatically defined. Stepping out of my building, I am surrounded by a Spanish ghetto with all the cover-story problems (crack, unwed mothers, welfare dependency), but walking west just half a block brings me to a solidly middle-class row of cooperative apartments, and just another hundred yards more brings on distinctly wealthy residents. In a three-minute walk, I have moved from poverty to Crabtree & Evelyn, a fancy goods store specializing in luxury soaps. I am told that if I were to move east from my building entrance (to Columbus Avenue), I would find myself among the notorious crack dens of the city. I have not yet walked on that avenue.

I can't think of a European city in which wealth and poverty exist in such close proximity. There are, of course, ethnic distinctions to be made. When I note "poor," it is a poor Hispanic and black population, and when I write "rich," it is predominantly white, though Japanese investment has made its presence felt here, too. (The buzzers on every other door of the co-ops along Riverside Drive have signs written in *Kanji*.)

I have started asking some of the older residents (often a gold mine for the field-worker) about the evolution of the neighborhood. I learn that until the late 1960s this was a predominantly Irish neighborhood. It is hard to believe that all traces of that presence have been eradicated. After strolling around, I find one last defiant marker of that Irish legacy: the Kennedy Funeral Home. (I guess it's appropriate that the last establishment to stay deals in the dead and dying.) The establishment stands out. It has a faux Cape house façade with white embroidered curtains. The owner is still a Mr. Kennedy, but he has hired a Hispanic consultant to maintain ties to the community.

I have been feeling many of the same frustrations in New York that I had during the first few months of fieldwork in Australia because I cannot speak the language of the streets. I keep thinking about the halting conversation I had earlier in the week with my Puerto Rican neighbor, Tony. He has an English vocabulary of perhaps fifty words. English does not get one very far in the *bodegas* and *carnecerias* that dot Amsterdam Avenue.

Fluency in the neighborhood is generationally distinguishable. The younger population speaks English and Spanish fluently, so I converse with them. But for Tony and other first-generation immigrants, communication with English-speakers is almost all gesture. Once in a while whites need to talk to the superintendent, whose command of English is practically nonexistent. Usually one of his children comes to help everyone reach some kind of understanding.

A typical view from my window includes clutches of young women (girls, really) tending to babies, the heads of older women poking out of windows, and men on the street pitching pennies, fixing unfixable cars, and drinking beer out of green bottles or rum from a shared brown bag. It is rare to see groups of men and women together.

THIRD WEEK

I went to a number of social events this week. As usual, everyone at the gathering was, like me, white and middle class. I was amazed how tight a network of friendships and professional links emerged during the meal. I have clearly stumbled into the American equivalent of the French intellectual elite. The same schools, the same vacation spots, and the same books are constantly mentioned. There are differences, however. French intellectual life is played out on a more intimate scale, so that in France the country's top lawyers, actors, writers, and filmmakers often intersect at various social events.

That is not the case here in New York. There are book parties for writers, museum openings for art critics and artists, and movie screenings for specialists in cinema. Of course I am moving in a slightly less stylish circle, but the point remains that there is a professional and ethnic homogeneity in the social gatherings I have attended.

I must now add another topic of obsession to the list that previously included only real estate and security. The obsession surfaces in the question asked before all others and pursued with the greatest intensity: What do you do? It seems that acquaintances need to know the nature of your professional life in order to feel at ease. In France it would be considered rude to initiate a conversation on such a topic. Conversations in France are introduced by discussions of family origins. White Americans seem less concerned by such genealogical inquiries.

I had an interesting conversation with a group of five women all roughly my age. I say "interesting" not because there were any overlapping interests but because I felt so alien. Most of the discussion centered around their bodies. I was amazed to find them absolutely at ease discussing their weight, how much they were going to lose, and how they were going to lose it. There was a detailed conversation on the relative merits of aerobics, swimming, and tennis, all activities that had as their goal weight loss. I wrote to a friend of mine in France about the discussion, and in the correspondence that followed we agreed that such intimacies would never be revealed in such a setting. Talk about the imperfections of one's body is limited to closest friends and mothers.

The commitment to keeping fit is visible everywhere in the neighborhood outside the Spanish community where I live. Athletic supply stores can be found every few blocks, and the reservoir a mile from my building is regularly circled by joggers in various states of fitness (I once saw a father jogging while pushing a baby carriage).

Although the American women I talked with are comfortable talking about the physical condition of their bodies, discussions of sensual condition are taboo. Again, comparison with the French experience is inevitable, where strangers are perfectly comfortable talking about the satisfaction and the limitation of their sexual liaisons. Maybe such discussion makes my American women friends uncomfortable because it suggests prefeminist roles. I know that my more traditional "feminine" interests such as cooking and knitting have frequently gotten me into trouble with professional women who find such activities frivolous and counterproductive.

These last few weeks in New York recalled the first lecture I had in cultural anthropology. The professor stressed the need to avoid cultural relativity that denies the uniqueness of the community under investigation. The more I learn about New York, the less comfortable I become with the terms and conclusions I have made. I suspect that if I gave the community in which I live the same attention I applied to the Warlpiri Aborigines, it would take many years to find answers to the questions that constantly confront me. What is the relationship between "black-magic candles" sold at the Haitian botanica and the Catholic religious figures? Why do my neighbors play the illegal numbers games on the street that pay much lower dividends than the state-sanctioned lotteries? But on a more theoretical level, I would like to know how much this Hispanic community adopts the values of white America, how it resists assimilation, and how it adapts elements of the society that surrounds it. Each question provokes twenty more questions.

FIRST MONTH

I gave my first dinner party. I was fascinated to see what people brought in the way of gifts: two bottles of wine, a dessert, and even a head of broccoli the guest thought I might want to toss into the salad. Each of these gifts, different as they are, share one common element—consumption during the meal. In France, such gift giving would be considered somehow inappropriate. Flowers are the most common offering to the host or hostess.

A few guests expressed surprise that I actually cooked the meal instead of ordering from a restaurant or preparing some microwaved delicacies. When I asked them if they ever cooked, they said proudly that they had never turned on their oven (they had been living in the same apartment for the last three years). After the party I had expected some reciprocal invitations, but none came. When I asked why the party was received so unilaterally, I discovered that many New Yorkers are reluctant to reveal where they live. The reasons are complex and diverse. One fellow I spoke to admitted he was embarrassed by the size of his apartment: It was too small a space in which to entertain. Another woman made a point never to invite anybody to her apartment. "It is my sanctuary," she said, "why would I reveal it to anyone?"

Subsequent dinners with these acquaintances were held at restaurants (except once in the home of close friends). The guests, each on separate occasions, called me up and proposed that we get together again with other friends in a restaurant. The effort of getting together for a meal at a restaurant is one facet of New York hospitality among people in their twenties and early thirties. But we often all share the bill!

SECOND MONTH

I attend my first women's studies seminar at a New York university. I have no idea what to expect and so arrive early to gather my thoughts. The participants start to enter, and I quickly realize that no men will be attending. The mood is warm and supportive, with a lot of high-pitched salutation and kissing. The seminar starts, and the speaker begins her lecture on "The Roles of German Jewish Women During the Second World War." The woman next to me shakes her head while the paper is being delivered. Another woman sucks her tooth, and still a third objects out loud. When the lecture is over, the listeners begin an open assault on her ideas, challenging not only her data but her premises as well. I am surprised by the vehemence of these condemnations. In seminars I attended in Britain and Australia, I never saw anger and argumentation. In France, where the pleasures of disputations are legendary, such a conflict would have been the start of a long-standing feud. That's not what happened here in New York. The seminar ended, smiles returned to the faces of the participants and the lecturer, and the women kissed one another good-bye.

THIRD MONTH

Although the poverty is sometimes unnerving, I am constantly surprised by the intensity of community spirit among people in the neighborhood. Most of middle-class Manhattan exists on the nuclear family level, while West 107th Street is always displaying the entanglements, jealousies, and affections of the extended family. I have very little to do with these interactions, but increasingly the residents are recognizing that my stay may not be temporary. The triumphs of neighborliness are small ones. Yesterday, Tony helped me carry a heavy shopping bag to the front door of my fifth-floor apartment.

FOURTH MONTH

The temperature has dropped well below freezing. The men who linger on the street corner have retreated into cars they keep heated, into the lobby of the nearby funeral home, into grocery stores, and into basements that reveal the glow of old color TVs. Bottles of rum are generally passed around.

There is clearly a generational separation in the male population. Rum is not an adequate stimulant for the younger men of the community. I regularly walk over the tiny plastic envelopes in which crack is sold. The dealing can be observed from my living room window. The transaction itself is a complex pirouette marked by dropoffs, cash exchanges, coded negotiations, and the ultimate sale.

One young entrepreneur has hung a pair of shoes over a lamppost. This marker is to alert out-of-town drug buyers to the availability of his wares. The cars stop, and after brief discussion he pulls the little plastic bag from his sock.

Missing from the street life are the women. They can be seen at the windows of their kitchens throughout the neighborhood. The apartment two floors below, which is occupied by the family of the building's superintendent, has no fewer than four generations of women coming and going. Disposable diapers, baby carriages, and small children are carried up and down the staircase. Women spend most of their time in kitchens with their children and female friends and relatives. Each sex relies on the emotional support of their friends and relatives of the same sex and the same generation level.

FIFTH MONTH

I spend the day taking a casual survey of the building's thirteen apartments. The ground-floor apartment is occupied by three Columbia college students with a serious commitment to hard-rock music. There is a sort of music war that takes place between Led Zeppelin and the Latino tunes. The second floor is occupied by a young, low-paid editor at a publishing house and a family from the Dominican Republic living in two apartments. The nature of this family must be defined in the anthropological literature as matrifocal. The third floor has an extended family from Ecuador, another one from Cuba, and three brothers from Puerto Rico. The fourth floor is occupied by a white American actor, a nuclear family of jazz musicians, and an extended family from Bolivia. The fifth floor is occupied by three Puerto Ricans, a white student from Columbia University, a freelance journalist, and a cultural anthropologist. One apartment is empty now. It used to be a "crack house," as white people refer to it here. One morning, the police raided the apartment. The only objects left in the apartment are a sword and Latino American saints, the heads and bodies lying separately on the floor. Maybe the police pulled the statues apart because they thought that the drug dealers were hiding the white powder inside them.

SIXTH MONTH

The windows of my office look out on a Spanish funeral home. Quite often I see grieving women. They scream, roll in the street, and sob uncontrollably. They show their grief to the entire community. The men tend to be less demonstrative. Once the coffin is brought out of the funeral home, it is quickly taken away. Death is not allowed to linger in New York. When a woman in a building adjacent to mine committed suicide by jumping off the roof, her body was taken away by the police less than fifteen minutes later. I am amazed to discover that there is no place to be buried in Manhattan.

There are two churches on 107th Street. One is a Catholic church, which is the most popular, and the second is called the Kingdom Hall of the Jehovah's Witnesses. Proportionally, white people attend the Pentecostal services more than the Catholic services, though they represent a small proportion of the people who attend services in both places. White people go elsewhere.

People cross themselves as they pass the statue of Jesus Christ that stands outside the Catholic church. Often several coins lie at the feet of the statue, and they are later picked up by homeless people. I have seen this done in Italy or Spain and even in some parts of rural France. But people's religious habits are not so simply defined and limited. In fact, within a few yards both from the church and from the Kingdom Hall, there is a strange store in which they sell all kinds of natural or health food and all the necessary apparatuses for magic religious practices as performed in parts of Latin and South America and the West Indies. Their collection of objects and of statues of saints (like those lying on the floor across the hall from me) is impressive. There, one can also buy candles to keep black cats away or to charm a lover. The Korean grocery store had to adapt, and they are now selling spray cans against black cats (considered bad luck among the Spanish-speaking people).

SEVENTH MONTH

It is much warmer outside. The men both young and old are back in the streets rolling dice, listening to loud music, fixing cars, and selling drugs. The women in the community emerge briefly in the late afternoon to join in the streetside discussions. Chairs and even a couch have been put on the sidewalk in anticipation of summer.

I am amazed by the variety of street games that are played by the older men. They can pitch pennies and roll dice for hours at a stretch. (Dice are played when the men of the street are cash rich; pennies are pitched when they are poor.) Occasionally a checkerboard or sets of dominoes will make a brief appearance. There is one man— the fellow who brought out the couch—who comes every day and calls out for mates to play with him—to play for money, of course. He seems to live off his winnings from the games. The only time of the week he cannot be found is on Sunday when he attends mass.

The increase in temperature marks a switch from rum drinking to beer drinking. The men in the neighborhood have a strong preference for Heineken, and though none of the men is rich, the bottles are never returned for deposit. Monday mornings are marked by dozens of empty brown bags littering the sidewalk. When the men are low on money, they pitch pennies and drink Budweiser.

The bottles are usually picked up by the neighborhood Hispanic homeless man named Junior. The people who live here also give him food, drinks, and money. One of the superintendents has given him access to a basement so that he and his dog can seek shelter for the night. Once in a while, often under the influence of crack or heroin, he becomes violent and insults some of the men who look after him. The victims usually ignore him and to get rid of him give him money or a beer. Here people take care of their "mads" and drug users.

Each time I try to characterize the community in which I now live, I am struck by the diversity within what is often perceived to be Latino cultures. I am referred to by the Spanish-speaking people on 107th Street as one of *los Americanos*; they do not even know that I am French.

I live in a building not of Hispanics but of Bolivians, Ecuadorians, Dominicans, Puerto Ricans, and Cubans. They are not fully integrated in the larger American society, and they are not fully integrated in their homeland either. They seem to be very aware of what is happening in their respective countries through radio programs, television, news that new migrants bring with them, and visits home every two years or so. They seem to construct their identities in relation to both environments, here and there, and so construct a unique environment that includes other cultural groups they may never have met in other circumstances.

The tendency to judge must still be fought. I still make comparisons, but less often.

REFERENCES

Banton, M. 1983. *Racial and Ethnic Competition*. Cambridge: Cambridge University Press.

Bastide, R. 1966. *Les Ameriques Noires*. Paris: PBP, Payot.

Bourdieu, P. 1979. *La Distinction*. Paris Les Editions de Minuit.

Hall, S. 1985. Religious Ideologies and Social Movements in Jamaica. In *Religion and Ideology*. R. Bocock and K. Thompson, Eds. Manchester: Manchester University.

Lévi-Strauss, C. 1961 (1955). *A World on the Wane*. New York: Criterion Books.

STUDY QUESTIONS

1. In reading this personal account, try to totally immerse yourself in Professor Dussart's situation, a foreigner in New York City moving into a mixed ethnic area of questionable personal safety. How comfortable would you be in this area? How would you feel about your sister or girlfriend living in such an area?

2. What topics of conversation tended to prevail among the author's neighbors and female acquaintances that were markedly different from appropriate topics in France?

3. Why was the author not invited to any of her dinner guests' apartments as a polite gesture of reciprocity?

SEVENTEEN

Life and Cultures: The Test of Real Participant Observation

E. L. CERRONI-LONG
Eastern Michigan University

Studying other cultures from afar, from books and in the classroom, should prepare one for the contrastive principles of living in a new culture. However, when Professor Cerroni-Long, an Asian Studies scholar from Italy, visited Japan, she discovered that intellectual preparation does not protect one from culture shock. For her, the need to understand, to lend predictability to the cross-cultural encounter, became a necessity for mental equilibrium. The conscious application of cultural anthropological techniques provided her with the foundations for both survival and understanding.

From having earned a Ph.D. in Anthropology at an American university, in combination with her experiences in many other cultural settings, Professor Cerroni-Long is able to explore some American culture patterns from an entirely different perspective.

E. L. Cerroni-Long is a professor of Anthropology at Eastern Michigan University in Ypsilanti. She was born and raised in Italy, where she received a Doctorate in Oriental Studies from the University of Venice (1970). She was a postdoctoral student at the University of Kyoto, Japan, from 1970 to 1972. She received a Ph.D. in Anthropology from UCLA in 1986. Dr. Cerroni-Long specializes in the study of intercultural relations and in the last twenty years has conducted research in various areas of Europe, Asia, and North America.

One of the students in my field methods class—slightly exasperated by the seeming intricacies of the ethnographic enterprise—said it best: "It's easy for you to be an anthropologist! . . . You are a *foreigner!*" Indeed, I have been a foreigner much of my life, and I consider myself a "professional stranger," not just because of my disciplinary specialization but truly as a result of life experiences that came about quite fortuitously but that I think have contributed in a crucial way to the depth of my anthropological perspective.

Growing up in northern Italy, in a family of artists and scholars passionately dedicated to the study of Italian intellectual traditions, I had a limited experience of "foreignness." Italy is an ethnically homogeneous society, poor enough not to attract—until recently—any sizable groups of immigrants from abroad and bourgeois enough to create extremely effective regional and occupational cleavages, so that differences in behavior are seldom experienced within one's own social circle. When differences do arise, they can be easily explained away. Actually, my own extended family harbored sharp regional differences—with my father's side being committedly Roman, my mother's side just as adamantly Friulian, and various other members having allegiances to the Venetian region in which we lived. But I always attributed the continuous conflict in styles of behavior to personality factors or simply to the tiresome unpredictability of grown-ups, and I spent little time analyzing it. I was too busy dreaming of faraway times and places—Asia, ancient Arabia, Africa—places I had never visited but with which I felt a great affinity, possibly having been inspired by family lore of glorious colonial experiences in Libya, by the exotic Northern African heirlooms I played with as a child, or by the intangible but very real "Oriental" flavor one can still find in Venetian architecture, art, history, and traditions.

Also, coming of age in the heady 1960s, when the West was enthusiastically rediscovering the "wisdom of the East," I could strengthen my interest in Eastern civilizations with a growing appreciation for their aesthetic and spiritual expressions. I can now see that my love for Zen Buddhism was stimulated by the prose of Alan Watts, my understanding of Islamic civilization was built on Burton's and Lawrence's descriptions, and my fascination with Indian thought was heavily dependent on Eliade's popularizations. But, my interest in Eastern civilizations was genuine, and when the time came to choose a graduate program of study, I was very excited to enter the newly created "Oriental Institute" of the University of Venice. There I spent several blissful years exploring all sorts of arcane areas of knowledge, with the freedom of choice and the instructional guidance that are the mark of truly outstanding academic programs. As time went by, I restricted my interest to the "Buddhist area" of Asian civilization, and later I decided to specialize in Japanese studies, writing a dissertation on the relationship between certain aspects of contemporary Japanese literature and the Japanese philosophical tradition. When I obtained my doctorate, in 1970, I felt I was quite knowledgeable about Japan, and when I received a two-year research scholarship to be pursued at the University of Kyoto, I left Italy without the slightest doubt about my ability to adjust easily to my research setting and to work on my project—the analysis of Japanese social change through literary expressions—easily and successfully.

DISCOVERING ANTHROPOLOGY

It took all of three days in Japan, the time necessary for me to make my way to the foreign researchers' dormitory to which my sponsors had assigned me, to change my outlook in a most dramatic way. My excitement about exploring "the Orient" started to dim by the time the plane landed at the Hong Kong airport, on its last stopover before reaching Japan. I had been flying for many hours and tiredness was certainly affecting me, but I remember looking around the transit lounge and having the distinct feeling of being on a different planet. It was not just that the physical appearance of the majority of the people surrounding me was so markedly different from what I was used to, it was also that they acted so strange! To begin with, so many people were squatting down—rather than sitting or standing—that I automatically scrutinized the floor to see if they were looking for something. Also, it disturbed my sense of propriety that so many people had taken off their shoes or were wearing them as if they were sandals, their feet halfway in and with the heels flattened out. Above all, though, I could not shake the feeling that people's gestures, their facial expressions, the interpersonal distances they kept, and the overall noise level their interactions created were somehow "all wrong."

Things did not get any better when I finally arrived in Japan and spent a short orientation period in Tokyo before proceeding toward my assigned destination, Kyoto. The fact that people seemed to have the greatest difficulty in understanding what I thought was fluent Japanese puzzled and irritated me—I discovered only much later that I was using linguistic expressions as obsolete as Chaucerian English. But what I kept finding most disturbing was the general noise level characterizing public places, the size and density of the crowds, and the frequency with which people waiting for a bus, using a public phone, or simply hanging out would adopt a squatting position.

By the time I finally made it to my room in Kyoto, exhausted by the long trip and in the grip of what I later came to recognize as a classic case of severe culture shock, I was determined never to leave it again, unless it was to go to the nearest airport, homeward bound. Two days later, my despondency diminished by ample rest and my determination somewhat weakened by the dictates of hunger and thirst, I decided that I could at least check out the place before leaving, and I timidly started exploring my surroundings. This brought me in contact with another resident, and the severity of my culture shock can be gauged by the fact that in realizing that he was a "fellow European" I felt such a sense of joy, relief, and gratitude that I practically never again left his side, and three months later we were married.

In retrospect, I think that my culture shock was actually amplified by this experience, since it compelled me to try to contemporaneously negotiate two cultural realities that were both quite alien to me: the Japanese one of day-to-day living and the English one my husband represented. At the same time, though, having a partner providing continuous emotional support gave both of us the opportunity to dispassionately analyze our reactions to the Japanese milieu, while the discovery of cultural differences between us increased our sensitivity to nuances of behavior and schooled us in the tolerance for diversity and sense of humor that alone can successfully lead to overcoming culture shock.

In my case, though, the reactions I found myself experiencing in Japan touched off an intellectual chain reaction. My culture shock filled me at first with surprise and then with indignation. How could a Japan "expert," as I still considered myself, find herself so totally lost in a culture lovingly studied for years? How could my knowledge of Japanese language, history, literature, and philosophy be of no use in helping me adjust to a setting I thought I was quite familiar with? How could I react so negatively toward a society I considered a sort of spiritual "second home"? But, above all, how was I ever to find a way to sort out the blooming, buzzing confusion that seemed to surround me and try to get on with the research required by my project?

The answers to these questions did not come quickly or easily, but I increasingly found help through a disciplinary approach I had known only vaguely before arriving in Japan, the approach of cultural anthropology. By becoming familiar with some of this discipline's concepts, not only did I start to understand and resolve my culture shock, but I also began formulating strategies through which I could successfully negotiate the reality of Japanese culture. As I began to recognize the cultural matrix of particular patterns of behavior, I came to see their connectedness and to accept their "necessity," and all the frustration and irritation I had experienced in dealing with them became diluted in the sheer pleasure of solving an intellectual puzzle. As time went by, I actually found myself looking for circumstances that would test my understanding. As I gradually trained myself in the fundamental anthropological skills of "attending, observing, registering, and correlating," I discovered that I could now look on cultural misunderstandings as a pleasurable challenge rather than a source of stress.

Predictably, the area in which I had experienced the greatest difficulties—much more serious than the discomfort initially created by the noise and the crowds—had to do with role expectations, particularly in relation to my scholarly activities. I had arrived in Japan as a young professional, with specific projects to accomplish. I expected to fit easily into an academic community where mutual intellectual stimulation would be freely exchanged, on a collegial basis. Instead, I soon found that my comparatively young age and the circumstances of my residence in Japan had automatically labeled me as an "apprentice." As such I had been assigned to a number of senior scholars whose role was not only to aid my learning but also "to look after me" in every sense of the word. Furthermore, their instruction would not be imparted through the scintillating intellectual exchanges I had so often engaged in with my Italian professors but through what first looked to be endless, aimless sessions of small talk, typically shared with a group of other "disciples," who seemed chiefly interested in providing a passive audience and were not even trying to discuss their knowledge, opinions, or ideas.

Although I felt it my duty to fulfill my hosts' expectations and I tried to play the "disciple" role to the best of my ability, for almost two years I found this experience utterly bewildering. It was only when my anthropological investigations led me to see the connection between socialization practices, sense of self, and definition of social role that I began to see how the Japanese teaching/learning style—through personal contact in the context of a hierarchical, paternalistic relationship—fitted so well with other aspects of Japanese society. In fact, I then became convinced that in Japan the teacher-student relationship encapsulates so many facets of the overall cultural "script" that it is perceived as a general model for interpersonal relations. Consequently, I believed its study would provide critical insight into the fundamental characteristics of Japanese culture, and I started to study it in earnest by becoming an "apprentice" to a number of "masters." In this area of behavior, as in several others that had created profound puzzlement, anthropology had led me from frustration to understanding, and I felt privileged to have found such a useful "key."

I really believe that the way I discovered anthropology gave an unusual twist to an experience that could have been lived very differently. Not having been formally trained in this discipline, I was able to explore it in an idiosyncratic way, picking and choosing concepts and approaches totally on my own and having the opportunity of immediately testing them in a "total immersion" situation. Being in Japan not as an anthropologist doing field research but as an Orientalist pursuing a literary project, I never developed the type of ambiguous rapport with "the natives" that cultural investigations often engender. My desire to understand Japanese society was not a requirement of research but a prerequisite for mental equilibrium. Thus I never resented the enormous investment of time and effort it required, and I never tired of doing it. Above all, I never perceived any aspect of Japanese culture as a "problem" to be studied; rather, I clearly recognized *myself* as the problem, insofar as I needed to learn to fit into Japanese society to be able to pursue my scholarly project. I did a lot of participant observation in Japan, but it hardly was the application of a particular disciplinary technique; I was as a child growing up, badly wanting to participate in the culture in which I found myself. Observation and relentless analysis were simply the only ways to earn an admission ticket.

As a consequence of all this, I never looked at cultural anthropology merely as an academic subject or as a field of professional specialization. Rather, I came to consider it a sort of "intellectual life preserver," an eminently applied science through which I could understand my husband, get on with my studies, and learn to live comfortably in a foreign country. At the same time, I also think that the fact that I "discovered" anthropology in Japan colored my disciplinary orientation. First, it strongly biased me toward a "cultural" rather than "social" approach, and second, it called my attention to the overall homogeneity and integration of cultural patterns, particularly as expressed in nonverbal and paraverbal behavior. Because I had to figure out the organization of Japanese culture "from the inside," through description and interpretation of details rather than through the abstract comparison of general characteristics, I found the model of culture originally developed by Boas, and still at the basis of the American anthropological tradition, much more useful than any other. Furthermore, this model proved especially effective because Japanese culture lends itself particularly well to an inductive, behaviorally focused analysis.

Japan is a very homogeneous society in which strict conformity to standardized rules of behavior is highly valued and commonly practiced. Partly because of this, the Japanese are experts at carrying on "silent dialogues" through the sophisticated modulation of nonverbal behavior, and they are extremely skillful at extracting symbolic meaning from the most varied aspects of experience. Japanese behavior is simultaneously so ritualized and rich in symbolic nuances that an outsider observer cannot escape an overpowering feeling of being in the midst of a high-level balletic performance, where everyone knows exactly how to contribute to the overall effect. As a result, in becoming increasingly familiar with Japanese culture, one comes to associate it with the image of a *tableau vivant*, a pattern of patterns, the best possible illustration for Ruth Benedict's concept of "cultural configuration." Furthermore, in dealing with the Japanese, someone with a growing interest in anthropology as a discipline—like me at the time—is strengthened in the belief that a culture can truly be studied and understood simply by observing and analyzing the behavior of its members.

ENCOUNTERING ETHNICITY

While the insights of cultural anthropology helped me considerably in adjusting to Japan, just as the experience of Japanese culture molded my basic anthropological perspective, what finally convinced me to pursue this discipline professionally—and to do so in the United States—was a trip to Hawaii. I went there from the East, since at the expiration of my scholarship I had decided to stay on in Japan to teach and do research. I stayed on for more than seven years, and the trip to Hawaii was just a holiday. But again, a chance experience gave a powerful spin to the trajectory of my life and of my intellectual growth. What I found in Hawaii was the phenomenon of ethnic variation. Obviously I was already aware of the reality of ethnicity, but it was only by seeing it correlated to minority status in the context of a truly multi-ethnic society that I perceived its great relevance to the understanding of culture.

Arriving in Hawaii from Japan made me look at the Japanese-Americans I came to know there with particular interest. Clearly they were neither Japanese nor American but something new and unique. What particularly struck me, though, was that what made them unique was not the superimposition of new patterns of behavior on the Japanese but rather the subtle way their Japaneseness had been—in my eyes at least—both subtly transformed and reinforced.

This conclusion was reached, I believe, because being attuned to Japanese non-verbal behavior I could see it reproduced faithfully, albeit in a simplified form, in the behavior of the Japanese-Americans I met in Hawaii. What *had* changed, in some cases quite dramatically, was verbal behavior, especially as a vehicle for the expression of values and beliefs. However, it seemed to me that a recognizable Japanese behavioral style was very much present and that among in-group members the decoding of its underlying symbolic meaning proceeded undisturbed by possible superimposed verbal disclaimers, as if it were operating below awareness and ahead of any conscious labeling process. I would see, for example, Japanese-American women forcefully argue for female equality and independence just as they nonverbally gave out messages of docility, other-directedness, and submission to male authority—messages that seemed to set the "tone" of interaction with other Japanese-Americans much more strongly than their verbal counterpart.

The observations I gathered during my visit to Hawaii considerably strengthened my inclination toward looking at culture as a system of communication and also gave me some basic ideas on how to define ethnicity in relation to culture. In particular, I remember becoming very excited about thinking that if indeed the original patterns of nonverbal and paraverbal behavior are maintained across generations of people born and raised in a culture different from their ancestral one, then they may constitute the very core of cultural behavioral style and thus be the key to understanding the dynamics of cultural membership and identity.

Subsequent research experiences in various parts of Asia, England, and Italy confirmed my original feeling that no matter what level of assimilation an ethnic group achieves, group identity is essentially maintained through the perpetuation of a set of microbehavioral patterns that are learned during the very early years of life. Although largely unrecognized as bonding factors, these patterns seem to determine both self-identification and group cohesion by generating a recognizable behavioral style that can be called on to establish group boundaries when necessary for ideological reasons. I also concluded that if we could trace the trajectory by which behavioral style changes during the process of acculturation, we would reach a better understanding of how it comes into being in the first place. As time went by, I increasingly felt that to test many of these ideas I needed to do firsthand research among ethnic groups living in a typically multiethnic society; that is when I decided to come to the United States.

Ethnic diversity is not, of course, a peculiarly American phenomenon, but the type of ethnic groups one finds in America and the ideological definition of ethnicity that has been developing within the context of American society warrant special attention. Most of the latent, emerging, or established ethnic groups I had occasion to study in Asia and Europe have not experienced relocation. They live in areas ancestrally theirs, and the characteristics of the land they inhabit are very much a part of their sense of uniqueness. Often, as the advocates of separatism among them argue, they are simply "nations without states," groups that have become part of larger national systems to which they do not feel they really belong. The situation I found in the United States is very different. With the exception of the Native Americans and of the Mexicans originally living in what has now become the American Southwest, all of the ethnic groups one finds in the United States are the result of migration. Furthermore, as a consequence of the civil rights movement and the nationwide social unrest of the 1960s and early 1970s, there has emerged in the United States a "minority group" ideology. According to this, the political elite has recognized the cultural diversity of a few ethnic groups, has regulated their existence through the creation of well-defined boundaries around them—first and foremost by declaring them "official minorities"—and has institutionalized the presumptive process of their assimilation through a program of majority-selected incentives for socioeconomic advancement. As a result, ethnicity and minority status—with all the socially uncomplimentary connotations of these terms—have become equated in the minds of many Americans, just as the latent consciousness of ethnic hetero-geneity leads many to believe that there is no such thing as an "American culture." These contradictions seem to *demand* anthropological analysis, and from my first days in America I believed that any kind of research conducted here would prove particularly rewarding. Furthermore, having decided to formalize my interest in anthropology by entering a graduate program at UCLA, I found that my excitement about doing research in the country in which Franz Boas had developed the anthro-pological approach I considered so attractive was compounded by that of studying in an academic setting that had actually produced a number of distinguished Boasian anthropologists. Because of all this, I saw coming to America not only as an opportunity for exciting research but also as both the fulfillment of a fantasy and the repayment of an intellectual debt. I did not know, though, that this experience would lead me to insights that entirely redimensioned my views of culture and of anthropological research.

CULTURAL PARTICIPATION AND ANALYSIS

After leaving Japan and before coming to the United States, I had gone back to Italy for a while, and I had lived for a period in my husband's home country, England. Also, over the ten years preceding my journey to America, I had visited a score of Asian and European countries. With this experience to back me up and with the knowledge provided by years of anthropological study and research, including pro-fessional involvement in intercultural training, I fully expected to be "vaccinated" against culture shock, but I learned soon enough that this is one reaction not assuaged by training. Besides, if now I at least had the consolation of being familiar with the symptoms of culture shock, this time they were combined with a psycho-logical crisis for which I was not at all prepared.

My decision to study anthropology in the United States had not been anchored to any amount of practical knowledge of the American educational system or even of the current characteristics of American intellectual life. With the ethnocentrism typical of someone making an emotional choice, I had expected that my study experience in America would closely resemble those I had already undergone in Italy and Japan, with all their characteristics of elitism and exclusiveness I took so much for granted.

I most definitely was not prepared for the atmosphere of an American public university campus, set by what seemed to me an incredibly large number of incredibly young undergraduates. I was not prepared for the frank and democratic American acceptance of the characteristics of mass education, including what I considered an enormous amount of bureaucratic complexity. I was not prepared to find that educational quality could be so openly and directly linked to its financial cost. I was not prepared to see such a large portion of both the undergraduate and graduate student population consist of foreigners. I was not prepared for the businesslike, impersonal way students were treated by campus staff and even by many professors. Most especially, I was not prepared for being considered "just another foreign graduate student" and to have to deal on a daily basis with people who were unknowingly belittling my background and experience—including years of fieldwork and university teaching—and whose behavior I so often found either patronizing or dismissive.

With hindsight I now think that this was an extremely useful experience, but its value was paid in frustration, humiliation, and exasperation. Again, I was lucky in being able to share it with my husband—who had also entered a graduate program—and in having the help and support of an outstanding group of academic mentors. The chair of my sponsoring committee, the late Professor Hiroshi Wagatsuma, was particularly instrumental in helping me maintain a measure of mental health. He himself, Japanese-born and trained at the most elite Japanese institution, Tokyo University, had undergone experiences similar to mine when first entering the United States, and after many years of teaching and living here, he was still vividly aware of the difficulties created by cultural dissonance.

Talking with Professor Wagatsuma was excellent therapy, but more important, in listening to the anecdotes with which he could so brilliantly exemplify his analyses of American culture, I started to realize that my problems were essentially *cultural* and that this experience, albeit painful, was also providing me with a great chance for reaching new insights about the craft of anthropology itself. After I had suffered greatly from what I considered attacks to my sense of personal worth, I finally realized that this was happening only because I had not framed this experience in anthropological terms. Why was I taking "native" definitions—of friendship, scholarly work, or success—so very seriously? Had I not learned the lesson of relativism and of the inevitability of ethnocentrism? Where was my use of the fundamental anthropological skill of balancing the emic and etic points of view? Why was I getting irritated by the Americans making fun of my accent when I had taken perfectly in my stride the Japanese incessantly pointing and laughing at my Roman nose or at my overall foreignness? These were all questions I found myself "stonewalling," until I realized that I was embarrassed by their simple answers. The fact was that, because American culture was typically Western, I had related to it as if it were my own and was then cut to the core by its "betrayal."

The whole problem emerged from the question of participation: Since I had come to America as a student, I wanted to fully participate in the culture in this role, but according to *my own* culture-specific definition of it. Thus, I had encountered great problems in areas of behavior particularly related to the definition of that role. The quantification drive underlying the educational system baffled me; the profound anti-intellectualism of even the most dedicated American student bewildered me; and the prevalence of anecdote over analysis, of simplicity over complexity, of concreteness over abstraction, and of detail over depth in the teaching and studying of social science vexed me. Here I was, in one of the best anthropology programs in the country, and all my peers would talk about whenever we met socially were other people, sports, money, or sex. If professional matters were ever discussed, they would concern grades, number of publications, or job prospects. If one became involved in a research project, people seemed interested in knowing only who funded and administered it. If one took a new course, people would want to know what the instructor was like.

While my initial adjustment problems in Japanese academia had to do with the acceptance of my role as the feudal retainer for munificent intellectual lords, now I felt plunged back into the nervous, immature atmosphere of my junior high school days. But whereas in Japan I had managed to detach my sense of self from the behavior that was required from me, and I had in fact taken pride in becoming an "impeccably cultural performer," now I could not seem to do the same. This realization led me to a long process of cultural self-analysis, at the end of which I came to better understand not only the salient characteristics of my cultural background but also all the hidden epistemological agendas that had colored my research until then. In turn, this made me look at the ethnographic enterprise from a new point of view, and I came to see in sharp relief some of its more common limitations: the concentration on the study of exotic, marginal, or socially deviant groups, clearly different from the ones we, the researchers, belong to; our common practice of "the field trip," always implying a physical demarcation between "our" territory and that of the people to be studied; and the use we make of our study of cultural specificity to acquire prestige within academic worlds that are themselves culture-specific. Indeed, a certain kind of anthropological research started to seem to me at this point a rigged intellectual game with limited possible returns. On the other hand, I also came to appreciate that once the test of *real* participant observation is successfully negotiated, anthropological analysis can provide the deepest understanding of the human experience.

Now I fully realized for the first time that culture is not a sort of house we can enter and leave at will. Culture defines the parameters of all human expressions, and, like a chronic disease, we always carry it with us. Thus, there are no extracultural standpoints from which to do cultural analysis. My understanding of Japanese culture had been filtered through the lenses of my Italian background, and the whole process was being repeated in America. However, both in Japan and in the United States I had not had the wish and the opportunity to distance myself emotionally from the setting of my cultural analysis. In Japan, for a variety of reasons—including the extreme physical "foreignness" of the setting—I had managed to become a real participant and to maintain an ethnographic detachment. But in America I had fallen into the trap of fully validating native categories and then resenting them.

Understanding the dynamics of this process helped me resolve most of my day-to-day frustrations and made me realize that anthropological practice, per se, does not necessarily lead to overcoming ethnocentrism. In fact, by "institutionalizing" the distance between the researcher and the people being studied, anthropological practice may subtly reinforce ethnocentrism. But, if anthropological practice is supplemented by the test of real participant observation, one can begin to comprehend the enormous scope of cultural constraints. At this point the anthropologist truly becomes an impeccable "professional stranger." From this point, however, one neither can "turn off" the anthropological lenses through which all experiences become framed nor "go home again," simply because the very concept of "home," as a privileged native culture, has been totally deconstructed through ethnographic detachment.

EXPLORING AMERICAN CULTURE

Figuring all this out took the best part of my first four years of residence in the United States, including a lengthy trip to Italy at the end of the third year. By the end of this period I had completed my coursework and taken my doctoral qualifying exams, and I was doing exciting research on several fronts.

As I mentioned previously, my original project had to do with trying to trace the trajectory of change affecting the communication patterns of ethnic group members living in a multiethnic society. Because of my previous experience, I had initially planned to study the acculturation of the Japanese-Americans. However, the very hypothesis at the basis of my research—that ethnicity is perpetuated through the maintenance of microbehavioral patterns acquired so early in life that they become almost unconscious—led me to consider the necessity of selecting for my analysis an ethnic group *not* labeled as a minority, to demonstrate that retention of an idiosyncratic ethnic style has nothing to do with social labeling or group militancy. Also, particularly under the influence of Professor Wagatsuma, I had become increasingly interested in the issue of "native anthropology," and I was intrigued by the way it related to the study of ethnicity. Specifically, being Italian myself, I started wondering what it would be like to study the Italian-Americans. Would my perceptions of this group be different from those of Italian-American scholars, and if so, how? And how would my observations compare with those gathered by researchers of totally different ethnic backgrounds, such as, for example, members of the Anglo majority?

While I was still trying to decide the focus of my research, I was lucky enough to become involved with a project investigating the health maintenance practices of various American groups of Asian ancestry. As I was able to use my "Asian expertise" within that context, I decided to concentrate on the Italian-Americans for my doctoral dissertation research. For the next several years, these were the two areas of investigation in which I was formally engaged. At the same time, however, the exploration of American culture as a whole remained my informal, but no less exciting or demanding objective. I soon learned that revealing this objective to American fellow anthropologists-in-training was not a good idea. In particular, my asking for their professional insights into their own culture seemed to create great embarrassment. In line with this, the unwritten rule about anthropology graduate work in most of the academic institutions I came to know during this period was that "real" anthropological research is done abroad. On the other hand, foreign students— especially from "exotic" Asian and African countries—would be encouraged to study aspects of their own cultures. Furthermore, I noticed that even discussing the topic of my formal research on ethnicity would create quite a bit of uneasiness; Americans, including American anthropologists, simply did not seem to expect that a foreigner may be here to study their culture, and ethnicity was certainly one of the aspects of the culture they least wished to discuss.

As for my Italian-American research subjects, while fully informed of the aim of my project and of the observation techniques I would employ, they were quick to let me know how they thought ethnicity should be studied. Although they always put up very graciously with my observation sessions, they also ended up "convincing" me that I should really interview them about their values and beliefs. In effect, all through my explorations of American culture, I repeatedly found a common popular concern with the ideational realm, an attitude almost opposite to the Japanese preoccupation with behavioral norms. A great many Americans seem to believe that "ideas make the person" and because ideas can and do change, people can continuously reinvent themselves. Perhaps because of this belief, the idea of American culture as a stable configuration is not commonly accepted, and even members of minority groups feel that their identity is a matter of "negotiation."

On my part, however, I found that applying a complex set of microbehavioral observation techniques, I not only could document the remarkable retention of an ethnic-specific behavioral style across generations of Italian-Americans, but I was also able to find relevant commonalities in the behavior of people observed in random social settings, from a doctor's visiting room to a barbecue party and from a department store to a university campus, thus gathering evidence of a system of recognizably American behavioral patterns. Also, the academic program I had joined gathered a large number of advanced foreign students, and it was very instructive and therapeutic to exchange notes with them on American culture in general and on the subculture of American academia in particular.

I especially enjoyed monitoring the reactions of Asian students, since I was often able to predict them, and I sometimes came to share these reactions. One of these had to do with American humor; neither I nor my Asian fellow students—especially the Japanese among them—could get used to the constant barrage of sarcastic putdowns Americans seem cheerfully to accept as "joking." After being caught in a particularly virulent exchange of wisecracks, one of these friends once told me he privately referred to it as "jockeying," as in jockeying for power and control, and I still think this is an accurate definition of what goes on behind the smiles. I recognized a distinct continuity between American humor and its Anglo-Irish counterpart. I had experienced problems with a certain brand of British joking all through the time I had lived in England. But what I found most surprising in the American penchant for sarcasm is its use by people who seem typically characterized by great personal vulnerability and a very shaky sense of self-worth, so that humorous repartee becomes a sort of voluntary "social flagellation."

Actually, I have often wondered whether Americans do harbor a streak of Puritan masochism; "No pain no gain" sounds profoundly suspect to my Mediterranean ears. Certainly the dictates of extreme individualism, combined with ideological rigidity *and* social heterogeneity, seem to lead almost inevitably to a "culture in pain." During my years in graduate school, I observed many casualties of the enormous pressure people live under. After maintaining a decent GPA while putting up with all the wisecracking, the showing off, the self-promotion, the undercutting of potential competitors, and the sexual and ethnic tensions, some students would just suddenly "disappear." "Oh, he moved to the Coast. . . . She has found a good job . . . . He ran out of money. . . . She just dropped out," people would say, and in a few days, the person would apparently be totally forgotten. When confronted about this cavalier attitude toward evident casualties of a ruthlessly competitive system, people would reply, "You gotta learn not to care too much. People move, start new lives, don't keep up. If you care you get hurt." To me it all sounded like the rationalizations of people hardened by life in a war zone.

Foreigners often comment favorably on the "energy" one senses in this country. It is certainly real, but its flip side is tension. When I first came here, one of the things that particularly struck me was that strangers who accidentally make eye contact—in the street, in shops, on public transportation—will speak or at least smile to each other, something unthinkable in either Europe or Japan. Americans say it is just a way to be friendly, but to me this always seems a touching effort at establishing an amicable truce with potential enemies, as if to avoid a likely confrontation. Similarly, I now find it "normal" that American public speakers almost inevitably begin their presentations with a little joke, but from a European point of view, this is a strategy that seems to betray both performance anxiety and a clumsy attempt at courting favor. It is certainly a very different opening gambit from the British one, which requires a strong statement of fact, or the Italian one, which can be either an idiosyncratic statement of opinion or an outright complaint.

Once I started to teach, the level of performance anxiety American students live with really became evident. To comfort my classes, I often tell them that in Italy examination results are always publicly posted, that most university exams involve a personal interview—at which the professor frankly expresses her or his overall opinion of you, whether positive or negative—and that most of these interview sessions are large public events, so that there may be a lot of witnesses to your downfall. They listen in disbelief and groan in real pain. Certainly, the characteristics of American society that critics traditionally bemoan—the personal isolation, the psychological insecurity, the ruthless competition, the liability of social status, and the intolerance for diversity—justify this anxiety. But, in my view, there are two factors that uniquely handicap the pursuit of a contented life in this culture. One is the commitment to ideological integrity over interpersonal harmony, and the other is the lack of cultural self-awareness. Obviously these perceptions are strongly influenced by my comparative framework, in turn created by my Italian background and Japanese experience. However, the "natives" themselves are ready to admit that ideas, values, and beliefs are taken very seriously in this country, and, in so doing, the human factor is repressed or trampled over and much personal unhappiness results. Shortly before arriving here, I briefly visited the Soviet Union, and I cannot shake the impression that American and Soviet cultures are unexpectedly similar in this respect. At a deep level not influenced by political changes, they share a penchant for "radical utilitarianism," a tendency toward measuring everything in relation to ideological goals, disregarding human and aesthetic values in the process.

What seems to me uniquely American, however, is a profound disbelief in systemic social constraints and, in particular, in the reality of an indigenous culture. For years I have been systematically polling students, acquaintances, and miscellaneous informants on their perceptions of American culture, and I must conclude that denying that an American culture exists seems to be one of the most consistent local cultural traits. But Americans are very interested in themselves, and if a foreigner asks about seemingly peculiar cultural characteristics—Why do people eat popcorn at the movies? Why do coffee cups often get refilled free in restaurants? Why do people always get invited to social events in couples? Why is ethnicity only recognized in minority groups? Why is youth considered better than maturity? —they take pause and seem willing to start looking at their behavior from a new perspective. That is when teaching anthropology becomes truly exciting. By openly discussing my perceptions of American culture and by encouraging students to analyze how these perceptions may be related to my cultural background, I can lead them to turn their ethnographic lenses to various aspects of their own daily experience.

The point of all this is that I have come to believe that the anthropological perspective is a "way of life," as well as the outlook of a specific discipline. Being an anthropologist can simply mean getting a certain type of diploma and performing certain prescribed activities according to the expectations agreed on by a certain professional community. But it can also mean trying to understand the very matrices of our behavior and being able, if not to escape the mazeways our native culture has trained us to walk, at least to analyze the entire process, dissect its formulation, and contemplate its results. Anthropological knowledge can certainly increase mutual tolerance but only if we are prepared to train the field glasses on our own cultural peculiarities and define them as such. To achieve this, it helps to undergo the test of real participant observation, but I believe that with the right guidance, aspiring anthropologists can be trained to reap the rewards of "continuous ethnographic alert" without having to suffer the pain of prolonged cultural dissonance.

There is, however, one potentially disturbing fact that must be taken into serious consideration when embarking on the ethnographic enterprise. That is the realization that if culture determines the framework of all our expressions, it must also affect our cognitive processes. This implies that any intellectual endeavor, including anthropological theorizing (or writing about anthropological experiences, as in this article), is culturally colored. Fortunately, human beings have an adaptive capacity for thinking they understand each other even when they are instead steadily mistranslating incoming messages. But this does not have to be the only way to keep intercultural interaction open. I am quite convinced that if anthropological research methods can be clarified and systematically applied, if we develop careful guidelines for the cultural self-analysis of aspiring anthropologists, if we relentlessly explore the process by which behavioral style emerges, and if we find a way to elucidate the boundaries between culture and ethnicity, our discipline can live up to the promise its founders felt assured it had.

I also believe it is particularly important to analyze cultural settings not usually considered "for anthropological consumption." Ethnographic reports on French or American culture have a very different impact on the Western reader than, say, descriptions of the Ik or Yanomamo cultures. Whether we want to admit it or not, the latter tend to become, at best, abstract metaphors for the human condition. The pervasive reality of culture can only be truly appreciated when you call people's attention to its local expressions, and if this can be done by native and nonnative researchers in a position of real participation, so much the better. Bronislaw Malinowski once said that anthropology is the discipline of the sense of humor. This is a particularly nice definition, I think, if we complement it with the lesson of real participant observation. If we can identify our own cultural foibles and still smile at ourselves, we can also learn to live with the strangeness of assorted "cultural others," since we will be able to see the culture as just a reflection of our own. This is the perspective I gained from my exploration of American culture, and how much value I give to it is self-evident: I am still here.

STUDY QUESTIONS

1. Aside from the fact of having to adjust to distinctly different cultural surroundings, how did having a partner from another culture effectively help the author in adjusting after her initial culture shock?

2. What problems relating to the applicability of studying a culture from afar and then finding oneself totally enmeshed in that culture became evident to Professor Cerroni-Long?

3. How were anthropological principles, the author's "intellectual life preserver," helpful in leading to the understanding of Japanese culture?

4. What did the author learn from her research in Japan, Hawaii, England, and Italy about the bonding factors of cultural identity?

5. If the author is correct, what can we presume are the social consequences of institutionalizing minority statuses?

6. Do you believe that anyone can ever completely overcome ethnocentrism?

7. What does the author imply by "a culture in pain"?

8. Do you believe that it is true that Americans live at a level of performance anxiety? What features of American culture does the author indicate to support this view?

9. In what novel and insightful ways does the author view anthropological perspective as a "way of life"?

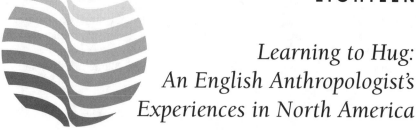

EIGHTEEN

Learning to Hug:
An English Anthropologist's
Experiences in North America

GEOFFREY HUNT
Institute for Scientific Analysis, Alameda, California

Expecting to make an easy adjustment to American life, the author is shocked by the differences between English and American cultures. He analyzes alcohol and drug addiction treatment, exploring the beliefs and practices of the therapeutic bureaucracy as reflections of American culture.

Geoffrey Hunt *grew up in England. He studied anthropology at London University, doing fieldwork with a West African religious group in urban South London. He came to the United States in 1989, and after twenty years of academic work, he began a new career as an applied anthropologist working on drug and alcohol addiction.*

Anthropology today is in deep turmoil. Starting in the late 1960s and the early 1970s, anthropologists have been involved in questioning the very foundations of their chosen discipline. Initially, the questioning concentrated on their geographical focus: Third World societies. As liberation movements in these countries ripened, and intellectuals within these countries began to analyze the intellectual dominance of the West, so anthropologists found themselves identified unfavorably with forces of oppression, colonialism, and imperialism, and even highly respected "founding fathers" were discovered to have collaborated with the colonial powers. As the anthropological research terrain shrank and anthropologists became persona non gratae, so also did the basis of anthropological thought come increasingly under scrutiny. Marxist and more radical anthropologists laid siege to the functionalist paradigm developed by Radcliffe-Brown and Malinowski.

Today, attention has shifted, and the discipline is involved in examining the holy grail of anthropology, the ethnographic text. These texts on which anthropology teaching was based have become the focal point of some very deep divisions. Partly as a result of critical thinking in all the social sciences, the motives of anthropologists and their writings have been questioned. Instead of accepting the text at face value, contemporary anthropologists have begun to reexamine the motives and the cultural assumptions of Malinowski, Evans-Pritchard, Firth, and Benedict. Such intensive questioning of the ways in which anthropologists construct the text is clearly a double-edged sword, for although on the one hand it has produced important and, in some cases, liberating assessments of possible ways of producing the ethnographic text, it has at the same time had the effect of making both neophyte and experienced anthropologists nervous about how they present their material. Today, authors can no longer remain hidden behind the narrative, but instead must reveal themselves in all their cultural nakedness.

Although some still decry such a development, anthropologists no longer need to have their personalized accounts published posthumously, as in Malinowski's case, or hide behind a pseudonym, as Laura Bohannan did.[1] Although trained in the ways of traditional anthropology, I have always found a "confessional" style of narrative more appealing, and hence the current debate has provided greater legitimacy for me to discuss fieldwork experiences. Such a discussion, however, should not be viewed as merely an example of personal indulgence or, as Llobera (1987) has called it, "navel gazing," but instead as a serious attempt to examine important current anthropological issues.

ANTHROPOLOGY TRAINING IN ENGLAND

Anthropologists have always involved themselves in somewhat ludicrous tasks, especially seen through the eyes of their fellow social scientists. Unlike other researchers, who are perfectly satisfied to conduct controlled experimental tests or design questionnaire surveys, anthropologists have been keen to explore far-off cultures and isolate themselves in relatively hazardous fieldwork circumstances. Until very recently, especially in England, which has a long tradition of Malinowskian fieldwork, a trainee anthropologist would never gain acceptance into the discipline unless he or she had gone through the traditional "rite de passage" of extended fieldwork in an "exotic" and often isolated society. This designated route of anthropological apprenticeship was not for me. Although Third World societies and their respective cultures were of interest, my chosen research focus lay within my own society. I had always been intrigued by cultural frameworks, but unlike others who sought to study them within distant societies, I wanted to look at them within my own. A West African religious immigrant group in South London was my chosen topic. Such a choice, however, was not received altogether enthusiastically by my teachers in a very traditional anthropology department at London University. The department was the home of Mary Douglas and also of Phyllis Kaberry, a student of Malinowski; Edmund Leach and Evans-Pritchard were regular visitors. On first learning that Camberwell in South London, and not India or Africa, was to be my fieldwork destination, my Professor informed me that Camberwell was neither exotic nor strange enough for fieldwork and that I was clearly playing at being an anthropologist. In spite of my efforts to emphasize the extent to which a syncretist West African religious group was culturally distant from my own white middle-class culture, he was not impressed and told me that to be taken seriously in anthropology I must remove myself completely from my own culture and conduct fieldwork in a far-off place. Promptly ignoring this advice, I set off, without their approval, for the uncharted urban terrain of South London. So began a checkered anthropological career.

My abiding interest in culture led me from immigrant religious groups to socially diverse drinking groups. In pursuing this latter topic, I began to confront the difficulties of attempting to decipher the culture of drinking among the middle class.

For the first time, I encountered rituals, symbols, and meanings that I knew well. Nevertheless, sharing a common culture with people whose practices I wished to understand created new difficulties. Rarely had I given much thought to my own rituals of drinking and entertaining, and I had never conceptualized these practices as symbolic arenas.[2] Moreover, little of the anthropology literature discussed how to examine one's own culture, or engage in self-reflexivity. Although anthropology had indeed begun the process of "coming home," much of its attention, at least within England and Europe, still focused on "peripheral" groups, and few anthropologists studied mainstream middle-class culture. Most academic anthropologists and sociologists, socialized within the middle class, saw their own culture as normal and natural, with little implicit anthropological interest. To understand middle-class meanings and values, I was obliged to become self-reflexive, suspend my preconceptions, and imagine myself to be an alien researcher come "to study the culture of the English natives." Culture, through such a process, would become anthropologically strange, and what had previously been taken for granted would become culturally alien. Learning such a process of self-reflexivity and enforced cultural strangeness would become even more important as my career in anthropology suddenly took an unexpected change in direction.

MOVING COUNTRIES

In 1989, after nearly twenty years of academic research, I decided to leave England and start a career in the United States. I saw my decision to move as relatively straightforward and thought only of the many possibilities that would open up for me. Because of an increasing specialization in research on alcohol issues, the prospect of continuing in this area in the United States seemed favorable. The United States federal government was well known for its extensive research funding in both the alcohol and drug fields, and a number of specialist research institutes existed. Furthermore, the recent start of the "drug war" seemed to point to a political climate that saw both drug and alcohol issues of some importance. Moreover, having never shown any flare for mastering foreign languages, moving to the United States seemed a sensible transfer, and integration into the society seemed easy. It was not that I underestimated the possible differences between England and the United States, but I saw those differences as resulting from different levels of economic development and mass consumption, and not arising from deep cultural divides. Aside from minor readjustments, I assumed that my moving to the United States would be culturally straightforward. Such a belief stemmed in part, from the existence of a common language, and a three-hundred-year history, in which the two countries were inextricably linked. But whatever the origins of my naivete, I soon found myself facing a system of different cultural values and expectations. From day one, seemingly simple everyday occurrences shocked me. For example, I would become confused when a shop assistant greeted my American partner with such a warm and personal welcome that I assumed they must be close friends, only to discover later that they had never met. I also reacted with surprise when telephone sales staff called me by my Christian name, a custom rarely practiced in England. Such simple cultural differences exasperated me, not merely because I was unprepared, but also because the very existence of the shared language had an effect of lulling me into assuming a false sense of cultural familiarity. If I had moved to France or Italy, the necessity to talk in an alien language would have been a constant reminder of cultural differences. In the United States, the shared language created a false sense of cultural security that, suddenly and unexpectedly, would be disturbed by minor cultural misunderstandings. For an anthropologist who had studied cultural frameworks for nearly twenty years, such experiences seemed ironic. Yet, whereas in England my attempts to make sense of alternative cultural systems had been contained and compartmentalized under the heading of research, here in the United States they pervaded my day-to-day existence. Such cultural conflicts soon became heightened in my professional work.

THE ANTHROPOLOGIST AS LOCAL GOVERNMENT BUREAUCRAT

Initially, unable to obtain an academic research position, I began working for a county government alcohol treatment bureau that administered local residential and day care services for alcoholics. My rationale for working for local government was that it would teach me how to tailor my theoretical research interests to the needs of social policy. I anticipated an environment within which a fruitful interchange of ideas would take place. A world where, on the one hand, I would lay out the academic and theoretical parameters of a particular issue, and on the other hand bureau officials would point out important practical modifications. No such interchange occurred. Instead, I found myself confronting a belief system in which the official idealogy had to be followed despite personal or professional beliefs. Within this setting it was not surprising that my detached and analytical training and perspective was not well received. The director and approximately 99 percent of the staff believed that the society was riddled with alcohol problems and alcoholics, and that if only alcohol could be removed from the society, many of its major problems would vanish. The staff, whether they were "in recovery" or just abstinent, believed that working in the alcohol bureau was not merely a job but a calling. They were there to pursue a mission to improve the society. This closed belief system viewed alcohol issues in a one-dimensional manner and allowed no discussion of alternatives.

This was my first encounter in the United States with the recovery movement, a mass movement that, although emanating from Alcoholics Anonymous, was no longer confined to providing solutions to alcohol problems. Today, as many writers have noted, the recovery movement offers panaceas for a whole host of personal and social problems. The near universality of this movement in the United States, propagated through individual groups, self-help books, criminal justice referral programs, television talk shows, docudramas, and seminars, is in marked contrast to its influence in England and other Western European countries, where its impact has been much less pronounced.

Into this environment, I arrived with views about alcohol diametrically opposed to both the personal beliefs of the staff and the official ideology of the bureau. Instead of an unquestioning belief in the idea of alcoholism, I held a cultural relativist position on alcohol problems and believed the Durkheimian principle that research on "normal" drinking was an essential prerequisite for understanding "abnormal" drinking. The disease notion of alcoholism seemed at best a very shaky concept, and the efficacy of the abstinent model of treatment seemed doubtful. A three-year study of alcohol treatment agencies in England had convinced me that "controlled drinking methods" were just as effective as those based on abstinence and the twelve-step movement.

Given the views of the bureau on the one hand and my own on the other, it was not surprising that a frosty atmosphere soon developed between myself, the director, and the staff. My brief stay at the bureau involved painful sparring matches. Although I tried to remain vague and noncommittal about my "heretical" views on such matters as the disease concept, controlled drinking, and alcohol use messages, the director became exasperated with my failure to become one of the team and was increasingly concerned that I might make an embarrassing public announcement on the disease concept. On one occasion, however, it was my *behavior* rather than my ideas that provided proof of my unwillingness to fit in.

The director, an ex-nun, who ran the bureau as a religious institution and administered large doses of moral guilt to her subordinates, decided to arrange an executive staff retreat to increase "team spirit." She believed that working in the bureau should not be just a job but that all members, and especially the executive staff, should be deeply committed to the philosophy of the bureau. The retreat, which lasted two days, took place at an expensive and secluded hotel and commenced late in the afternoon on the first day. During the first session, which, according to the agenda, was to be on the philosophy of the bureau, I realized that I would need to be especially diplomatic about my views. Fortunately, instead of a deep discussion of the bureau's philosophy, individual executive staff members took the opportunity to share with the group favorite poems, passages from novels, pieces of music, and even a short video of a balletic juggler. After the session, the staff met for dinner and as we sat around deciding what to order, the waitress asked if we wished to have something to drink. While the rest ordered iced tea, I chose a glass of red wine. Although I suspected that this gesture could be provocative, I felt that because this was now my free time, not bureau time, I should be allowed to drink wine at dinner as I normally did. My behavior disturbed the director, who, I later discovered, had wished to reprimand me. However, she decided that because I was European she should excuse my behavior. Nevertheless, she considered my openly drinking alcohol in front of two staff members who were "in recovery" to be "a failure of good conduct," and because of my unacceptable beliefs she sent me a sharp memo questioning my "organizational fit." Fortunately, soon afterward, having found alternative work, I left the bureau. But though the difficulties of matching my professional and personal views with the requirements of a local government department had been removed, new cultural conflicts soon arose.

THE ANTHROPOLOGIST AS EVALUATOR

I began a new "career" as an evaluator for a local nonprofit research company, hired to assess a federally funded substance abuse community prevention program. In England, I had little contact with evaluation or evaluators, and it was not until I commenced work in the United States that I encountered representatives of this new profession and realized that evaluation was a burgeoning career for unattached and out-of-work social scientists, and even anthropologists.

As the number of qualified anthropologists has increased and the number of teaching positions has declined, would-be researchers have found work in the field of applied anthropology. Here anthropologists are expected to apply their training and expertise to solving social difficulties or assessing the possible impact of social change. For these anthropologists, postmodern debates about anthropological writing may seem a theoretical fad that has relevance only in ivory towers. Such debates hardly concern applied anthropologists toiling in the trenches. Nevertheless, working as an applied anthropologist involves new problems and new conflicts. Forced to survive outside the academy, anthropologists have sought to balance their assessment of what is required, given their perspective as professional anthropologists, with the needs of the people who hired them. In these new environments and under these new pressures, they have learned to accept that researcher-centered research has to give way to client- or community-centered research and evaluation.

Following this new career path, I convinced myself that surely twenty years of academic research would enable me to take on this new role.[3] Once "on board," I would easily learn new techniques and acquire the appropriate terminology and jargon. Unfortunately, I was mistaken, for although the technical part of being an evaluator was straightforward and I quickly learned to use all the key terms such as *process evaluation, formative evaluation,* and *outcome measures* in all the appropriate places, I failed to comprehend clearly the requirements of being an evaluator within the drug and alcohol arena. It was not my inexperience of evaluation technique that created the difficulties; it was instead my total inability to understand and fulfill the cultural expectations of being an evaluator in the United States.

EVALUATING A FEDERALLY FUNDED PROGRAM

My task was to evaluate the impact of a federally funded community substance abuse program. In 1990, the Office for Substance Abuse Prevention (OSAP)[4] created by the Anti-Drug Act of 1986 began funding a series of community prevention projects. The projects, known as the Community Partnership Program, eventually totaled 251 nationwide. Broadly defined, the purpose of this grant was to encourage the formation, development, and, thereafter, the ongoing existence and vitality of grassroots, community-level organizations and initiatives aimed at preventing alcohol and other drug-related (AOD) problems within local communities. The basic premise of the Partnership program was that meaningful, long-term reductions in alcohol and other drug problems would be won only when the concerns, energies, and commitments of local communities are focused on this problem territory.

One requirement of this program was that a local evaluator should evaluate each individual partnership. This was my task, and I began to attend a series of local prevention meetings that took place at county health departments, government offices, and community-based organizations. I also attended a series of prevention trainings held both locally and nationally and a series of national conferences. In attending the various meetings, I began to realize that, besides any technical expertise, they expected that I do three things: (1) join in, (2) be intimate, and (3) believe.

JOINING IN

In previous research settings, I had been expected to participate in many diverse activities and situations. Some had been easy to fulfill, others not. For example, rolling across the floor while chanting religious slogans and pretending to fly was not easy, but my fellow West African church members had been impressed by my attempt, especially knowing that I was not a believer. They secretly hoped that through the process I would learn to believe. Drinking with the "lads" in a village pub as part of my "culture of drinking" research was much easier, except that I did not like beer. For my new drinking friends, this raised doubts about my masculinity and my character as a serious drinker. Nevertheless, as long as on occasion I drank distilled alcohol, they accepted me in their company. Such fieldwork activities taught me how to become involved while remaining detached enough, or occasionally sober enough, to be able to record what was going on. But these techniques of remaining detached were, I soon discovered, unacceptable in community prevention evaluation. There the participants wanted me, despite my evaluation status, to be a believing member of the team.

BEING INTIMATE

A key feature of joining in was being intimate. This was done in two ways. First, participants believed that joining in meant shedding any sense of formality or social distance and revealing both some personal information about oneself and one's harmful experiences with alcohol or other illicit drugs. This created serious dilemmas for me. Although willing to share personal information with friends over a long and indulgent dinner, I was extremely unwilling to confide any confidential information to a group of strangers. Furthermore, my experiences with illicit drugs were virtually nonexistent, and in relation to alcohol I often described myself as a "wino," consuming wine at every meal except breakfast. My love of alcohol meant that I was clearly different from the prevention practitioners who sought to increase societal restrictions on alcohol use. Far from seeing alcohol as an evil substance, I viewed it with a benevolence verging on deep affection. Having been raised within the environment of a large hotel, where drinking was a central feature, alcohol occupied a central symbolic and ritualistic position in entertaining and in the art of being sociable. Not only had my experiences with alcohol been entirely positive, so also had the experiences of my family. Therefore, whenever an exercise at a prevention meeting was called for that entailed revealing personal and painful information about myself and my relationship to alcohol and drugs, I would begin to feel terrified and extremely self-conscious and would desperately try to think of something I could say that would reveal little about myself while not offending the other participants. Although I believe that anthropologists should be honest in doing fieldwork, I do not think that the official evaluator should openly declare his doubts about the program at public prevention meetings. Therefore, if asked by the group why I was attending the meetings or what I needed from the group, I would avoid all references to personal details, adopt a businesslike attitude, and reply that my aim was to encourage better collaboration and coordination among prevention activities. Such terms were frequently used in local government parlance, and the participants accepted them. Thus, I survived another day as evaluator.

Second, being intimate required physical contact with fellow participants. At these prevention meetings participants expected that I would hug people I hardly knew, hold hands with perfect strangers, and even, once, fall limp into the arms of people I knew only superficially. For example, early in the project, at the end of one meeting, the leaders asked the group to stand in a circle, hold hands, and close our eyes. Then, one at a time they instructed us to squeeze our left hand when we felt our right hand being squeezed. The group facilitator started the exercise and told us that it would circulate around the group and eventually return to him. So there I stood with nineteen other leading and committed local prevention practitioners, supported by federal dollars, holding hands in a circle with my eyes closed and waiting for my right hand to be squeezed. As I waited, I truly wondered why I had moved to the United States. Would I have come if I had known that my lofty training as an anthropologist would have led me to this exercise of holding hands with strangers? On another occasion, at a team-building event in the redwood forests, to learn more about "risk taking," I and another seven participants were instructed to arrange ourselves in a circle. Each of us, in turn, was chosen to stand in the middle, with our feet together, hands across our chest, and fall back limply against the circle. The rest of us were told to catch the falling person and gently push him or her toward another part of the circle. This exercise, the instructor informed us, would help build a sense of trust and develop team spirit.

Such behavior meant that any formal or aloof stance was clearly unacceptable. As the child of a middle-class family raised within the formal confines of an English hotel and the enforced male bonding of a Catholic boys' boarding school, notions of propriety were clearly embedded in my psyche. Physical contact between boys at school was clearly frowned upon, in spite of all the jokes about English homosexuality. Because of these childhood experiences, I had developed a keen sense of dread of physical contact except with people with whom I had deep personal relationships, and even with these people, physical contact was limited. In fact, I believe my mother once said words to the effect of "Don't touch people, because you don't know where they have been." Yet here I was expected not only to touch people but to fall into their arms. As I stood looking at the trees, wondering how to avoid the exercise, I pondered ruefully why it was that the anthropological methodology books I had read as a postgraduate had not mentioned such fieldwork activities.

BELIEVING

A basic assumption of all those involved in the program was that they believed in the need for such a substance abuse community prevention program, and by definition they assumed that the evaluator would also believe in the program. Yet for myself believing raised many problems. First, I was skeptical as to the need for such a program. Notions of drug and alcohol problems are socially constructed and socially amplified. This is not to imply that drug and alcohol problems do not exist, but instead to assert that social and cultural factors determine the way that the problems and their solutions are conceptualized. Thus, I wondered to what extent this emphasis on alcohol and drug problems allowed federal sponsors, local government supporters, and local participants to avoid concerning themselves with other, more intractable structurally based social problems. This skepticism, which created difficulties, could have been overcome by adopting a detached professional position. But there existed other, more serious problems. To believe wholeheartedly in any program raises the danger of either falling into what House (1993) has called "clientism"—doing whatever the client wants—or failing to maintain any sense of objectivity. Although doubts have been raised about the researcher's privileged position of objectivity, having a detached outsider examine and assess a program is still beneficial. Such a position requires remaining at least intellectually distant from the program. This, in itself, did not mean that I should remain totally aloof from the participants, but did mean that I should refrain from believing in the program so completely that I failed to retain a sense of critical awareness. Only by being detached could I assess the extent to which the program fulfilled its own requirements, whether they be those of the local participants, the federal government, or the local government that financially administered the program. Evaluators and researchers who champion participatory research often underestimate the difficulties of assessing a program objectively, while being part of the team. Finally, I found the pressure to believe in the program to be culturally disturbing. Why was it that the participants felt I should believe? Was it, as in the recovery movement, that they refused to contemplate alternative beliefs? Such questions reminded me of my research on the West African church. Unlike the prevention activists, the church members were willing to accept my not believing, and never did they exert pressure on me to believe. Why then was there this difference?

In the initial months of the project, although unable to find satisfactory answers, I came to understand that the culture of the program and the participants' expectations of the evaluator were connected in some way or another to the society's belief that team and community building were the way to solve society's problems. In my desire to find answers, I eagerly awaited my first national Community Partnership meeting in Washington, where I would meet other local evaluators who, I was convinced, would supply me with answers.

MEETING THE EVALUATORS

The start of the meeting in Washington did not bode well. The organizers gave each attendee a name tag on which his or her Christian name appeared three times larger than the surname—a clear indicator of future enforced familiarity. To those who were to present papers, name tags with bright green ribbons were provided, which made the presenters look like prize cattle at the local agricultural show. In addition, all participants were given a black plastic conference bag on which was emblazoned the slogan "Prevention Works." The slogan seemed a little premature since the prevention program had only just begun and its effects only recently monitored. Having received our gifts, all one thousand of us trooped into the hotel's main ballroom. The opening speaker, the director of the federal agency, began by telling the participants to stand and say to each person on either side of them, "Hello, neighbor." She then informed the assembled group that they "were truly a beautiful audience and part of a changing landscape," and because of that we should applaud ourselves. The audience, acting like a group of well-trained seals, proceeded to clap enthusiastically. After her speech, in which she praised the audience for their prevention work and told them they were clearly developing a bonding with each other, she introduced the next speaker, an African-American pastor. He also made the audience stand, but this time instead of acknowledging their neighbors, he instructed the participants to give thanks to God. Again, the audience obeyed with enthusiasm, ending their praise of God with a resounding "Amen." What followed was in essence a revivalist sermon, in which the pastor attributed drug and alcohol problems to a decline in moral and spiritual values. Toward the end of his talk, he instructed the audience that before leaving the conference each of them should bond with someone. When he had finished, the audience spontaneously stood and rapturously applauded. As I looked around, few in the audience seem in any way surprised at receiving a religious sermon at a federally sponsored conference. I assumed that the event had been provided primarily for the local activists, and I was sure that once the evaluators met on their own, many would voice their surprise and concern at the appropriateness of such an event.

This, however, did not occur. When the evaluators met, most of them noted that they had enjoyed the speech. Their response, and the extent to which it differed from my own, made me feel confused and isolated. I wondered how these social scientists could have been anything but amazed at the tenor and message of the talk, which seemed contrary to much of the social science thinking on drug and alcohol abuse. A growing sense of cultural isolation overtook me as I observed them and listened to their responses to the opening evaluation session. The head of the prevention program and the chief evaluator outlined their vision of the role of evaluation and the work of the local evaluators. After informing us that we were "on the cutting edge" of prevention work, they told us that our primary task was to work closely with the program managers to ensure "program plausibility and, whenever possible, act as advisers to the program." According to them, evaluation was to be an integral part of program planning, and the evaluator must see himself or herself as part of the program team. In emphasizing this perspective, they showed that their view of evaluation inclined more to program guidance than to critical research. Being told to work closely with the program participants and staff was not a problem in itself nor was it a problem for evaluators like myself, trained within anthropology, who, unlike other researchers, always worked in close contact with the people. However, what was troubling was the impression that critical assessment was not welcome.

During the session, my colleagues sat, listened, took notes, and asked only technical questions. Never did any of the approximately ninety evaluators question the perspective of evaluation. Never before had I experienced a meeting between government officials and social scientists where the latter not only accepted the government view but in fact welcomed it. Where, I asked myself, were the critical thinkers, the skeptics, or even just the suspicious ones? Not only was there no critical questioning of the philosophy of the program, but also a great deal of enthusiasm was expressed. As a group, the evaluators celebrated the program, seemed honored to have been chosen, voiced their belief in its efficacy, and stated how important it was that the program be a success.

Even after the meeting, in private conversations, where one might have expected some dissension, little was expressed. Whenever I communicated my own reservations about the program and its rationale, my colleagues viewed me with some surprise, and I began to feel as though I possessed a contagious disease. On occasion, their looks conveyed a sense that they thought I was a troublemaker. Some, having discerned my nationality, would listen patronizingly with a bemused look to the theories of the misguided foreigner who clearly did not understand the purpose of the program. One evaluator, having overheard my questioning of the program, even invited me to lunch to hear more. He was very pleasant, listened with respect, and assured me that I had a very "interesting" perspective.

As I sat in my hotel room and thought about the day, I realized that of course they were right; I was indeed a foreigner and a stranger in my newly adopted country. I also began to understand that by suggesting that social scientists, whether in the guise of federally designated evaluators or not, were there to ask critical questions, I had naively assumed that having a shared professional designation inferred similar cultural and professional values. In making such a cultural assumption, I was behaving like many other anthropologists, who on first encountering the "natives," committed a series of cultural faux pas. Just as my experiences with the program participants had illustrated the cultural divide, so also did my interactions with the evaluators.

Through these encounters and my continuing involvement with the program, I began very slowly to perceive a common thread in my experiences since I had arrived in the United States. Just as in the alcohol bureau I had failed to comprehend the strength and rigidity of the belief system, which brooked no questions, doubts, or alternatives, so now I realized the comprehensiveness of a belief system that saw the whole society gripped by an epidemic. Illicit drugs, alcohol, and, later, tobacco had become the evil substances that were undermining the community and gnawing at the society's moral fiber. Into this crisis I had arrived, and instead of believing, or at least remaining silent, I had expressed disbelief.

Nevertheless, more than just failing to comprehend the extent to which the society had become gripped by the rhetoric of the drug war, I also began to realize the extent to which I, a cultural anthropologist, had failed to think like one. Instead of examining both the latent and manifest functions of the community prevention program, I had chosen to consider only the latter. I had completely failed to see the program and the role of evaluation as part of a cultural and "symbolic universe" (Berger 1967). The Community Partnership Program had been developed within a social climate that believed that the social and moral fabric of the society was under threat. The reasons for the malaise were identified as drug and alcohol problems. The period that began in the sixties and continued into the seventies had led to an indulgence in the personal use of drugs. This indulgence had now got out of hand and led to a situation of disorder. Social order had now to be re-created and reestablished. The Community Partnership Program had been given the task, and through a therapeutic process and a series of ritualistic practices, each local program was to regain a sense of permanence and a sense of order and reaffirm community.

Unlike previous social problem programs, for example the War on Poverty, the Community Partnership Program reaffirms community not necessarily by doing any real community building, but instead by creating community as a psychological phenomenon. As Sennett has argued, community can be built not by any physical activity but by developing a sense of shared "imagery and feeling." "What matters is not what you've done but how you feel about it" (quoted in Rapping 1996: 124). A therapeutic belief in a "change of heart" had been transplanted to the community level. No longer were the participants expected to change society, they only had to change themselves. In other words, social change was no longer structural change; it was instead "establishing relationships with people." Within this framework, it is therefore not surprising that "hugging" had become such a crucial element.

This view that sees social change as resulting from a "change of heart" is not specific to the partnership but can be traced to more general themes within U.S. culture. For example, Skolnick argues that these ideas result from a strong sense of religiosity that "promises that we can solve our problems through changes of heart rather than through the difficult and divisive route of political and social change" (1991: 203). Other writers have noted the importance of this view within the recovery movement. For example, Kaminer, in her particularly caustic and insightful analysis, shows how the movement sees the process of reforming ourselves and our families as the way to reforming society. According to Kaminer, this view is the "movement's party line," a point neatly captured in the quotation from Bradshaw, one of the gurus of the codependency and recovery movement, who suggests that "recovery will save us as a society . . . you have only to recover and the world recovers with you" (Kaminer 1992: 94).

When seen from such a perspective, activities that had appeared strange if not bizarre, seemed now to make sense. The local participants' desire to have me join in, be part of the team, hold hands, hug, and fall into waiting arms were all understandable when seen as part of a process of therapeutic community building. Sharing experiences on the evils of alcohol and drugs were necessary if individual members and newcomers were to become bonded. Even religious sermons at federal conferences no longer seemed out of place when viewed from the perspective of a reaffirming ritual intended to galvanize the audience into feeling special and part of a nationwide team.

From such a vantage point, it also became more clear why CSAP should promote a view of evaluation that was inherently uncritical. If the underlying purpose was to develop a psychological community, then the official monitors must also be part of the team. No longer were they to play the role of "critical observers"; instead, evaluators were there to be "facilitative participants" within the collaborative model. As one evaluator noted, evaluators should become more like therapists. If evaluators are to be highly collaborative and part of the team, then they must also join in and believe, both in the program and its activities, and, like the program participants, proudly display the conference slogan "Prevention Works." Given such a viewpoint, uncritical evaluators appeared less reprehensible when viewed as believers in the pursuit of building community.

In part, some of my inability to think like a cultural anthropologist lay in the difficulties I faced since my arrival in the United States, and especially in relation to cultural differences around drinking and the use of alcohol. As a European, I am still struck by the way in which alcohol and the influence of Alcoholics Anonymous pervade day-to-day life. Why is it, as Peele (1989) has noted, that approximately 90 percent of Americans believe that alcohol use—an accepted part of social life in most European countries—is a disease over which millions of people have no control unless absolute abstinence is adhered to? This cultural belief in the inherent dangers of a substance is significantly different from views about alcohol in England and parts of Europe, where in general the problem is regarded as inherent in the drinker, not in the alcohol. For example, an alcohol ban in Italy during the 1990 World Cup competition was acceptable because "fans" or "supporters" were already regarded as potentially disreputable and, admittedly, alcohol makes bad behavior worse. However, the average citizen can distance himself or herself from the kind of person to whom such restrictions must be applied, their views about alcohol remaining unaffected.

In spite of the seeming "sameness" of the cultures, different sets of cultural values and meanings surround alcohol and drinking behaviors. In the United States, people scrutinize an individual's drinking behavior for signs of problematic social and health developments. In my own situation, I soon discovered that my social drinking practices, considered perfectly normal within England, had become a point of issue. Levels of consumption defined as acceptable by the British Ministry of Health's "Sensible Drinking" guidelines became, in the United States, indicators of problem drinking. Even innocent statements such as "I need a drink" (which often expressed my feelings after having attended yet another prevention meeting) were judged by some as signs of alcohol dependency. No longer did I live in a society where alcohol occupied a generally positive position; instead I lived in a culture where it possessed increasingly negative characteristics. The harmful effects of alcohol are seen everywhere, and the club of recovering individuals grows larger every day. In fact, to be in recovery or to be an ACOA (adult child of an alcoholic) confers status and bonds the individual with others who have been through a similar experience. In casual conversations or even chance meetings, it is often one of the first pieces of information supplied. Supplying this information, individuals make public their position regarding the alcohol issue and pledge their allegiance. In so doing, they resolve any issues of ambiguity, a trait that Wasserfall (1993) has suggested is seen within America as untrustworthy.

Rather than submit to the societal pressures to conform, I decided instead to assert my cultural differences. As I began work in the United States, first at the alcohol bureau and then as an evaluator, I became increasingly defiant about my own views about alcohol and my drinking practices. But my personal reaction interfered with my professional perspective. Rather than adopting a position of intellectual detachment on issues of alcohol and alcohol problems, I took sides, and in so doing failed to be self-reflective. Instead of examining those times or occasions when I felt "uncomfortable" or "out of place," in order "to map the dark side of others' worlds" (Willis 1978), I merely bristled. Instead of attempting to understand the meanings that the society attributed to alcohol, and hence the symbolic purpose of the program, I saw only differences between the cultural position of alcohol in England and the United States. Fortunately, in using ethnographic techniques to evaluate the program, and especially in producing extensive fieldnotes, I gradually regained a position of detachment from which I could analyze the underlying purpose of the prevention program and the sociocultural context of alcohol and drug problems.

CONCLUSION

In hindsight, the experience has taught me the difficulties of retaining a professional anthropological stance while attempting to settle in a new country. Unlike anthropologists who begin fieldwork and are warned of "going native," I had chosen to move to a new country not to study the "natives" but to create a new life with a new partner. Soon after arriving, I began to realize just how culturally dissimilar England and the United States are, and to recognize the informal pressures placed on immigrants to conform to the dominant culture. The process of dealing with those pressures and maintaining my own identity emphasized my cultural isolation. In fact, whenever a visitor from Europe arrived at our house, we spent considerable time comparing notes and discussing what we saw as strange U.S. customs or activities. The sense of cultural isolation was exacerbated by working in a culturally alien nonacademic work environment, whose ideology seemed diametrically opposed to my own. Taken together, these factors contributed to my inability and unwillingness to accept a series of cultural practices that irritated me and against which I reacted. In so doing, I became unable to make sense of the culture into which I had arrived, even when as an anthropologist I was assigned the task of evaluating a prevention program.

Today, though still reacting negatively to such everyday forms of familiarity as "Have a nice day" or "My name is Joseph, and I'll be your waiter," I see more clearly some of the threads that weave together the cultural fabric and that help explain the connections between notions of individual and community identification, substance abuse problems, perceptions of societal malaise, and federally funded prevention programs.

NOTES

1. See Smith Bowen 1964.
2. See Hunt 1991 and Hunt et al. 1988.
3. Although relatively few anthropologists can be found working as evaluators in the drug and alcohol fields, ethnographic evaluation has made a significant impact, especially in the field of educational evaluation (Wolcott 1987; Fetterman 1986).
4. The name of the agency was subsequently altered to the Center for Substance Abuse Prevention (CSAP).

REFERENCES

Berger, P. 1967. The *Sacred Canopy*. Garden City: Doubleday.

Fetterman, D. M., and Pitman, M. A. 1986. *Educational Evaluation: Ethnography in Theory, Practice and Politics*. Thousand Oaks, CA: Sage.

House, E. R. 1993. *Professional Evaluation*. Thousand Oaks, CA: Sage.

Hunt, G. 1991. The Middle Class Revisited: Eating and Drinking in an English Village. *Western Folklore* 50, October, pp. 401–420.

Hunt, G., Mellor, J., Satterlee, S., and Turner, J. 1988. Thinking about Drinking. *Surveyor* 22, 20–32.

Kaminer, W. 1991. *I'm Dysfunctional, You're Dysfunctional: The Recovery Movement and Other Self-Help Fashions*. Reading, MA: Addison-Wesley.

Llobera, J. 1987. Reply to critics. *Critique of Anthropology*, VII, 2, pp. 88–90.

Peele, S. 1989. *Diseasing of America: Addiction Treatment Out of Control*. Lexington, KY: Lexington Books.

Rapping, E. 1996. *The Culture of Recovery: Making Sense of the Self-Help Movement in Women's Lives*. Boston: Beacon Press.

Smith Bowen, E. 1964. *Return to Laughter*. New York: Doubleday Anchor.

Wasserfall, R. 1998. Gender Encounters in America: An Outsider's View of Continuity and Ambivalence. *Distant Mirrors: America as a Foreign Culture* (2nd ed.). P. DeVita and J. D. Armstrong, Eds. Chapter 11. Belmont, CA: Wadsworth.

Willis, P. 1978. *Profane Culture*. London: Routledge.

Wolcott, H. F. 1987. On ethnographic intent. *Interpretive Ethnography of Education: At Home and Abroad*. G. Spindler and L. Spindler, Eds. London: Lawrence Erlbaum Associates.

STUDY QUESTIONS

1. Whether an anthropologist, sociologist, or student of American culture, what problems can you imagine you would face in attempting to conduct research in your own culture?

2. What is meant by "self-reflexivity" and "enforced cultural strangeness" as research requirements in one's own culture?

3. In Professor Hunt's first encounter with an American alcohol treatment bureau, how did his views and those of the program differ? What are your own feelings on these operational and philosophical differences?

4. What personal and cultural experiences and beliefs posed problems with the requirement that the author become intimate within the prevention program?

5. What were the author's practical and objective concerns about uncritically "believing" in a program that he was hired to evaluate?

6. The author portrays the meeting of the evaluators as a comic opera. How conscientiously did this federally funded agency concern itself with issues of critical social research?

7. In what important ways did the author reassess the symbolic structure of the therapeutic communities? What were the cultural value differences toward drugs and alcohol between England and the United States that had to be reconciled?

NINETEEN

A European Anthropologist's Personal and Ethnographic Impressions of the United States

EMANUEL J. DRECHSEL
University of Hawai'i at Mānoa

In this wide-ranging and personal essay, Professor Drechsel discusses the American penchant for viewing ourselves as culturally European. Using his European background and long-term familiarity with the United States, he argues convincingly that there is a unique American culture strongly influenced by non-European sources, especially the Native American culture. For the author, this culture includes elements of a Wild West mentality but is best understood as a "creole" in which non-European elements are not always obvious or distinct. He concludes the essay by offering the compelling comparison of American culture to a circus.

Emanuel J. Drechsel *was born and raised in Switzerland. He studied anthropology with a focus on Native American languages of the eastern United States and received a Ph.D. from the University of Wisconsin-Madison in 1979. He has lived and done anthropological research (including fieldwork) in the upper Midwest, the South (especially Louisiana), and Hawai'i. Married to a native Hawaiian, he currently resides in Honolulu and is professor of Liberal Studies at the University of Hawai'i at Mānoa.*

INTRODUCTION

The careers of anthropologists, as those of other professionals, reveal distinctly personal dimensions and reflect such diverse influences as individual experiences, sociocultural roots or a certain disillusionment with them, and often an interest of a romantic nature. Such individual traits are evident in biographies of two intellectual ancestors of mine, *Wilhelm von Humboldt* (Sweet 1978/1980) and *Edward Sapir: Linguist, Anthropologist, Humanist* (Darrell 1990), as in those of other scholars. Accordingly, I have always been aware of a distinct personal dimension in my own career as an anthropologist and linguist and in my perspective as a foreigner living in the United States. My sociocultural background and personal experiences not only explain my areas of interest and even my reasons for coming to the United States but obviously have also colored my views of this country.[1]

Thus, examining the personal backgrounds of anthropologists—particularly the backgrounds of foreign anthropologists—is an important part of understanding their professional views. Such a review is warranted for reasons no less significant than realizing their presumptions, misconceptions, and even prejudices, for the recognition of any personal bias can help both the anthropologists and others to revise their understandings of a foreign society. Yet, beyond this basic reason, there is another justification—perhaps equally important but rarely recognized explicitly—for considering the personal dimensions in anthropologists' perspectives, experiences, and observations. Anthropologists' personal experiences not only may reveal the subjectivity and limits of their observations, but also may provide different angles and serve as inspiration for new ideas that a native might ignore or miss. In short, the anthropologists' personal backgrounds may add—so to speak—twists to their observations, with positive as well as negative consequences.

To help the reader unwind any "personal twists" in my observations below, I first offer an autobiographical sketch including information on my upbringing, sociocultural background, and personal experiences. These, I contend, relate directly to my experiences as a foreign anthropologist in the United States, even if such a connection may first appear insignificant. What follows leads to an informal account of personal impressions and ethnographic observations I have made as a European in this country. They specifically consist of personal experiences, informal observations in and out of the classroom, systematic fieldwork with Native Americans and other ethnic groups, and ethnohistorical research over a period of some twenty years.[2]

ROOTS, UPBRINGING, AND YOUTH

I was born in Switzerland in 1949 and grew up in the northeastern part in a little town by the name of Romanshorn, located on the Lake of Constance in the canton of Thurgau. My mother and her side of the family have always reminded me in a kind of ancestor's myth that we were Appenzellers, descendants of small but sturdy peasants in the hills and mountains south of the lake, recognized for many "peculiar" traditions among other Swiss. Descent has indeed tied my family to a small community in the half-canton of Appenzell Outer-Rhoden through my mother's father, who, however, was the only immediate ancestor with ties to northeastern Switzerland.

In reality, I can maintain little claim to an Appenzeller identity, for I never met my maternal grandfather, apparently a most remarkable man, who had unfortunately died before I was born. Significantly, he had not even lived in his native canton, nor has anybody else in my immediate family for that matter. My mother's mother had roots in French-speaking Switzerland and in France. A maternal aunt, my mother's oldest sister, always presented herself as American, as she had settled in the United States as a young woman. On my father's side, I have had roots in Germany, about which I have never learned many details but some of which supposedly extended even farther to Sweden and Russia. As a boy, I also acquired ties to the United States through my American godfather, who eventually married my mother. An inspiring model and a gentleman in the truest sense of the word, he has always enjoyed my admiration, for he never assumed the role of a stereotypical stepfather and—sociologically speaking—has always remained more of a magnanimous uncle with his calm, nonimposing manners than an authority figure.

There is even less of a justification for an Appenzeller identity on a social basis, for my family has shown little sympathy for one of the Appenzellers' characteristic traditions, their long-lasting resistance to granting full political rights to women. (These rights were finally installed in the last holdout of institutionalized male pre-dominance, Appenzell Inner-Rhoden, by a recent order of the Swiss federal court.) Although not exactly feminists by modern standards, the women in my family on the maternal side have always been quite independent and have pursued their own goals and careers, far more so than average Swiss, let alone Appenzeller, women. In the 1920s, my mother's mother, although not an architect, designed her own house, which has stood out because of its simple beauty. My maternal aunts likewise distinguished themselves in one fashion or another. One was among the first women in Switzerland to acquire a driver's license at a time when only men were behind the wheel. But instead of turning into a "car freak," she became engaged in promoting public transportation and environmental protection when few people had even heard of ecology. Most important, my mother developed her own business designing and manufacturing jewelry, for which she won several national awards, and successfully switched to health therapy after "retirement."

Indeed, I grew up with little exposure to Appenzeller traditions. My only familiarity with Appenzell has been from sporadic hikes and skiing trips into the nearby mountains, which lead up to the dominant peak known as Säntis with a height of some 8,200 feet, clearly visible from my hometown on a nice day. But I have found mountains with all their imposing beauty as rather confining my horizon literally as well as metaphorically—not to mention that I remember mountains as the prime location of natural disasters in Switzerland (avalanches, floods, and earth slides). Since youth, I have also taken exception to the widespread Heidi mentality of identifying Switzerland with the Alps, especially the Matterhorn and the Lucerne areas that the Swiss tourist and other industries have much promoted. I have further objected to the accompanying philosophy of political conservatism as reflected in the Wilhelm Tell mentality of the mountain cantons[3] and as revealed again in recent disclosures of an unconstitutional underground branch of the Swiss army in the mountains. Counter to the common cliché, Switzerland has been much more than a beautiful rock in the midst of Europe, fine chocolate, handy army knives, precision watches, or secret bank accounts (see Gonseth 1989–1990).

The major geological landmark of my native country, the Alps, has thus had little positive emotional significance for me. For my home, I have always preferred the shore of the Lake of Constance with the adjacent lowlands and hills, the primary environment of my childhood. My emotional association with the lake has remained so strong that today I have retained few early memories, happy or sad, in which the lake does not figure if only in the background; in contrast, the mountains simply do not figure in my recollections, except for two or three. My orientation has thus been away from the mountains, that is, northward and northwestward, which also included a regular glimpse beyond Switzerland's national borders into the neighboring Federal Republic of Germany (FRG) or nearby Austria. A ferry has connected my native town, Romanshorn, with Friedrichshafen, the home of the first zeppelins. Once vehicles to the wide world, they flew again overseas to America in my imagination, inspired by old photographs and by my aunt's memories.

My multinational roots exposed me to things foreign in my early youth. My German father, an engineer by profession, acquainted me with different technologies—at first cars and trains, then redesigned sailing ships and windmills as examples of an alternative, ecologically responsible industry. He warned me of nuclear energy, environmental disasters without national borders (as in the case of Chernobyl), and fascism, which he had experienced personally.

My horizon widened literally as well as metaphorically when, as a teenager, I moved to Basel, the country's second largest city, located on the Rhine River in northern Switzerland in a triangular corner facing France and the Federal Republic of Germany. The river not only draws much of its water from the Lake of Constance, but has also been Switzerland's major lifeline to the world at large. Because of its unique infrastructure, Basel has long been a center of transportation, industrialization, and international financing in Switzerland and has enjoyed a rich tradition of culture and education. The city also forms the heart of a larger international area known as *Regio Basiliensis* (Latin for "Basel region"), a socioeconomic area that extends across national boundaries from northern Switzerland into the Alsace (France) and Baden (FRG) and is bordered by the Jura and Vosges mountains and the Black Forest. This region has been the home of more than two million people sharing traditions in a common dialect, literature, architecture, and other characteristics and has successfully pursued across-the-border trinational cooperation independent of farther-reaching efforts at European economic and political integration such as the European Free Trade Association (EFTA) and the European Community (EC).

The reason for my move to Basel was to attend *Gymnasium* (an institution of secondary education equivalent to high school and at least the first few years of college) and later the university. I could conveniently join my stepfather, who as editor of the English magazine of a major pharmaceutical company was professionally engaged in this city during much of the week and maintained an apartment there. Through him and his American, British, and Anglophile Swiss friends, I acquired a taste and fascination for Anglo-Saxon "things" ranging from technology (such as the caboose at the tail of American freight trains, airplanes, skyscrapers, and suspension bridges) to food (like peanut butter, pumpkin pies, pancakes, and sandwiches). With a growing appreciation for baroque and classical music, I learned to relish modern "serious" American music in the form of blues and jazz, which resounded from Basel's concert halls, museums, and smaller establishments. Jazz concerts during these years, such as the big-band swing by Count Basie and Duke Ellington, the cool music by the Modern Jazz Quartet, and free-jazz experimentations by Don Cherry, have remained part of my cherished memory until today. I even adopted some "Anglo-Saxon" mannerisms such as carrying change loosely in my pocket instead of in a wallet and wearing white socks with dark long pants (only to shock some Americans with my "low-class" attire years later on my first visit to the United States). Moreover, I identified my stepfather's calm and relaxed manners as characteristically American and also eyed smoking the pipe as an expression of Anglo-Saxon sophistication. Thus, I experienced eye-opening but protected years of *Sturm und Drang* by enjoying an ideal combination of home and freedom.

But my multinational roots and "mixed" sociocultural heritage went deeper than an interest in foreign technology or a few teenage fads. I grew up diglossically in Swiss and Standard German, which are mutually unintelligible, and had many years of formal and intensive instruction in German, English, French, and Latin. I heard all these languages (except the latter) and others spoken at home, as my parents regularly received guests from other parts of Europe, the United States, and elsewhere. My parents also adopted a Tibetan boy, who attracted the family's entire attention and through whom I became acquainted with a sizable Tibetan refugee community in Switzerland. My older sister and her part-Chinese boyfriend introduced me to Chinese food, including the use of chopsticks, and to Asian designs. Moreover, my "foreign" fathers exposed me to liberal political ideas and alternative interpretations of both past and current world events. In fact, dinner-table conversations in my family have often included discussions of politics, religion, and other controversial topics, which, over a glass of wine, could occasionally become rather spirited.

Whereas "the grass across the fence often appeared greener" to me, I also learned early that the big wide world was not always so rosy. A major event in recent history to leave a deep impression on me, as if I had experienced it in person, was World War II, which regularly assumed reality through my family's memories of it: my father's encounters with Nazi terror in his native country, my mother's and my maternal aunts' accounts of the bombing of the lake's German shore by the Allies at night (including their fear of errant shells hitting the Swiss side), and my stepfather's unpretentious, but all the more impressive, descriptions of his experiences as an Allied soldier on duty in Europe. These recollections gained in reality from occasional visits to the neighboring Federal Republic, where the destruction of World War II still was very much evident through the 1960s. War has remained one of the most terrifying events for me until today, which is why I could not develop any enthusiasm for my (involuntary) military service in the Swiss army.

With my multinational roots, I increasingly came to understand myself as a citizen of Europe rather than of Switzerland. The cosmopolitan and liberal perspective that I have enjoyed and have taken for granted at home has always appeared to me the only valid answer to today's many transnational problems such as war, economic exploitation, and environmental destruction. In frequent disagreement with popular opinion, I have argued that Switzerland's international responsibilities could not be limited to membership in a few "nonpolitical" international organizations concerned with emergency aid and relief, economic development, science, or culture (such as the International Red Cross as well as selected European and United Nations organizations). My own international roots have specifically led me to support an active role for Switzerland in Europe's unification and full membership in the United Nations beyond minimalist international agreements. I have even taken the unorthodox position that my native country should take the initiative and leadership in Europe's political unification. This plan has seemed to be the sole feasible long-term solution for a peaceful Europe. The alternatives in which the European Community either dictates the conditions for Switzerland's eventually unavoidable admission to the union or leaves the country isolated like a hole in the center of the continent are realistically unacceptable, as an increasing number of Swiss citizens and government officials have apparently come to recognize in a recent *Euro-Initiative*. The common claim by fellow citizens to Switzerland's political neutrality has long appeared to me a weak argument, questionable by a long history of partiality as evident, for example, in dubious international trades of arms and various unconstitutional approaches to NATO.

I today envision an international confederation of states analogous to the national one of the Swiss cantons as a model for a unified Europe. Such an association of European states would be characterized by a modern liberal constitution, a political system of direct democracy (including the right to referenda and initiatives), an explicitly multilingual and multicultural constituency, and circumscribed federalism. I would also hope for such a unified Europe to assume true armed neutrality, committed to nonoffensive international politics.

My views have corresponded to what Adolf Muschg has perceptively described in *Die Schweiz am Ende—Am Ende die Schweiz* (1990), a collection of essays on Switzerland's recent history and future role in a unified Europe, whose title translates as "Switzerland at the End—In the End Switzerland." Yet, counter to official tenet and public opinion, the author has argued that what makes Switzerland (including its political system of direct democracy) unique is not Tellian in tradition, in fact is not even Swiss in origin. Instead, it is the product of foreign immigrants such as Friedrich Engels, who completed the civil revolution of 1848 in Switzerland. Hence, Muschg has proposed that, to maintain its identity, Switzerland must open its doors to Europe, just as it could serve as a multilingual and multicultural model for a European confederation.

In my search for a more intact world, I had originally had in mind a political system for Europe like that of the United States of America, only to switch to a Muschgian view over the years. But the United States has continued to exert on me a strong fascination in other ways, especially for its size and multiethnic composition. Blues and jazz have mesmerized me not only for their artistic value but also because of their social implications; in a world of so much conflict, this music has offered an alternative art by successfully blending different cultural traditions into a new "international" one.[4] Following a long romantic tradition in Europe, I developed an interest in the native population of the United States. Native Americans had already played an important role in my youth, shaped by juvenile fiction of little literary or ethnographic value, only to grow beyond the interest of boyhood into a serious anthropological concern.

Eventually, I had an opportunity for overseas travel on student exchange programs—first to Great Britain during a summer while still in *Gymnasium* and then to the United States after I had obtained my Swiss university entrance degree, the *Maturität* (a cognate of English *maturity*). My visits to both countries proved exciting beyond all expectations. While living with local families for several weeks, I could experience and participate in their daily lives and could also undertake some traveling, especially in the United States. On a visit among Caddo in Oklahoma, I also came to meet Native Americans for the first time.

In the fall of the same year, I entered the Universität Basel, which with its international atmosphere seemed a sample international community. For my major, I chose ethnology, which not only provided a better understanding of cultural differences and seemed to hold all the answers to the world's problems but also fed my enduring curiosity about the alien and different, especially Native Americans. There kept lingering in my mind the question of what had really happened to the Native Americans, so often presumed to be absorbed into modern American society or else extinct. My early university studies thus stimulated an interest in acculturation, which I have always understood as a reciprocal (if often uneven) process between members of two or more societies rather than a one-way street. I developed a particular fascination for the creative ways by which communities merged elements of their own traditions with foreign influences into new creations (as in jazz music), and I soon turned to such phenomena as cultural revitalization movements among Native Americans and native peoples of the Pacific. When I expanded my academic horizon to include linguistics, my interest translated into a fascination for language contact and contact languages including pidgins and creoles.

In considering all these topics, I never forgot my own multicultural background, and I like to think today that it provided me with awareness for cultural differences as well as mutual accommodations in acculturation.

MOVE TO AND RESIDENCE IN THE UNITED STATES

My university studies in Switzerland instilled in me a growing desire to return to the United States for the purpose of gaining special expertise in Native American ethnology and doing an ethnographic field study in a native community.

In the fall of 1972, I transferred to the University of Wisconsin at Madison as a special graduate student in anthropology with generous financial support by a private Basel foundation. Originally, I had no intention to obtain a degree in the United States. But as I met the university's academic qualifications in spite of fundamental differences between the Swiss and American systems of higher education, I took the opportunity to pursue a Ph.D. in this country rather than returning to Switzerland after a year or two of special studies.

While solidifying my interest in cultural anthropology, I expanded my studies to linguistics, especially the topic of language in culture and society. A major concern of mine has since been ethnologically defined models of language change that incorporate a broad range of sociocultural factors. Much of my research has subsequently focused on the applicability of sociolinguistic models derived from the study of pidgins and creoles to Native American languages. Drawing on both field and archival research, my dissertation project consisted of a sociolinguistic and ethnohistorical study of Mobilian Jargon, a Native American pidgin of the lower Mississippi valley (Drechsel 1979, 1986).

Likewise, far beyond my original plans, I had met during the 1973 Linguistic Institute at the University of Michigan a woman who did not remain just a casual acquaintance but became a close friend and eventually my wife. Rather than returning to Europe after obtaining my Ph.D., I followed an academic career in this country, again by invitation rather than by plan. One position provided the stepping stone for another. Over the years, I lived in Georgia, Louisiana, and Oklahoma aside from Wisconsin and other parts of the upper Midwest. On visits to the Atlantic and West coasts, I have moreover become acquainted with both the city and state of New York, the New England area, Texas, northern California, and Hawai'i. Although my research has focused on Native Americans and I have visited various Great Lakes, Southern, and Plains communities, my field projects have also acquainted me with many of their non–Native American neighbors such as Acadians ("Cajuns") and blacks in southern Louisiana. Over the years, I have encountered people of other ethnic groups and social backgrounds in various circumstances—Americans of diverse European ancestries, African Americans, native Hawaiians, and Japanese, Chinese, and Filipino communities in Hawai'i. Currently, I again reside in Hawai'i, where my wife, a native Hawaiian, and I moved after several years of residence on the mainland.

I have now lived in the United States for some twenty years, during which I have pursued a variety of sociolinguistic and ethnohistorical research topics. At the same time, the larger society has not escaped my attention as I have become familiar with several areas and different communities. These have served as context for my personal experiences in this country and my ethnographic observations. I have also gained many valuable insights about U.S. society from teaching anthropology and linguistics at four state universities for more than ten years. The students' reactions to different and strange peoples as well as to their foreign teacher have revealed much about themselves and their society.

I have now been farther away from my original home than I ever intended or imagined to be. Having lived in the United States since the summer of 1972, I have also spent almost half of my life in this country. Yet I have not taken root beyond the acquisition of permanent residency. Whereas the U.S. Office of Immigration and Naturalization considers me an immigrant, I have not felt like a settler. Obtaining American citizenship has not been on my mind—not for any reason of personal variance or animosity but solely because of my identity. With all my interest in Native Americans and my appreciation for life in this country, I have remained a European at heart throughout these years. In this, my two fathers have probably served as role models, who—although residents in Switzerland—have always maintained their foreign citizenships and identities.

From a sociological perspective, I have remained a visitor, albeit an extended one, as is characteristic of academics and other highly mobile professionals. The purpose of my move to the United States was purely professional. Unlike so many preceding immigrants to this country, I did not have to escape from economic disaster, political persecution, religious oppression, or some other misfortune that would leave me with little or no hope, let alone desire, of ever returning home. I have thus had the luxury of escaping the intrinsic social pressures for settling and starting a new life in the United States that "true" immigrants experience when leaving behind their native countries.

In maintaining my European identity, I have continued looking at modern U.S. society from an outside perspective; hence I do not claim my observations to be emic. I also contend that, as a visitor, I have not necessarily shared the amenable attitudes of true immigrants, eager to start a new life, to settle down, to embrace their new environments without reservations, and perhaps even to forget their original home.

However, I would not make any claim to objectivity if such were possible in the first place; I fully recognize the influence of my own sociocultural environment and personal experiences on my perspective but in different ways. These have indeed affected my interactions with Americans. In all my gratitude for their hospitality, I have maintained differing views; with all due respect for my hosts, I have also taken the liberty to disagree with them. While occasionally critical, my observations are intended in honesty and ultimately remain sympathetic.

RECEPTION IN THE UNITED STATES

It would not have occurred to me to mention my "visitor" status had people in this country not again and again presumed me to be in political or other exile from my native country. Quite unexpectedly, many Americans—usually nonacademics and middle-class people of European ancestry—apparently thought of me as a refugee of some sort when they learned of my foreign origin. They often assumed that I had moved to the United States to escape a repressive society, to enjoy free enterprise, and to pursue "the American Dream." Amusingly, many Americans have also thought—quite erroneously—that, as a foreigner, I did not pay local or federal taxes, even if I drew a regular income from an American employer and a government institution such as a state university. This and other similar privileges again were presumably due to my special status as a refugee.

What has probably made my hosts' attempt at determining my national origin more difficult is my foreign accent, which has occasional British features but is otherwise undefinable to many Americans. Most apparently do not hear a remnant German accent that I notice in linguistic recordings of my own speech, and instead are primarily aware of Briticisms in my English, which still reflects the influence of my Swiss secondary education with BBC English as a model.

Judging by my English speech, many Americans have hence assumed my native country to be either England or—more often—one of its former colonies and new commonwealth associates. Numerous people have regularly guessed my home to be in Australia, which I first assumed they had simply confused with (German-speaking) Austria, but their references to "down under" in further conversation left little doubt about their intentions. Several Americans have also wondered whether I came from India—possibly because they have noticed a greater range in pitch in my English, similar to that of southern Asia when compared to American English, although the intonation patterns of the English spoken by East Indians and Swiss differ substantially from each other. In an extraordinary instance of national misidentification, a foreign-exchange officer at an Oklahoma bank, where I ordered a draft in Swiss francs drawn on a bank in Geneva, thought of me as the son of white settlers in Swaziland. Such preconceptions about my origin perhaps explain why some Americans have thought of me as a refugee.[5]

Americans have revealed other misconceptions about my origins. Many people have again and again confused my native country with Sweden, in which case conversation inevitably turned to free sex, democratic socialism, and cars. Once identified as a citizen of the Alpine republic in central Europe, I have encountered various other stereotypes. Americans have often thought of me as the son of wealthy watchmakers, chocolatiers, or financiers—with a secret bank account at home and on some private business in this country. That neither my parents nor I have been engaged in any of these enterprises or that Switzerland might have more diverse industries (such as precision instruments and machinery including sophisticated weaponry, chemicals and pharmaceuticals, jewelry, textiles, fashion, and foods other than milk products) has apparently crossed the mind of but a few of my hosts. The esoteric study of America's native peoples and their languages has appeared to them as even a stranger reason for leaving Europe.

When the discussion dealt with Europe, Americans have frequently expressed admiration for its "cultural wealth" as evident in fine cuisine, high fashion, time-honored architecture, distinct arts, and a rich history. In recent years, conversations have also dealt with topics of new technology as related to automobiles, trains, and airplanes. Many Americans have even expressed some sort of cultural insecurity or inferiority in relation to Europeans, with which I have taken issue—usually in vain.

I first interpreted such reactions simply as part of initial courtesies and relation building by Americans, especially in conversation with a European such as myself. But I have found the same indications to apply if my conversational partners had no previous knowledge of my European ancestry and in fact assumed my native country to be outside of Europe. Their surprise has usually been all the greater learning my true origin.

While appreciating approval for things of which Europeans and Swiss in particular can justifiably be proud, I have more often felt overwhelmed by Americans' praise to the extent of feeling embarrassed, for my understanding of Europe's modern history ranging from my parents' memories of World War II to my own experience of more recent events could hardly justify so much acclaim. To such expressions of enthusiasm, whether or not genuine, I have struggled to find an appropriate response. Neither full approval nor silence has seemed appropriate, and outright disagreements have appeared outright improper. Polite arguments suggesting that North America's history is equally rich, if only different, and that it in fact reveals greater diversity than Europe's have usually dispersed in the wind. Probably worst among my various reactions have been my tongue-in-cheek agreements. Those Americans not familiar with a kind of devil's advocate teasing, especially nonacademics, have regularly misunderstood such responses. I guess that they also interpreted them as typically arrogant European, and no follow-up explanations could alter their opinion. I have observed similar situations of unease or even miscommunications between Americans and other Europeans, which have in fact served as a telling mirror of my own interactions. Nowadays, I usually respond in a mumbled mixture of approval and disapproval as an unsatisfactory way out.

My experiences with Americans' perception of Europeans and reaction toward them have inadvertently made me wonder how Americans perceive themselves in sociocultural terms. In particular, I began wondering whether Americans socioculturally attempted to be Europeans instead of themselves and whether such behavior revealed an unconscious awareness of cultural differences that they did not recognize otherwise.

"AMERICA" AS A HOME OF TRANSPLANTED EUROPEANS?

From my informal conversations with many Americans of all ethnic and social origins over the years and on various occasions including fieldwork, class, and parties, there has indeed emerged a widely shared picture: a *perception* by Americans of themselves as culturally "Europeans transplanted to the New World," albeit politically independent.

Usually, phenotypically white Americans have cited their European ancestry and have neglected to mention non-European elements in their family history, as if their ancestors had lived in total isolation from their various non-European neighbors. I cannot recall any European American voluntarily sharing information about any of their non-European ancestry. Only on learning about my interest in Native Americans have some people occasionally come forth and made a reference to a Native American predecessor, many by responding that their grandmother had been Cherokee. In most instances, their answer was rather stereotypical, and they could not provide any further details about their Native American background such as their grandmother's name, language, and so on. No white American has ever admitted to any African elements in his or her ancestry although such are evident throughout the South.

On the other hand, if the physical appearance of Americans revealed any obvious non-European ethnicity as in skin color, facial features, or hair, they would usually provide an explanation of considerable detail about their Native American, African, Asian, or other ancestors. Many "non-European" Americans, among them Native Americans and African Americans of Louisiana, have freely shared information about their European descent along with their non-European and have done so without denying their Indian or African identity. Similarly, kin of my wife's mother, most of them phenotypically Hawaiians or Asians, see themselves in part as descendants of a nineteenth-century German or possibly Dutch settler by the name of Elderts, and they even attribute specific family characteristics to his ancestry. Also indicative of U.S. Americans' view of their own society as fundamentally European is the widespread concern about the change in ethnic composition of the United States in favor of a growing nonwhite population, as reflected most eminently in a recent issue of the national news magazine *Time* (9 April 1990).

There are various other indications for Americans' cultural identification with Europe. Historically, the United States would not have shown such an extensive commitment to fighting two world wars in Europe in the first half of the current century had the country not felt some sense of close kinship with it. Likewise, neither the American public nor the government would have paid as much attention to the recent developments in Europe, quite possibly at the expense of the Third World. In terms of their geographical perspective, the urban area on the upper Atlantic Coast area (including Boston, New York, and Washington among others) has remained the economic and political hub of the United States in spite of major economic problems and overall has sustained an Atlantic orientation with a focus on Europe. The federal government, Wall Street, and the United Nations as indications of political and economic power have retained their offices on the East Coast and have no immediate intentions to move to California with a corresponding 180-degree switch in orientation. Cities of the same northeastern area have also provided major resources for this country's education, the arts, and—in many significant ways—industry. By their mere location, other major urban centers east of the Rocky Mountains such as Chicago, Atlanta, and New Orleans have had long-standing ties with the Atlantic and, by extension, Europe. New Orleans's ties to the Caribbean and to Central and South America and its close link to the Pacific via the Panama Canal cannot hide its partiality toward Europe, especially its former colonial master France.

There are obvious exceptions to my generalization about a basic European orientation by much of U.S. society, but they actually strengthen my argument further in the form of negative evidence. Traditional Native Americans, various other minority groups, and recent immigrant communities such as Vietnamese maintain their own distinct identities and are perceived by the larger public as socioculturally marginal. Apparently, they do not "count" until they are presumed to be successfully acculturated to the "European" way of life. Then there are the states west of the Plains, especially the West Coast and even more so Hawai'i, with their orientation toward the Pacific and Asia. But they have not succeeded in fundamentally changing the established perception of the United States as a culturally "European" nation. While competing with the East Coast in terms of education, popular culture (such as film and music), and industry (for example, computers), California has yet to become the nation's hub in international politics and economy. Much of Hawai'i is a prime exception by its mere geography, island ecology and history, revealing distinct Polynesian traditions and Asian influences and as such has remained unique among the fifty states. Ultimately, not even the islands have been immune to Europe's lures, as when the state's governor John Waihe'e, the first of part-Hawaiian ancestry, visited various European countries in 1989 for the purpose of expanding and improving business contacts and when state officials make repeated references to the islands' long-standing ties in trade, education, and culture to Europe. A conspicuous sample of such European influence is the Royal Hawaiian Band with its distinct Prussian accessories and a substantial repertoire of German tunes, a carefully maintained institution going back to Hawai'i's imperial era in the nineteenth century. The Pacific Age, until recently predicted to be just around the corner, still seems quite far away.

The widespread, overall cultural identification of U.S. Americans with Europe has obvious roots in this country's history—the European's dominance in the colonization and historical settlements of North America and the United States in particular, accompanied by the subordination, enslavement, and extermination of non-European peoples (natives, Africans, and Asians). On the other hand, there is a common but vague notion that, after Columbus's "discovery," Europeans came to the Americas, found a mostly empty land, settled, proliferated, established their first democracy, and eventually expanded—all presumably under God's directions. Not even the major events that people recognize in U.S. history, namely the American Revolution and—in the South—the Civil War, have ever put into question the separatists' presumed cultural roots in Europe. The American Revolution merely severed the country's political dependency on England, and the Civil War would at best have led to another independent political entity in North America in people's minds without changing its fundamentally "European" sociocultural orientation. As I have found from conversations with past and present students as well as professionals, orthodox history has continued presenting the United States, one-time colonies of European powers, as a historical extension of Europe. When stripped of names and ethnic identifiers, conventional accounts of American history read just like historical tales of European history such as my Appenzeller ancestral tales or the Swiss' very own Wilhelm Tell legend. Yet, just as I along with other Swiss cannot claim a single line of ancestry, U.S. Americans are not simply transplanted Europeans but share a history of multiple cultural traditions.

A EUROPEAN'S PERCEPTION OF U.S. SOCIETY

Myths of origin as gathered by anthropologists among peoples around the globe have raised questions about the ethnographic and historical validity of such accounts. Thinking about how U.S. Americans perceive themselves has stimulated reflections of my own about this country, in which I have examined my experiences and my observations from an anthropological perspective.

In contrast to their own perception, Americans have in fact appeared to me as socioculturally different from Europeans since my early youth and have been distinct from the British as well, although for all practical purposes they speak the same language. My first impressions were based largely on juvenile stereotypes. Yet as I came to rely on my own observations and experiences while living in the United

States, my view changed to one of this country as socioculturally even more unique, that is, distinctly American and correspondingly less European.

After the initial excitement about the United States's width, diversity, and novelty had worn down, I also experienced moments of boredom, frustration, and even homesickness in this country. In spite of exciting new American dishes such as bigger and juicier cheeseburgers, many delicious pies, spicy Blackened Redfish, and fine Mexican cuisine, I have regularly longed for a "hearty" *Röschti* instead of its American counterpart of onionless and half-fried hashbrowns, various Swiss cheeses (of which there is not just what Europeans identify as Emmentaler but a great diversity of others), a glass of Fendant (a dry Swiss white wine, rarely exported to the United States because of its limited production), or simply a "warm" beer with a "spicy" flavor. On the other hand, I have missed a regular spirited discussion of topics close to my heart (like philosophy, politics, or history) in place of gracious dinner-table conversations on the weather, the job, or sports, the latter for which I have not developed any more enthusiasm since my youth. Americans', and especially American men's, preoccupation with sports, as evident from their pervasive presence in high schools and colleges and from all their attention in the media, seems distinctly American. In contrast, a German newsweekly that I regularly consult, *Die Zeit,* and other European newspapers carry no section on sports or discuss them solely as sociohistorical phenomena on rare occasions. The continued avoidance of the metric system as official measurement in this country renders it likewise unique. But most significant, there is something of a surviving Wild West mentality as demonstrated by Americans' rejection of a national gun law and support for the death penalty.

Such experiences of American sociocultural distinctness have not been uniquely my own but are shared by other Europeans and foreigners because of their different sociocultural backgrounds. In all these instances, it has helped little that I had been exposed to U.S. American culture in childhood and while still in Europe. Also, I could hardly deny my emotions, positive or negative, about my new surroundings, although as an anthropologist I can rationalize about such differences and my reactions toward them. Drawing on my own cross-cultural experiences, I would actually doubt any anthropologist or other social scientist who—however marginal to his or her own original home—claimed immunity from any similar reactions about a new social environment. I would suspect that he or she was either dishonest or mentally ill.

Yet to some social scientists, my experiences may reflect minimal or superficial sociocultural differences between the United States and Europe and would not justify an ethnological interpretation of American society as anything other than fundamentally European. After all, so might go the argument, I could experience differences of a similar kind in another part of Europe or possibly even within Switzerland in another language area. In actuality, there are more substantial sociocultural differences between the United States and Europe, albeit underlying and less obvious.

A good but rarely cited example is humor. After twenty some years, I still wonder about much American humor as presented in comic strips, on television, and in films. There are some aspects of "Doonesbury," "M*A*S*H," Bill Cosby (but not his coactors) in "The Cosby Show," and Cookie Monster of the Muppets that make me laugh. But I experience little or no amusement in most American comedies, especially slapstick humor, that an entire audience in a movie theater may find hilarious. Instead, and to the embarrassment of my wife or other American company, I am often entertained by scenes that, as judged by the audience's reaction, apparently were not intended to be absurd. A drastic example of such comedy might even be sermons by fundamentalist television preachers, were I not fully aware of their questionable motivation and practices. Conversely, my and other Europeans' sense of humor has usually resulted in bewilderment in my wife and most of my American friends. For this reason, I have consciously avoided making jokes, especially in the classroom, for fear of simply not being understood or inadvertently offending my audience. Quite unexpectedly and to my pleasant surprise, I have occasionally made my classes laugh when I had absolutely no intention of making a joke.

American humor need not escape me for linguistic reasons, for I have had considerably less difficulty in following British humor as available in magazines like *Punch* or on television broadcasts such as "Monty Python's Flying Circus" and "Spitting Image." If the linguistic argument applied, the reverse would in fact hold true because I have now had considerably less exposure to British than American English. Instead, I believe there is a nonlinguistic difference in the form of a much stronger political dimension in my and many other Europeans' understanding of humor as compared to that of Americans, who regularly shun such in accord with their avoidance of politics and religion as suitable topics of dinner-table conversations. There may yet be another, more substantial difference between their definition of the absurd, which I am not prepared to pinpoint here. However, our mutual reactions have reminded me time and again that these sociocultural differences are real even if they escape full description.

An even more significant example of characteristic American culture in my own experience has been blues and jazz music. Besides giving me a great deal of personal pleasure and excitement, this art form has pointed the way to my perspective of the United States as socioculturally American rather than European. Often misrepresented as uniquely black American, blues and jazz music has obvious African and European roots and is an exemplary representation of what in my mind has been distinctly U.S. American—a creative integration of diverse cultural traditions into a new form of art. If seen in their larger sociohistorical context, including their impact on modern "classical" as well as popular music, blues and jazz music no longer remains that apparently marginal tradition surviving in more or less stereotypical presentations of Dixieland music in New Orleans's French Quarter, in sterilized dance music presented as swing, in a few select and smoky clubs of New York City or San Francisco, or on "elitist" public radio stations.[6] That blues and jazz music has long had a worldwide impact and that there may now exist a more lively scene of jazz music outside the United States alters little in my argument and only demonstrates its attraction as a result of its creative power. It has proved to be a great disappointment not to hear as much jazz in concerts and the media as I had expected. I also remain astonished about how little public recognition modern jazz musicians such as the fate John Coltrane have enjoyed, although his characteristic phrasing in tenor and soprano saxophone playing reappears in imitations throughout today's popular music.

Rather than dismissing blues and jazz music as a sociocultural epiphenomenon, I hold it as a key to our understanding of U.S. American culture, representative of the neglect, if not disregard, of nonEuropean traditions or a reinterpretation of these, if recognized, in terms of some vague European history. This typical American art form has in fact inspired my interest in acculturation in general, which has extended all the way into the ethnology of Native Americans and into anthropological linguistics, as evident in my research on pidgins and creoles. The example of blues and jazz is only one among many that make me think of the United States as a society fundamentally different from Europe in spite of obvious and many significant historical interconnections. Just as Dixieland is not simply brass music performed by a European military marching band, American society is not Europe transplanted to North America; rather, it is a historical almagam of diverse cultural influences including Native American, European, African, Asian, and others.

Among various instances, there are some that reflect distinct Native American flavors. Usually interpreted as a Pilgrim or even Judeo-Christian holiday and celebrated with full fervor, the prime American holiday of Thanksgiving is by all indications Native American in its roots—in terms not only of a typical menu consisting of corn, sweet potato, turkey, cranberry sauce, and pumpkin pie but also of the overall idea of expressing gratitude around fall. Thanksgiving probably was a European immigrants' partial adaptation of the Green Corn Ceremony once widespread among the native peoples of eastern North America, who gave thanks for successful crops of corn in either summer or fall in a kind of new-year celebration (see Witthoft 1949). That most Americans hereby happen to express their gratitude to a Judeo-Christian god today is incidental.

It is tragic that Thanksgiving, whether or not recognized as a Judeo-Christian tradition, has not become an occasion for acknowledgment of the native peoples, to whom this country and the world at large owes so much. When Europeans first set foot onto the North American continent, it was not that vast area of wilderness inhabited by a few "savages" as still imagined in the minds of many history teachers. As archaeologists have demonstrated repeatedly, American history has built on a long and solid prehistory, to which there appear more connections than disruptions in spite of the Europeans' enslavement and systematic genocide of native peoples. In addition to the stereotypical Thanksgiving produce, Native Americans have contributed many other items of food. What would gumbo and many other local dishes of Louisiana be without *file,* an indigenous spice consisting of pounded sassafras? The indigenous peoples of North America have also made significant contributions to technology, such as the canoe and toboggan as means of transportation, the adobe as insulator, and the pueblo as architectural design. Moreover, the horticultural and agricultural traditions of Native Americans have been the basis for numerous pharmaceutical and chemical products of today, just as much of the modern cultural geography of the United States, including the infrastructure, has built on traditional indigenous settlements, trails, and waterways. Many place names with unconventional spellings, including Mississippi, Wisconsin, Chicago, and numerous others, reflect Native American linguistic influences. *Bayou,* a term that refers to a marshy and sluggish tributary to a river or lake in Louisiana and adjacent states, is not French in origin as we might surmise from its spelling or pronunciation; instead, it derives from Mobilian Jargon or the Chickasaw-Choctaw trade language and ultimately from Choctaw proper, that is, *bayuk* (river, creek). Native Americans on the Atlantic Coast may even have invested early European settlers with egalitarian, revolutionary ideas of liberty and democracy that their descendants now claim as their own. Acadian ("Cajun") music with its obvious elements of European folk music and blues reveals some characteristic native scales as well. I often wonder whether typical American ball games such as football and baseball do not likewise draw on Indian influences. It has even occurred to me at the risk of unduly stretching my argument that the long American tradition of warm hospitality and generosity may reflect a native heritage. From my ethnohistorical research on Indians of eastern North America, I inadvertently recall the many early accounts of their magnanimity toward Europeans and other immigrants, their open-arms reception and even full adoption of the newcomers into native societies, often culminating in the latter's transculturalization (see Hallowell 1963).

Reflecting my special areas of interest, these examples are but a select and isolated few among many other native influences on American culture that anthropologists and ethnohistorians have recognized for some time (for a recent survey, see Axtell 1981, especially Chapter 10). Yet, whereas the European impact is widely recognized in Native American societies, U.S. Americans—including social scientists and historians—usually neglect or fail to recognize reverse influences in their own society or history except perhaps in negative terms. For this one-sided picture of the United States, Americanist anthropologists and historians bear some responsibility because, in our studies of acculturation and culture change in general, we have yet to give equal and methodical consideration to the question of the indigenous impact on the U.S. American society. Unfortunately, much Americanist ethnological and ethnohistorical discussion has remained superficial in this respect by listing single examples of influences, as I have done above, or by focusing on selective borrowings rather than taking into account the overall process. It is sad but indicative that, for instance, Volume 4 of the *Handbook of North American Indians,* entitled *History of Indian–White Relations* (Washburn 1988), does not offer a separate, systematic discussion of this question. On the other hand, long-needed popular publications such as Jack Weatherford's *Indian Givers* (1988) often present oversimplified and tenuous reasoning. Unfortunately, such studies, although commendable in intention, may only reinforce long-held stereotypes of Native Americans as "the noble savage."

Similar arguments of substantive non-European cultural influences in American society extend to Africans, Hawaiians, and Asians among others, as is evident in food, speech, folklore, music, and so on. From a historical perspective with a time-depth extending back into "prehistory" and with greater attention to ethnic diversity, it becomes increasingly difficult to imagine how the United States could *not* have drawn on or incorporated other, non-European traditions. Orthodox Americanist social science actually owes an explanation of how this country could have remained as European as it is usually presumed. In dealing with this issue, we might open our eyes toward non-European elements in U.S. American history and society.

With proper attention to prehistory, the historic role of non-European peoples, and mutual interethnic acculturation, the United States no longer appears socioculturally as European as commonly assumed. Yet U.S. society is not simply a loose and disorganized mixture of European and non-European cultural elements but a different sociohistorical entity that forms an integrated whole in spite of numerous internal discrepancies, conflicts, and external influences. In other words, U.S. American culture is a *creole,* interpretable in either traditional terms or as a metaphor borrowed from linguistics. In the first instance, a creole can be a person of partial or even predominant European descent, born and raised in America with a tradition of his or her own including distinct non-European influences. *Creole* also refers to the first language of a multilingual community that derives from an interlingual medium technically known as pidgin with characteristically diverse influences from many languages including non-European ones (see, for example, Romaine 1988).

In analogy to the linguistic analysis of creole language and in contrast to related European languages, the sociocultural as well as linguistic similarities between the United States and Europe appear more superficial and their differences correspondingly deeper and more substantial than commonly suggested. The differences refer not only to sociocultural traditions passed on by Native Americans or introduced by immigrants from outside the Americas and Europe but also to newly created, modern American traditions such as blues and jazz music. As in creole languages, such non-European elements are not always obvious or distinct; nevertheless they are not any less real than the widely acknowledged European influences. One reason why they are more difficult to recognize is that they have been submerged in what may superficially appear as a European heritage—in analogy to non-European features in creole languages such as African elements in Caribbean creoles and even in black English or Hawaiian features in Hawaiian creole ("pidgin"). In the latter case, note for instance the characteristic Hawaiian syntactic pattern of predicate and subject in a conventional phrase like "Good da food," not to mention other Hawaiian influences evident, for example, in the vocabulary. A recognition of such underlying differences adds a complementary dimension to our understanding of American history and culture that will make it considerably more diversified and richer.

In short, European traditions have blended with non-European ones into a sociocultural almagam with characteristics and a history unique to U.S. American society. Like America's other historical societies, this country has been substantially different in its culture from Europe even though the latter has selectively adopted various old and new American inventions since its "discovery" of the Western Hemisphere.

THE ETHNOGRAPHIC METAPHOR OF "CIRCUS"

Whereas this can hardly be the place for an ethnography or ethnohistory of the United States, a metaphor—that of "circus"—offers an interpretation of U.S. society in terms of a separate sociocultural entity, as it may *appear* to outsiders. This metaphor solely is a figure of speech or a summary of ethnographic impressions and does not provide an explanation of historical development for any U.S. sociocultural characteristics. This analogy not only draws on experiences and observations of my own but also relies on impressions by fellow foreigners in this country, conservative Native Americans, and other "marginal" Americans, who in spite of substantial sociocultural differences among themselves have shared similar reactions to their larger sociocultural surroundings.

The circus metaphor proposes an intentional association of U.S. society with a typical traveling show including various actors such as clowns and exotic animals performing special acts in a large tent. Further, it is intended to draw on fond childhood memories, which I assume the reader holds. The circus metaphor has no negative, secondary implications in terms of "disorder" or "confusion," nor does it necessarily suggest exclusive applicability to the United States. In reverse, Americans may experience any modern foreign society, including my very own native country, in similar terms.

Principally, the circus metaphor suggests that to outsiders Americans are more "theatrical" in appearance than their common self-image of rationality, business, and science makes them believe. At the same time U.S. American culture, while remaining strange, is alluring, perhaps even fantastic (in the literal sense) to outsiders, just as the circus world exerts fascination on its audience. Yet aside from this general allegory, U.S. society exhibits numerous specific circuslike traits and includes among them some exotic and esoteric elements.

First, U.S. American culture is youth-focused, as evident in advertising, fashion, and the consumer market at large. Like a circus, Americans constantly appear to be "on tour," as reflected in the rapid changes in fashion, fads, and moods among their younger generations. These changes reveal uncertainty about Americans' sociocultural identity and little of any deeply rooted sense of history, but they also reveal a willingness for social experimentation, comparable to new acts in the ring.

At times, the United States even comes across as a huge Disneyland, which lives in a circus dream world with its newspaper comic strips, television cartoons, the unrealistic world of Hollywood, fantastic toys, and entertainment and theme parks. A distance to reality comes through in the dominant emphasis on "fun" in primary and secondary education with all its attention to sports and nonessential areas such as military preparation programs, usually at the expense of basic academics. There are still other aspects that reflect a dream world: school and military parades; elaborate graduation ceremonies and parties, including such extravagant features as the students' rental of fancy limousines;[7] much clamor and hoopla accompanying sports events with the raising of flags, the singing of anthems, public invocations, and performances by mascots and cheerleading troupes; and political gatherings with all their show and pomp.

Like the circus as a small world in itself, U.S. American society has exhibited a kind of island mentality, as reflected in its isolation from the larger natural and social environment. There is the continuing reliance on natural resources as if they were limitless. The country's weak or absent commitment to dealing with other major issues, ranging from a national health policy and public education to public transportation and the balancing of the national budget, serves as an example of withdrawal. An island mentality further comes forth in the nation's failed adoption of international standards or its refusal to recognize any international authority (such as the International Court in Den Haag) unless convenient. Even the widespread use of the term *America* in media, education, and the public to refer specifically to the United States rather than the entire hemisphere is a linguistic reflection of unfortunate insensitivity to the country's neighbors, close and distant. From this perspective, the so-called "open" society paradoxically appears quite closed.

Corresponding to magic and other "unreal" acts in a circus, U.S. society exhibits much behavior related to the make-believe or supernatural domain. In light of the constitutionally granted separation of church and state in this country, I have always been surprised about the great permeation of religion in modern U.S. society as evident in prayers or invocations at many government and public-school events, whose appropriateness has usually remained unchallenged without any action by the American Civil Liberties Union. The contrast to my own social background is all the more striking in light of the fact that Switzerland and other countries that do not recognize a strict separation of church and state make far less reference to the supernatural on public occasions.

Yet the wonderworld of the United States with its "circus" orientation has also been the source of much creativity. Americans have obviously demonstrated true imagination and pioneer spirit in the arts and sciences, technology and industry, and other forms of human expression. Examples are so numerous as to make a selection difficult. Yet in a random choice of just a few, there come to mind not only music as in blues and jazz but also national parks, architecture, suspension bridges, J-boats, computers, and space exploration. In their youthful spirit, Americans have moreover surprised me again and again with their seemingly unlimited generosity, ingenuity, and optimism.

Hence, there remains fascination for this country comparable to that of children for the circus. Just as American youngsters abroad feel deprived of the many "fun" things that they had available at home, children of foreigners in this country often have a difficult time returning to their native country and adjusting to what they consider a meager and boring life once they have tasted the "forbidden fruit" and "the greener grass across the fence." This observation by no means applies just to societies with restrictive political or religious ideologies, but to liberal ones of Europe as well. This "dream-world" orientation also exerts an extraordinary fascination on grownups from far and wide. I suspect that, on a long-term visit to Europe, I would similarly miss many of the amenities that I have come to enjoy in this country.

CONCLUSION

Rather than leading me astray and into an academic dead end, my interest in Native Americans, their languages, and their societies has led me to a different understanding of the United States, if perhaps via a detour. On the basis of my own multicultural background and through my studies, I have gained a broader perspective of U.S. society and a valuable dimension that might otherwise have escaped me— the country's creole history, including a substantial non-European heritage as exemplified here primarily by its Native American traditions but evident in others such as blues and jazz. Their study inadvertently offers a more comprehensive understanding of American society and history in anthropological terms, which I have interpreted in terms of the metaphor of "circus," an ethnographic profile of U.S. American society from an outsider's perspective.

There even is a moral, although hardly a new one, in this story: Americans may and should be proud of their amalgam heritage and their creole history and need not pretend or attempt to be Europeans. On the other hand, non-Americans, including Europeans, must recognize Americans on their own sociocultural terms. A better mutual understanding of cultural differences between Americans and Europeans obviously is a necessity in our rapidly changing relationship and desire for true peace.

Notwithstanding substantial cultural differences from Europe, the United States also remains of interest for comparison as the functional model of a modern multiethnic, multistate society to an emerging unified Europe because of their sociopolitical and economic similarities—better than any other modern, multistate and multiethnic society such as the Union of Soviet Socialist Republics, the People's Republic of China, India, or Brazil. With the United States' previous experiences as a modern multiethnic, multistate society to guide Europe, a unified Europe has the benefit of avoiding major errors in national policies on health, environment, public education, infrastructure including public transportation, and languages, for which

Europe ought to be grateful. Commission of similar errors by European nations thus has become much less excusable.

Yet the United States need not serve solely as a negative sample but can still stand as a model with its constitution, many environmental policies, higher education, ingenuity in computer and aerospace technology, and artistic creativity. Certain areas of this country, such as Hawai'i, may also illustrate ethnically diverse communities with substantial social balance and comparatively little discrimination or interethnic strife, which must become a major concern to Europe with its increasing ethnic diversity resulting from a growing immigrant population. Like Americans, Europeans must learn to accept and recognize the increasing creolization of their society with multiple, diverse traditions as a creative development in their future. *E pluribus unum—et plures in uno!*

NOTES

1. I dedicate this essay to my parents—my mother, Rita Hubbard Banziger (Swiss), my late father, Armin Drechsel (German), and my stepfather, Stanley L. Hubbard (American), all of whom have significantly shaped my life. I also wish to recognize three major teachers of mine, who happen to represent the same cultural traditions as my parents: the late Hans Ehrenzeller, Meinhard Schuster, and William W. Elmendorf. Furthermore, I must acknowledge the Werenfels-Fonds der Freiwilligen Akademischen Gesellschaft der Stadt Basel, whose generous support made possible my dream to study in the United States and built the foundation for much of what was to follow. I also thank my wife, Teresa Haunani Makuakane-Drechsel, and my Indian colleague, Jaishree Odin, for many helpful suggestions.

2. I recognize that, in presenting autobiographical information, I run the danger of adding a metatwist that ideally requires closer examination as well. But this issue will not receive any further consideration here.

3. Tell is a mythical and literary figure who according to legend shot an apple from his son's head in challenging Austrian usurpers in the thirteenth century and who has served as a patriotic symbol of independence for Switzerland until today.

4. From this perspective, the popular cousins of blues and jazz, namely rock and roll, beat music, and their modern descendants, have mostly appeared melodically pale and rhythmically sterile to me.

5. If in short encounters I did not wish to present a long and complicated explanation about my origins or the reasons for my coming to this country and if I made a conscious attempt at avoiding Briticisms in my speech, I could identify myself with Wisconsin or the upper Great Lakes area, at least in the South, without anybody taking exception or challenging me. Actually, there are formerly German-speaking communities in the upper Midwest (including Swiss-American ones such as New Glarus in Wisconsin) that have maintained more or less of a distinct German or Swiss accent in their English. Similarly, there are communities of Scandinavian ancestry that exhibit the distinct intonation patterns of their first language's with a greater range in pitch that is similar to mine in some ways.

6. In analogy, we can extend the same reasoning to corresponding musical traditions in other parts of American such as reggae in Jamaica and samba and bossa nova in Brazil.
7. Graduation ceremonies obviously are a form of initiation rites, which seem to reach a peak with high school students. Afterward, the nature and extent of graduation festivities seem to be inversely related to the value of the student's degree.

REFERENCES

Axtell, James. 1981. The European and the Indian. *Essays in the Ethnohistory of Colonial North America.* Oxford: Oxford University Press.

Darnell, Regna. 1990. *Edward Sapir: Linguist, Anthropologist, Humanist.* Berkeley: University of California Press.

Drechsel, Emanuel J. 1979. Mobilian Jargon: Linguistic, Sociocultural, and Historical Aspects of an American Indian *lingua franca.* Doctoral dissertation, Department of Anthropology, University of Wisconsin-Madison. Ann Arbor: University Microfilms International.

_____. 1986. Speaking "Indian" in Louisiana. Linguists Trace the Remnants of a Native American Pidgin. *Natural History* 95 (9): 4–13.

Gonseth, Marc-Olivier, Ed. 1989–1990. Images de la Suisse/Schauplatz Schweiz. *Ethnologica Helvetica* 13/14. Berne: Schweizerische Ethnologische Gesellschaft.

Hallowell, A. Irving. 1963. American Indians, White and Black: The Phenomenon of Transculturalization. *Current Anthropology* 4 (5): 519–531.

Muschg, Adolf. 1990. *Die Schweiz am Ende—Am Ende die Schweiz. Erinnerungen an Mein Land vor 1991.* Frankfurt am Main: Suhrkamp Verlag.

Romaine, Suzanne. 1988. *Pidgin and Creole Languages.* London: Longman.

Sweet, Paul. R. 1978/1980. *Wilhelm von Humboldt. A Biography Volume 1: 1767–1808, Volume 2: 1808–1835.* Columbus: Ohio State University Press.

Washburn, Wilcomb E., Ed. 1988. *Handbook of North American Indians. Volume 4: History of Indian–White Relations.* Washington: Smithsonian Institution.

Weatherford, Jack McIver. 1988. *Indian Givers. How the Indians of the Americas Transformed the World.* New York: Crown Publishers.

Witthoft, Rachel. 1949. Green Corn Ceremonialism in the Eastern Woodlands. Occasional Contributions from the Museum of Anthropology at the University of Michigan, No. 13. Ann Arbor: University of Michigan Press.

STUDY QUESTIONS

This article is so wide-ranging that it is more practical for the individual teacher to develop a list of study questions to fit his or her own programmatic format.